An Introduction to
HTML5 Game Development
with Phaser.js

Travis Faas

CRC Press
Taylor & Francis Group
Boca Raton   London   New York

CRC Press is an imprint of the
Taylor & Francis Group, an **informa** business

CRC Press
Taylor & Francis Group
6000 Broken Sound Parkway NW, Suite 300
Boca Raton, FL 33487-2742

© 2017 by Taylor & Francis Group, LLC
CRC Press is an imprint of Taylor & Francis Group, an Informa business

No claim to original U.S. Government works

Printed in Canada on acid-free paper
Version Date: 20160404

International Standard Book Number-13: 978-1-138-92184-9 (Paperback)

Library of Congress Cataloging-in-Publication Data
Names: Faas, Travis, author.
Title: An introduction to HTML5 game development with Phaser.js / author, Travis Faas.
Description: Boca Raton : Taylor & Francis, CRC Press, 2016.
Identifiers: LCCN 2016008918 | ISBN 9781138921849 (alk. paper)
Subjects: LCSH: Computer games--Programming. | Internet programming. | HTML (Document markup language)
Classification: LCC QA76.76.C672 .F335 2016 | DDC 794.8/1526--dc23
LC record available at http://lccn.loc.gov/2016008918

**Visit the Taylor & Francis Web site at
http://www.taylorandfrancis.com**

**and the CRC Press Web site at
http://www.crcpress.com**

Contents

Preface

If I had to give another title to this book, it would be "All the things I wish I had known about HTML5 game development before I started." New and emerging technologies make mastering game development rather difficult. Typically, there is a flurry of motion as people create new technologies, experiment, and solidify best practices. I spent a lot of time during the writing of this book delving into this storm of creation. I examined how people were making their HTML5 games and what tools and technologies they were experimenting with, and I was digging into the source code for the Phaser framework. I have written this book to accumulate all this knowledge into one place with the hope that another me out there is spared the fate I chose for myself.

Anyone who is technically competent will tell you that writing a book on technology, especially if it is new and evolving, is a losing game. Oftentimes the technology will change so quickly that by the time a large scale project is finished the new version of the game engine will be incompatible with the original project. This remained true for this book, to the effect that every chapter I wrote was rewritten with each new monthly release of Phaser. I highly recommend that you take a look at the official Phaser website while you read this book in order to see how the framework has progressed.

Knowing that technology will progress ever onward, I have attempted to write a book that focuses on game development techniques and tooling, using a specific build from the Phaser game engine as its base framework. The intention is that you learn the basics of HTML5 game development from this book and then you can apply it with Phaser or other similar game engines out there. To help you with this process, this book has been broken down into two major sections. The first section covers the basics Phaser's game engine, which can apply more broadly to a multitude of HTML5 game engines. The second section then takes these basics and applies them in the construction of a series of different example games. The purpose of the second section is to show the basic building blocks that Phaser provides in use inside of fully working game systems. This will give you both a better understanding of how these elements can be used and you will have some projects that can be used to kickstart your own development.

Like most human endeavors, this book has been a group effort. Many people contributed to the content of these pages, sometimes directly, other times in a more intangible manner. My biggest thanks must go to my wife, who was kind enough to give up weekends and nights with me as I sunk into the terrible depths of HTML5 game development. Claire, your wondrous patience with my madness is always appreciated.

On the technical side of things, major thanks to Alex Porter for letting me know I was mostly on the right track with my book. And sorry to my media applications students. I told you all that you were just guinea pigs for my ideas. I probably learned more from you all than you learned from me, and this book shines because of it. One last technical thanks both to Adam Saltsman for getting me into game programming originally with the wonderful Actionscript 3 Flixel library and Richard Davey for making and leading the development of Phaser.js.

Working with such wonderful art made the creation of these games in these books a true pleasure. My wife, Claire, provided the lovely robot and glitch for the shoot 'em up, and Steve Brand did the great speedy fox platformer game art. In the tower defense style game, I took the approach of using free game assets to quickly prototype the game. The tileset is from Kenny Vleugels, who makes a huge array of high-quality and free game prototyping graphics. I highly recommend checking out his site, http://www.kenney.nl/assets. Finally, the skeleton and human sprites were produced by Kacper Woźniak, who has a lot of lovely work ranging from free to a few dollars per asset on his site http://thkaspar.tumblr.com/.

As I previously mentioned, I like to think of this book as partially a message to my previous self. I'd like to include my last bit of advice I would give to my past self if I were so lucky to meet him: Don't wait to make a game. I say this simply because the world of game development is complex and is quickly changing. Making a game is time consuming and requires hard work. It is going to take you a long time to make something you're happy with, so it is best to start at it early. Once you get in there, you will learn that there is no better feeling than putting everything together and having a little world come to life on your screen. So go start making games. Every little one counts.

Author

Travis Faas has taught game and app development at Indiana University–Purdue University Indianapolis (IUPUI) for half a decade. Before switching to a different career as a teacher, he spent some time making cutting-edge interactive websites for local, regional, and national clients. He loves the multidisciplinary trait of game development because it keeps things fresh and can engage people on a broad spectrum. For him, game development is just another way to express oneself, and he wants to see as much variance and creativity in those expressions as possible. When not teaching, he's tinkering with new and emerging technologies.

CHAPTER 1

Introduction

HTML and JavaScript (JS) are technologies out to change the world. Or, more likely, they already have and have simply not given up on the change. Hardly a single day goes by without a new capability being added to the presentation powers of JS and HTML5. In a few short years, the web browser has gone from being relatively slow to a media machine capable of rendering games that people would swear were on modern gaming machines. Today it is even possible to play games inside a web browser using only a game pad one might use to play later on an XBOX or Playstation (and they will even look as good). JavaScript and HTML have come a long way since their early days as simply document markup and display.

1.1 Web Technologies

HTML5 and JS have a low enough learning curve and such a low barrier to entry that many people have found they can quickly and easily find a an outlet for their creativity using these technologies. Because the only requirement for viewing HMTL5 projects is a modern web browser, one's output is easily shared across the web (and increasingly on mobile devices).

For slightly more complex creations, the developer might require a specific web browser, but that is increasingly becoming the only limit on what is needed to get someone up and running with an interactive web-based project. This same limit applies to the creator—nothing more is needed to get up and running and making things beyond having a text editor and a web browser with the chops to make the code run.

Along with this easy-to-use environment comes a great community of other creators who are committed to making tools, tutorials, and inspirational media for the world to see and use. This community is excited about what they are making, quick to help a newcomer, and always looking for ways to make the creation of fun and interesting things easier and more enjoyable. While community is not often talked about when technologies are discussed, it is worth noting simply because as solitary as they may be, programmers and developers love company, and the better the community, the more enjoyable an associated technology tends to be.

The major web browser manufacturers—Mozilla, Microsoft, and Google—are astoundingly dedicated to bringing their users (and thus the developers who rely on these browsers for their capabilities) the latest and greatest features. It is getting quite easy to access some of the most powerful features of a device through easy-to-use APIs (application programming interfaces) made by the hardworking people who make our web browsers. Today we have access to things like geolocation, accelerometers, advanced audio, the canvas tag, and WebGL to make advanced interactions with (relative) ease. Additionally the browser manufacturers continue to improve JavaScript, the "glue" of the web. Each year brings new features to the language, making it more manageable to work with and easier to understand.

The aforementioned development community has not stopped with just what the browser manufacturers provided to them. Instead the community goes out of its way to build toolkits and frameworks that supply what the browser manufacturers could not make or decided was not within the scope of a browser API. While this book will be talking about building games using one of these frameworks, there are more available that can be used for games, business applications, or even artistic expression. There is the ubiquitous jQuery that makes web coding life easier in general. Angular JS and other frameworks are appearing to help make the production of interaction sites faster and more manageable. Each day offers something new in the JS world that shows just how powerful the simple scripting language really can be.

1.2 Important Advancements

The wealth of new, creative JS games would not be possible without several advances in web technology, notably the introduction of the canvas element and a general increase in JS performance. Along with the canvas element came two drawing contexts: two dimensional (2D) and three dimensional (3D). Both enable JavaScript to draw into a HTML element, but they rely on different technology to produce graphics. The 2D context enables per-pixel manipulation, while the 3D context allows access to lower-level graphics capabilities through the use of WebGL. These two advancements give the developer the ability to manipulate graphics at quite a fast speed, a necessity for games.

The HTML5 canvas is a combination of the canvas tag in HTML and a JS API to give a programmer the capability draw into the pixels inside the bounds of the canvas' width and height. The API provides some basic functionality like drawing rectangles, lines, and images. It is then up to the developer to figure out how to use the canvas, typically in some manner of animation loop. By creatively drawing to the canvas, clearing the drawn pixels, and drawing elements again in a slightly different place, a developer can get gamelike interactions onto an HTML page.

WebGL (or "web graphics library") is a subset of OpenGL that was used primarily in the development of desktop media. With WebGL, web developers gain access to the low-level graphics capabilities (notably the graphics processing unit [GPU]) of the device the web page is running on. In other words, with WebGL, a developer now can use graphical looks and capabilities that can rival any other game being released for the same device. Though it has had varying support, current trends indicate nearly all new browsers and devices will soon support this technology.

Finally, the hard work of the browser manufacturers has paid off with extremely fast JS execution times. The major browsers all compete in getting to the grail of "fastest JavaScript" engine. As the title swings between browsers, the public tends to benefit from faster web pages. Game developers benefit from a scripting language that can run games with less of a performance hit. Combining the quick speed of current JS engines with WebGL provides an extremely easy environment to make games, all thanks to the hard work and competition of our web browsers.

1.3 Where Games Are Played

The wonderful thing about making games using JS and HTML is that they are accessible nearly anywhere. Nearly any web browser your target audience may be using will at least be able to render a 2D canvas, and quite likely will get the speed (and graphical boost) from a WebGL context for the canvas. Today web-based games don't have to be restricted to just the desktop either. When it comes to deployment, one has a wealth of options where your games could be played including desktop, tablet, and phone devices.

Perhaps the easiest way to get an HTML5 game out to a potential user is to host it on a website. All a developer needs is a webhost and a URL. Once they have uploaded their game to the web, anyone who navigates to the page will load up the game and be able to play fairly quickly (assuming the game has been optimized for web deployment and the game is quick to pick up). This is of course a big pro simply for speed of deployment. However, one major detraction is that one needs to pay for the bandwidth to serve all the game files (sometimes multiple times per player, especially if they decide to come back to the game from another computer). Games, being fairly asset heavy in the art and sound department, can quickly become expensive to host.

Another method of game deployment, which might help mitigate the need for hosting dollars, is to take an HTML5 game and, through the use of some extra programs, "wrap" the game up with some more code and release it as an app for any of the big app stores (Windows, Google Play, and the Apple App Store being major contenders). The programs that turn your HTML5 games into apps often give one access to a host of features that are not available to a JS developer, such as access to the phone's notification system or the ability to post to the phone's game hub. Using these features can make it very hard to tell that the game was made originally for the web and keep your players coming back.

Two players in the HTML5-to-app field currently are Cordova (and the related PhoneGap technology) and Cocoon JS. The latter is focused primarily on enabling game developers to have access to the fastest and most robust wrapper for games and interactive content, typically accomplished by stripping away any unneeded parts of the browser and speeding up any graphics calls that are related to the 2D or 3D canvas context. In general, it would be the most preferred of the two, but keep your eye on each just in case they change in the future.

1.4 Web Development in the Modern Day

The past few years have brought tremendous changes to the web development profession. An influx of talented developers has descended on all parts of the technology to build frameworks and approaches to make the resulting sites and applications robust and easily maintainable. With technologies that range from the ubiquitous jQuery to growing new technologies like Node.js (and the multitude of libraries available in Node's package manager), it is a good, if a bit confusing, time to be a web developer. For example, a modern-day developer might find themselves using several different features of Node to run a webserver, break up their files into more easily edited pieces, and build their JS automatically.

All of this technology comes at a price. It takes some buildup time to understand all the moving pieces and get them set up properly. There is a lot of studying and reading of documentation before a particular technology can be employed, and, technology moving at the speed it does, there is a high chance that a library, approach, or framework that was chosen to be employed will change at least once during the development of a project of any significant scope. Thankfully, the benefits outweigh the costs (though it may not always feel like that), and it appears as if the pace of change is slowing.

Old web developers were used to simply working on their files with little technological help, uploading all of the source files of their project to the web, and sending the URL of that resource out to their client. In order to catch up with the modern day, web developers would need to learn how to get their computer writing some of the JS for them, how to run commands on their command prompt to test their project, and how to export their final build files before deploying. It is more moving pieces than before but becomes quick once one gets used to the process.

1.5 Who This Book Is For

This book is not a total basics introduction to game development. It is a bit more advanced in its approach to web game development and makes an assumption that the reader is not afraid to delve into technology to tinker from time to time. In general, there are two groups who would most benefit from this book, but general curiosity is a completely valid (and encouraged) reason to pick up this book.

The first group that could benefit from this book is the "current web developers" who have an interest in making games. This book uses a skill set that the current web developers already have and most likely strengthens that skill. If you're a web developer who has some skill in JS, this is the book for you. You don't need to leave your current area of expertise and you'll be making games rather quickly.

The second group that has a chance of finding good use of this book is "game developers" who are looking for a foothold in web development. This book will help a game developer who is used to another framework, perhaps an engine like Unity3D, to take their first steps into the web development world without leaving something that feels familiar to them. It is only a few more jumps from there to be making more robust HTML applications.

There are always others who will find some use of this book. If the content within gets your interest, then this book is for you. Books are cool like that.

Hopefully I've scared you off only a little bit from diving into modern HTML5 game development. For someone who is interested in JS and HTML5, learning how to develop games is a wonderful introduction to the practice of web development. It will get you used to how to set up your workspace and deal with modern libraries and how to build full working applications instead of simply "pages with some components dropped into them."

CHAPTER 2

State of HTML5 Games

Wherever computation goes, games tend to be quick to follow. And with good reason. Games provide a fun way for any programmer to practice their skills, and, if lucky, spread that joy and fun to other people as well. The web has proven itself to be a great venue for games due to the ease of deployment and the increasingly robust media capabilities of HTML. At the web's very beginning, web browser manufacturers didn't have the time or desire to make their media capabilities very robust. The resulting media on the early web was quite slow and developers often looked to other, faster ways to get games and interactivity onto their sites. These faster ways came in the form of "plugins" or separate programs that the web browser would load into a page and allow it to take over a section (or all) of the content in that region.

2.1 Growth of the Interactive Capabilities of a Web Browser

The two major plugins used on websites were Java applets and Flash Player (first developed by Macromedia and later Adobe). Java applets didn't fare too well as it had a tendency to have a long and painful loading time (a killer on websites even today). The Java programming language remains in use however for other media development such as Android applications. Flash, however, quickly took the lead in displaying interactive media to users on the web in part because of its easy-to-use vector animation tools and relatively quick download times for files. Over time it accumulated a strong developer mindshare and Flash quickly gained more advanced capabilities, including filters and masks, a stronger scripting language, and the ability to manipulate the individual pixels on the screen. For quite some time, Flash remained the only sensible way to get high-quality interactive media to a user on the web. Starting around 2008, it slowly became apparent to both consumers and developers that plugins were not going to cut it anymore, and the browser manufacturers began to play catch-up with Flash. New features and capabilities were introduced into browsers quickly, and today, it is safe to say that (save for a few features and hiccups) modern web browsers can do natively everything Flash was needed for originally.

In order to catch up with the capabilities of other plugins, the two primary areas browsers had to focus on were speed of code execution and graphical capabilities.

While one could argue that the execution time of code is always important, it is especially so when working with a user-facing system. Without fast code, complex interactions will feel sluggish, the user won't feel in control and will likely quickly give up on the system and look for something more responsive and rewarding. Early on, JavaScript (JS) did not need to be a fast language. For the most part, it was only used for simple page enhancements like form validation and little animations to catch the eye. Once it started getting used for very complex systems like Gmail or interactive online maps, the slowness of JS started to show. Browser based games require a similar increase in code execution time. Graphical updates need to be run, preferably, at 30 frames/s for a smooth user experience. In games with a lot of actors, particles, and physics, this quickly turns into a lot of calculations being done several times a second.

It is important to note that JS is not a compiled language, at least not by default. JS is instead interpreted and executed the moment it is loaded into the page by something called a JS engine. Each major browser has its own engine with creative names like the Chakra engine for Internet Explorer, V8 for Google Chrome, SpiderMonkey for Firefox, and Nitro for Safari. If you're interested in the current speeds of the different engines, searching for "javascript benchmark" will surface a number of pages listing speed benchmarks. In general, with each iteration from one engine, the others will redouble their effort to catch up, getting a fairly close speed for each of the major engines.

JS engines can boast some very impressive speeds now. The way they achieve this speed is through the use of a series of optimizations that take place at interpretation time. The major optimizations are just-in-time (JIT) compilation, ahead-of-time (AOT) compilation, and several optimizations to the instruction set of JS itself. AOT compilation is a series of actions that the

JS engine takes before actually running the code. The engine will examine all the code for anything that can be rewritten to faster instructions for the machine and do those transformations to the code before actually running the script. JIT is an applied approach to this compilation step, only doing the AOT when it is absolutely needed so as to not slow down the user's computer too much during the compilation step. When seen in JS, the command "use strict" at the top of a file has a tendency to force code that can be run faster. Mozilla has been pushing the subset of JavaScript instructions that are truly fast in JS with their asm.js technology, which limits JS to only instructions that are as fast as possible, getting as close to native performance as JS can currently. Asm.js is reaching speeds that enable the cross compilation of C code to JS, with game engines like Unreal being able to export their games to a JS runtime that can be run on a website.

Graphical speed is another key portion of the viability of a richly interactive web, especially when it comes down to something as graphically demanding as games. The early browsers were lacking in this realm, working with a fairly light Cascading Style Sheet (CSS) specification (once it was there) where even transparency was difficult to achieve and animations were sluggish when one tried to transition document object model (DOM) elements. Once rendering speed became important, the browsers rushed to catch up, speeding up their DOM updates, increasing their CSS support, and, perhaps most importantly, adding in support for the canvas tag. The canvas tag gives developers the capability to forego writing HTML and CSS to determine what to show on the page and instead just draw whatever they want into a box on the page. The canvas tag has two different ways to display graphics inside of its granted screen space. The first is 2D, which gives developers the capability to manipulate the individual pixels inside the canvas, allowing for games to be built in the way they were classically made. This original game development method copied pixels from offscreen spaces onto the canvas (a technique called "blitting"). These copied pixels could be used for player characters, backgrounds, and even fonts. The second context, 3D, provides a way for web pages to get access to the GPU of the device (and its significantly faster graphics capabilities), so long as the browser has enabled the support of this capability.

When running in the 3D canvas context, WebGL is used to render graphics to the canvas' space on the screen. WebGL is a specialized set of graphics commands that work well with graphics cards JS API (application programming interface) that is taken primarily from the OpenGL 2.0 (a graphics display language used on personal computers) specification. In order to actually change what is displayed in the canvas region, a shader must be written that tells the graphics card what is should be displaying. Shaders can be programmed for WebGL in the OpenGL Shading Language (GLSL) shader language and compiled at runtime. The total combination gives a web developer access to nearly all the graphical capabilities that modern games have.

As the browser got faster and better capabilities, it became clear around 2010 or so that JS and HTML would be the future of interactive content on the web.

New capabilities were slowly getting added into the browsers (faster than some could keep up), but there simply wasn't a lot of work done yet on the frameworks that a developer would use to make their own workflow acceptable. Not to mention the fact that not all users out there would be using these modern browsers. Many developers set out to fix this problem, and, in the process, developed a lot of different frameworks and tools to aid in making interactive applications on the web today.

2.2 Wide Selection of HTML5 Game Engines

Part of the explosion of JS frameworks included a multitude of different game engines. A quick look at html5gameengine.com lists a total of 22 unique engines and these are noted to be the "cream of the crop." There were many that were popular in 2010 that fell by the wayside as new ones arose. The major issue behind this explosion of game engines is that the basics of a game engine isn't too hard to get down into code, and it is possible to get a basic game engine up and running in about a day or so with dedicated work. Many developers, when jumping into making a game, are quick to simply write their own engine for the simple challenge of it. Unfortunately, even if a game developer wishes that it would be better to go with one of the already premade game engines, their work is not done.

One of the difficulties of any developer is finding the technology that best suits their creative goals. Each engine (and toolset) has a set of strengths and weaknesses, and some are known for being more *well maintained* than the others. Some engines will have a focus on mobile or an emphasis on a certain type of game. Others will have been built to work in tandem with a certain plugin or editor (the top HTML5 game engine, Construct 2, is like this).

In general, HTML5 game engines fall into three different categories, each with a different focus:

1. Pure JS and web development workflow
2. Customized editor with a native HTML5 export
3. Professional game development suite with optimized export

The first engine type, pure JS workflow, is the closest to the tooling that web developers currently use to build web pages and hybrid mobile applications. It is heavily reliant on Node.js for many steps of its process and keeps the user closest to the final generated code. While great for current developers, there is typically a requirement to pick up a few more programs (for things like animation and map editing) and understand more of the pieces before being able to hook everything together. Because this is more of a web developer's approach, compatibility with the widest range of web browsers is typically a priority for these frameworks. They will gracefully fall back to older technology when the latest and greatest browser features are not present.

The second approach is used by programs that are built for the graphical design of games, giving the user the capability to position elements on the screen and quickly add game logic to each of the game entities. While not as full featured as the modern game development engines like Unity or Unreal, these game makers are typically more approachable and stick to an easily understood 2D context. Game Maker and Construct 2 both fall into this category and are great for new game developers looking to get their feet wet and potentially continue on to make full featured games. There are a number of games built in Game Maker that are quite polished and have been released professionally to great acclaim. The scripting languages for these engines are typically specialized to the editor. While a simple and easy approach, if the game needs to communicate with the rest of the page via JS, the final result can get a little bit messy to deal with.

The final approach to creating web games is to use one of the big engines (notably Unreal Engine and Unity3D). The teams working on these engines have been working closely with the browser manufacturers to get exporters working that transfer their games to a JS and WebGL context. While still a bit slow, the engines will typically export games that have their code transpiled (or taking source code and turning it into another language's code) to JS via Emscripten. This transpilation step performed by Emscripten will optimize all the instructions for asm.js, ensuring the fastest execution times for the final output game. The games generated via this approach tend to be large and take some time to download, so a developer should take some care when selecting this approach. It remains an option for the latest and greatest web browsers, but is reliant on WebGL, potentially keeping a number of web browsers away from the final export. As the code that is written for the game is in the original editor and the final output isn't the most human readable, this could be seen as the least close to the "web developer" mindset.

With all the other engines and frameworks, why would one want to work in just HTML and JS? One of the major advantages (or disadvantages) of JS in the current day is simply that the language is so well adopted. Just about anywhere someone needs a scripting language, JS can be found. One can find it on websites, running robots, as a scripting language for web servers, and even behind some powerful game engines (like Phaser). Many people already know JS or, seeing its broad applicability, would like to know JS. Once learned, not only can JS be applied everywhere, but it also becomes a de facto tool for programmers to lean toward.

Another reason sticking "close to the gears" of JavaScript is good is to make it easy to customize the HTML page the game is displayed in after it is complete. Additionally, many developers who will be making web games will already be web developers and will be able to quickly get up and running in this new system, not having to step outside of their current capabilities. This often means better compatibility across different web browsers as well. Finally, because there is no in-between translation step to the game's programming, it is possible to have very lean games to send to users, great for when total download size is an issue like it is on the web.

2.3 Tools

Today a web developer's utility belt is swiftly growing to include a number of technologies that make their life significantly easier, most enabled by a program called Node.js. Originally Node was developed as a technology for creating server-side JS applications (bringing with it the strengths of JS's event model and combining it with a strong input/output module for filesystem manipulations). It was quickly adopted as a way to manage dependencies on other bits of JS (formalized through the introduction of the Node package manager), import needed code libraries (through a technique called common JS), and run a lot of behind-the-scenes lifting that a backend developer may need. As developers started playing around with Node, they quickly realized that it could be used to do file operations on the developer's machine as well, giving them a way to automate otherwise fairly complicated processes like and code scaffolding (or generating prebuilt sets of code). Eventually tools for quickly fetching needed code libraries for the front end were introduced, like Bower and Yeoman. This was a lot to manage, so some automation systems were also built (Grunt and Gulp) that run tasks for the programmer automatically so the developer can stay focused on writing and debugging code.

These tools will be explained in more detail in Chapter 4. One important tool to note is Babel (and the related Babelify). Each of these tools will let the developer write their game code in the most modern versions of JS (currently sitting at about ECMAScript 6, though 7's features are quickly approaching as well). Babel and Babelify will then transpile this code down to a lower level of JS (ECMAScript5 currently). This lets a developer create a codebase that takes advantages of all the great features of the future language without having to wait for browsers to catch up. And once the browsers have caught up, then the untranspiled code can be uploaded to get the benefits of a clean code base and a faster interpreter.

2.3.1 Phaser.js

Finally, we go to our game engine of choice. Phaser.js is an HTML5 game engine meant for use in creating graphically rich 2D games. Originally created by Richard Davey, it has had future contributions by other developers. Currently it ranks fifth on html5gameengine.com in terms of popularity. While that number may not seem impressive at first glance, two of the engines listed above Phaser (Easel.js and pixi.js) are not "full-featured" game engines. Instead these engines only provide a clear graphics API to work with but are reliant on the developer for things like game step updates, physics, or states. The other two (ImpactJS and Construct2) are not only game-focused engines, but they also come with a monetary cost associated with them. Phaser is the only free game framework that works via normal HTML and JS in the top five, making it a solid choice for any web developer looking to get their feet wet with game development without spending a dime.

One of the best features of Phaser is that Richard Davey uses it for professional projects (and engages with others who do the same). Because the framework has to be working for clients, the fixes made to get games working for deadlines are pushed to the Phaser framework as well, giving all the developers access to more power and a less buggy system. Phaser has a great community that has formed around it that helps drive its feature set and helps others who are also using the engine. The community is quick to get back on a question about a bug or quirk in the system and happy to discuss best practices.

Phaser's lineage is clearly inspired by the Flixel game engine that was (and remains) popular in the Flash game development world. Improvements have been added to the original Flixel approach since the earliest builds of Phaser, and it has been rewritten to work in a way that works best in a JS context. It has support for sprite animations, sounds, tilemaps, several different physics engines (and the capability to add in more as needed), and particles (and many other, smaller but still useful things). An important addition to Phaser is the capability to deal with touch input pointers and the ability to support screen resizing, which are considerations that have become quite important for mobile devices.

Another important feature of Phaser currently is its ability to quickly and easily switch between a hardware-accelerated (but slightly less supported) WebGL mode and a slower but widely support 2D context for its rendering. Following the principles of "graceful degradation," it is possible to have Phaser choose the best approach by default and fall back to slower but more supported approaches when needed. The rendering of game objects is actually done behind the scenes using another framework called Pixi.js, which simplifies the graphics calls in JS and provides a single API that will run for both WebGL and the canvas (save for some specialized items like shaders in the 3D context). It is actually Pixi that does the heavy lifting of animations and image rendering into the different contexts.

2.4 Basic Structure of an HTML5 Game Project

In general a HTML5 game is going to include these folders and files:

- Scripts/ (or js/)
  - Holds the framework file (in this case Phaser.js)
  - Often will have a file for the game code that uses the framework
- Src/ (optional)
  - A folder used to store the source files that will be compiled into the full game code
- Assets/
  - Images
    - Used for backgrounds and sprites

- Maps
  - The data for any tilemaps in the game
- Sounds
  - Sound effects for the game, often in multiple formats
- Music
  - Music for the game, often in multiple formats
- Misc
  - Any additional data (dialog files, runtime scripts, or special files used by the game)
- Index.html
  - The html file that sets up the game and starts the loading; the JS will handle all interactions after the basic setup
  - Often has some basic styling to position the game and set up a nice user interface (UI) around it

When the game is run the only files linked in index.html are typically the Phaser engine, the gameplay code, and the CSS needed to style the page. Phaser will handle the rest of the work of loading in the assets and putting them into the page. The only thing to note with this setup is that, especially when Phaser is running in WebGL mode, it cannot load these files from the local file system. Instead, due to a number of browser security codes, the files need to be loaded from a web server instead. This can be a bit of a pain, but with a little bit of setup, one can find that the process of getting a web server ready to go isn't too big of an issue. Most of the code in future chapters will be written in a series of separate small JS files that will be compiled into one final file. These smaller files will be included in a directory called the src directory, which is technically a folder that will not be included in the final deploy to the user. There will be more and more of these "development only" files and folders as the book progresses, but in general, this is the structure that you as a developer will be working with the most.

CHAPTER 3

A Simple Game

This chapter is going to walk you through the construction of a simple game in Phaser.js. Because this game is only meant to "get your feet wet," it will not delve too deeply into all the different parts of Phaser.

3.1 Game Goals

The player takes control of the unnamed hero, Cat Catcher. Using the arrow keys, they are tasked with getting their hero over to collect a cat on the screen. Sadly the hero isn't a shining example of an animal control employee, and the cat will always get away, but the player's score will increase. It's a race against the clock to run into the cat and get points for reasons only the simulation knows.

3.2 Setup

A good start for Cat Catcher, like many projects, will be the creation of a folder to hold all the associated files for the project. Go ahead and create a new folder and give it a name like CatCatcher. Inside this folder, create two more directories: img and js. Additionally make an index.html file inside the root folder.

3.3 Getting Phaser

In order to use Phaser on a web page, you'll need to download and include the script inside of your HTML markup. The download can be found at http://phaser.io/download (or, more specifically, http://phaser.io/download/stable). This page will give you a number of options to download, the easiest one for this walkthrough is to right click and download the phaser.min.js file from the stable page. If you know how to use git and are insistent on using it, it is possible to clone the repo with all the source, examples, and build files to your computer. If you go this route, make sure to find the minified Phaser file from the dist folder.

3.4 Getting the Images

Head to https://github.com/meanderingleaf/PhaserBookExamples/tree/master/CatCatcher2000/img and download the images folder. Move the images into your project's img folder.

3.5 Setting Up the html

With the folders and files in place, it is time to start writing some code. The first step is to get a web page setup, so it can hold the game and include the scripts required to run the gameplay. Open up index.html in your text editor of choice and write up the basic html boilerplate and a few extras to get Phaser ready to go.

```html
<html>
    <head>
        <title>Cat Catcher 2000</title>
        <script src="js/phaser.min.js"></script>
        <script>

            var game = new Phaser.Game(800,
                600, Phaser.CANVAS, { preload:
                preload, create: create, update:
                update });

            function preload() {
                //load in assets needed
            }

            function create() {
                //setup game
            }
```

```
            function update() {
                    //run game loop code
            }

        </script>
    <head>
    <body>

    </body>
</html>
```

The notable addition to the boilerplate is linking the Phaser library (before the other scripts) and the game setup code at the top. The game setup code is where Phaser begins to work its magic. The first line in the setup script tag sets up a Phaser game and will always be the entry point to every game written in Phaser. The first two numbers are the width and height of the game. The next call is to specify what rendering context should be used for the canvas. It is possible to specify to the Phaser if it should run on the canvas in 2D mode or in a 3D, hardware-accelerated mode. For this example, the (potentially confusing) Phaser.CANVAS option is supplied, instructing Phaser to run in a 2D context. This is the only time it will be used in this book, letting us run this simple example without having to launch a server to test. Generally, however, unless there are specific use cases, one should always supply Phaser.AUTO in order to render in hardware-accelerated mode by default and fall back to 2D if the browser does not support WebGL.

The final argument to the setup code is a Javascript object. Behind the scenes, this actually creates a simple Phaser state. States will be covered later in this book, but in short, they are an object with properties that specify functions to run throughout the state's lifespan. There are three phases defined in this state. "Preload" is used for loading in assets for the game before gameplay starts. Here one loads in the images, sounds, and other related pieces of the game. "Setup" is called once before the game starts running, providing a chance to get game objects ready and placed into the game. "Update" is set to the game's internal tick (or clock) and is called during the game loop. This is where most of the game logic will be written. Beneath the setup line are the actual functions that will be called by the state that still need to be fleshed out.

3.6 Preload Phase

The preload phase is used to load in any asset (whether it be audio, textual, graphical, or a specialized type) into the game before the game runs. This ensures the assets will be ready for use in the game and not suddenly appear only once the gameplay has begun. This phase can take some time and will generally be longer and the bigger and more numerous the assets will be loaded. Keep this in mind as the preload phase will continue until all the assets are loaded, stopping players from getting to the actual gameplay.

Longer preload times can have a chance of losing players before they even get to the game (and its hopefully catchy mechanics). Listed here is the code to preload three image assets that should be placed into the preload function.

```
game.load.image('cat', 'img/cat.png');
game.load.image('catcher, 'img/catcher.png');
game.load.image('bg, 'img/bg.png');
```

This is the general method for loading any asset into a Phaser game. The first argument is the "id" (or key) of the asset and must be unique. The second argument is the path to the asset to be loaded in. Other assets may take more arguments, but thankfully images are an easy one to load. Take note of the IDs, they will be used later to create objects in game based off the assets loaded.

3.7 Create Phase

The create phase is used to get the game completely set up and ready to run. This means creating the objects that will first appear in the game, setting up user interface elements, and generally getting anything out of the way that doesn't need an update timer but does need to be in the game. Because we're working in a basic Javascript tag, it is necessary to add a few variables outside of the other function scopes so they are accessible throughout the game. I've chosen to put them right underneath the Phaser.Game setup line.

```
var cat, catcher, cursors, txtScore, score;
```

In this particular setup function, the sprites will be created, the score text field will be added, and the input keys will be defined and readied. Because sprites are rendered in the order that they are added, the first sprite to be added should be the background. The line "game.add.sprite" creates a new sprite of the type specified at the end (this will be an instance of the bg image) and adds it at the x and y positions (in this case 0, 0).

```
game.add.sprite(0,0,"bg");
```

3.7.1 Setting Up the Player and Cat

The player sprite is after background, so that it will render atop our game's lovely backdrop. Here the player sprite is added to the game at the center of the page, and its anchor (the point that counts as the center for its rotation and scaling) is set to its top center. Centering the anchor will allow us to easily "flop" the player's sprite around for easy left and right animation. Finally, the physics for the player sprite is enabled. By default, sprites are not enabled for physics, so they will not be able to collide against other objects nor will the developer be able to specifically respond to collisions. There are different physics in Phaser, but arcade physics is an acceptable choice for this game.

```
catcher = game.add.sprite(400, 300, "catcher");
catcher.anchor.setTo(.5,0);
game.physics.enable(catcher, Phaser.Physics.ARCADE);
```

After the player, the code to add the cat should look quite similar. The only difference is that instead of a predefined x and y location, the cat is put to a random location inside of the game (based on the game view's width and height).

```
cat = game.add.sprite( Math.random() * game.width,
  Math.random() * game.height, "cat");
game.physics.enable(cat, Phaser.Physics.ARCADE);
```

3.7.2 Adding the Score Text

Phaser's text object comes in two parts: (1) the definition of the text style (defined in a subset of CSS) and (2) the addition of the actual text field. This text field is added near the upper left-hand corner, with a starting text of zero (from the score variable).

```
score = 0;
var style = { font: "20px Arial", fill: "#FFF" };
txtScore = game.add.text(10, 10, score.toString(),
  style);
```

3.7.3 Setting Up the Arrow Keys

Usually getting input from several keys would require a lot of code and setup for the keys and to store their up/down states. Thankfully, Phaser has a simple way to set up an object that will automatically track the arrow keys on the keyboard. We'll be referencing the cursor object in the update step, but this will set up listeners for the up and down states of the up, down, left, and right keys.

```
cursors = game.input.keyboard.createCursorKeys();
```

3.8 Putting the Gameplay in the Update Phase

All game engines are built upon this critical concept called the "game loop," which is the method that is called on a predictable interval that involves the calculation of all the simulation's code. The loop is the place where positions are changed, collisions are checked, input is taken, AI is calculated, and any other miscellaneous tasks are completed. In Phaser, the game loop method is named update. This particular update function will implement two components of the gameplay. First, it will move the player when any of the arrow keys are down. Second, it will check to see if the player has hit the cat.

```
if(cursors.left.isDown) {
        catcher.x -= 5;
        catcher.scale.x = 1;
}

if(cursors.right.isDown) {
        catcher.x += 5;
        catcher.scale.x = -1;
}

if(cursors.up.isDown) {
        catcher.y -= 5;
}

if(cursors.down.isDown) {
        catcher.y += 5;
}
```

The first step is to move the player character based on the input of the player, through the use of the cursor object made in the create phase. Cursors have the properties for the four arrow keys and self-manage the down and up states, so one only needs to check if they are currently depressed (using the isDown property of each). If any of the buttons are down, the player's sprite is moved from where it currently is five pixels further in the associated direction. While technically susceptible to the classic "moving diagonally is faster" cheat, it will be fine for this simple game.

The only other notable lines of code are in the right and left handlers. Changing a sprite's scale isn't often useful, but setting scale to −1 essentially "flips" the sprite to face the other direction (in this case horizontally). The point for the flip is based around the sprite's anchor point. If its center x point is not changed to the center of the sprite, setting the scale to −1 will make it appear as if the sprite had warped back its length, instead of just turning around. This is why, when creating the player sprite, the anchor is set to the center x. When scaling now, the transformation will be applied from the center of the sprites width, making it flip around its middle (see Figure 3.1).

Finally, the last line of the code checks to see if the player has hit a cat (they visually overlap). Should the player sprite and the cat sprite be overlapping, a collision handler function is run, which is entitled catHitHandler.

```
game.physics.arcade.overlap(catcher, cat,
  catHitHandler);
```

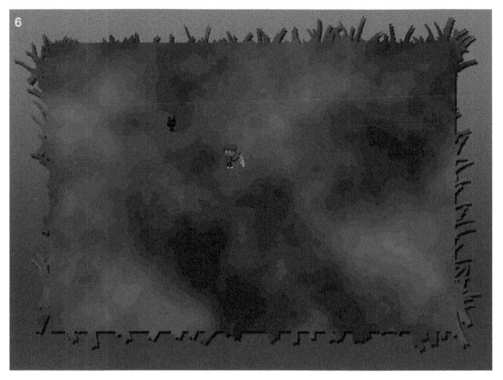

FIG 3.1 Screenshot of the finished version of Cat Catcher 2000.

3.9 Collision Handler

Collision handlers respond to an overlap between two display objects, in this case the player and the cat. All collision handlers in Phaser take two arguments, which will be references to the objects that hit each other. This function goes into the code at the same level as the create and update functions.

```
function catHitHandler(catcherObject, catObject) {
        catObject.x = Math.random() * game.width;
        catObject.y = Math.random() * game.height;

        score ++;
        txtScore.setText( score.toString());
}
```

Since this is just meant to be a quick jump into Phaser, the game simply moves the cat to a new place (using the reference passed into the collision handler). Then, the almighty score is incremented, and the score text is updated using the setText function. Nothing to fancy, but it still generates a basic type of game without a lot of work.

3.10 Testing

Finally, in order to test this game, find the index.html file on your computer and double-click to open it up. It will launch in your browser of choice and, with luck, your game will be inside of a nice canvas in the screen. Click on the canvas to make sure the browser has keyboard focus and use those arrow keys to catch as many cats as you can before you get bored.

CHAPTER 4

Workspace Setup

This chapter is one of the "necessary evils" of modern web development. For better or worse, more and more projects are becoming reliant on build script and configuration files for them to properly run. This means it is becoming increasingly hard to simply open up a text editor, maybe download a few files, and get to coding. Instead, there is often some time spent in a command prompt (or terminal), setting up the project and getting it ready to go. And even after the initial setup, it will be impossible to work without the command line open and running something. This chapter explains the tools that are used to get all this configuration done and the setup of a file that will get one working on the cutting edge of web development (though the web moving is fast as it does, it will not likely stay that way for long).

Don't Want to Deal with All This Configuration?

If you don't like walking through all the different steps of creating a build script and getting everything installed (not many do, to be honest), there are only a few steps you absolutely need to follow in this guide. First, install git as directed near the start of this chapter. Then install Node.js, right after git. Finally, install Yeoman as directed at the end of the chapter. Then you can simply use the Yeoman generator described at the end of the chapter to have your computer run through the rest of the setup in this chapter automatically.

Modern projects that use the web technologies of HTML, JavaScript, and CSS are becoming complex enough to need specialized scripts and configuration files for different projects. The reason why toolchains are needed is that modern sites need to take into account all the different people and devices that may be using their work and support as many of those as possible. Dealing with all the quirks and performance issues of the different browsers takes a lot of time and effort, which is mitigated somewhat by using the work of other web developers who have built tools to address the same problems others are having.

Speed of development is another major reason for making use of toolchains and build scripts. This is because using other's work (with their consent, of course) results in less work and thought that you need to take on. It may appear that taking some time before hopping into the development of a project can is a setback, or at least unnecessary, but that's not quite the case. Once an environment is properly set up and running, development will often progress faster now that the project can catch errors and do things automatically that would have had to have been done manually before. Oftentimes, a good setup will also lead to more structure to the code, helping speed up future additions or maintenance.

This chapter might feel like a parade of technologies, introduced in quick succession. While this is true, each has an essential component in the development of a robust Phaser game, and you'll find yourself happy to have this setup once you progress on to more complex games.

In this chapter we're going to look at the following:

- *Node.js* and how it has changed the development of websites
- *Grunt.js* to examine the various tasks that developers may want to run to speed up development
- *Babel, Browserify, and Babelify* that enables the creation of modules in a future-looking ECMAScript 6 fashion
- *Bower* that will install and manage user-facing libraries like Phaser
- *Yeoman* for when you might want to set up another project like this quickly (or skip this setup entirely)

In case you get lost, the end of this chapter has a way to quickly and easily set up this project base without having to go through all the steps described. This is a Yeoman generator that will scaffold out (or create the project structure and directories needed) for you automatically. It can be used to create new projects to work through the examples in this book or for personal use.

4.1 Installing Git

Git is a source control system and is commonly used by developers to collaborate on programming projects. It's a way for many different people to add to a single code base without having to go through the arduous task of sending over chunks of code and saying to a collaborator "Now this bit goes at line five in file whatever." A necessary part of the collaboration process is downloading the new files, and, if it is a new collaborator, that means all the files. The combination of source control being an easy way to download a library of code and easily get any fixes that are later added to the code has made source control systems a preferred distribution method.

Nearly all new publicly accessible code libraries are hosted on some sort of source control system and git is one of the more popular ones. While you won't need to know how to use git specifically to get through this book, you will need to have it on your computer for the next steps in this chapter to work properly. Thankfully, the process of installing git is quite simple: head to http://www.git-scm.com and download the installer. Once you run it, you will be set.

Note for Windows Users

Make to select the option "use git from command prompt" as you progress through the Windows installation process.

4.1.1 Node.js

After installing git, the next most important step in getting this environment setup is to install Node.js, which will open up the ability to install all of the other libraries explained in this chapter that rely on the Node being installed. Installing Node will also install node package manager (npm) that will make this process as simple as writing a few words in the command prompt. If you don't already have node installed, head to http://nodejs.org/ and click the download button to get an installer for your system. Once installed, you will have node on your computer. This will give you access to two terminal commands: node and npm.

4.2 Command Prompt

Before moving on in this chapter, we need to take some time to familiarize ourselves with the command prompt. For some time, a JavaScript developer could get away with not opening the command prompt and working in an integrated developer environment (IDE) like Adobe Dreamweaver or a lighter-weight editor like Textmate or Notepad++. Thankfully, the command prompt is not too complex to master, and it remains one of the basic skills of a web developer, especially one using Node. Here are some basic commands to get around the file system.

4.2.1 Opening the Command Prompt

First, you need to know how to access the terminal. It is a different program and process for different systems.

4.2.1.1 Windows

On Windows the program is called command prompt. The easiest way to find it is to hit the Windows key on your keyboard and type in "cmd." The search will eventually find the program and run it, though you can also go looking for it manually through your programs if so desired.

4.2.1.2 Macintosh

Access to the command line on Macs is done through a program called "Terminal." This program is inside the Utilities folder for the programs on your computer, or you can get to it via opening spotlight (by pressing command + spacebar) and typing "terminal" (see Figure 4.1).

4.2.2 Command Prompt Navigation

4.2.2.1 Location

Figure 4.1 is a picture of a command prompt. Note that to the left of where the user can input text is a directory path. This is the path that the prompt is currently pointing to and this path is used as a reference for any commands run within it.

It is important to know where you are in the file system when working in the terminal. Many commands throughout this book will only run in certain locations with other files present. Other commands might create new directories or files in the folder the prompt is currently situated at, so always be mindful of location.

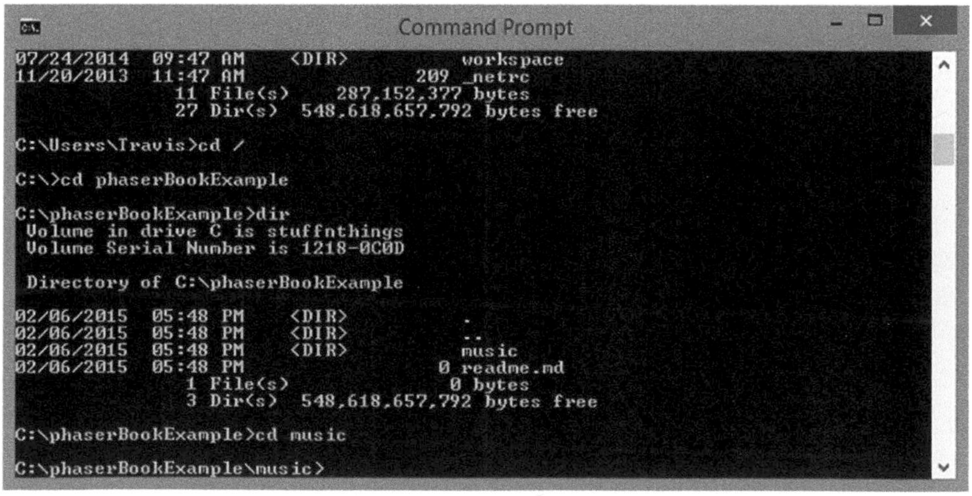

FIG 4.1 Example of a command prompt.

4.2.2.2 Entering Commands

The next few sections will list out some basic commands. Every command entered into a prompt needs to be followed by pressing the "return" or "enter" key for the command to actually run.

4.2.2.3 Viewing Directory Content

```
dir (on windows)
ls (on everything else)
```

Entering "ls" (or "dir" on Windows) lists the contents of a directory. Similar to looking at the window of an open folder, it will show all the files and folders inside of the current directory.

4.2.2.4 Changing Directories

```
cd nameOfDirectory
```

Entering "cd" followed by a folder name will move to the folder named, so long as it exists. For instance, typing **cd music** when in a folder that has a music folder will move into that folder. Once in the music folder, typing ls or dir will show the presumed musical content of the folder.

```
cd nameOfDirectory/nameOfSubdirectory
```

It is also possible to navigate through multiple directories by adding the slash in between them, just like typical file structure syntax.

```
cd ..
```

Entering cd followed by two dots will move the prompt up one folder.

4.2.2.5 Quickly Opening a Folder in the Command Prompt

The command prompt will always start at a user's home directory, which is usually close to the root of the filesystem. Oftentimes, a lot of changing of directories is necessary to get to a project's folder. A great shortcut that gets around having to navigate through the whole directory structure or type in a long path name is to *drag and drop a file or folder onto the command prompt*, which will fill in the path for you. In combination with the change directory command, it can be really handy for quickly navigating to a project folder by typing "cd" with the space after it and then dropping in the desired destination folder (shown in Figure 4.2).

4.2.2.6 Command Prompt Flags and Arguments

As seen in the changing directory examples, commands on the prompt can have more arguments and flags come after them. In general, if you see something with a dash or minus sign in front of it, then it means it is a flag that is telling the command to behave in a certain way, or do something special. Items that follow the initial command without a dash preceding them

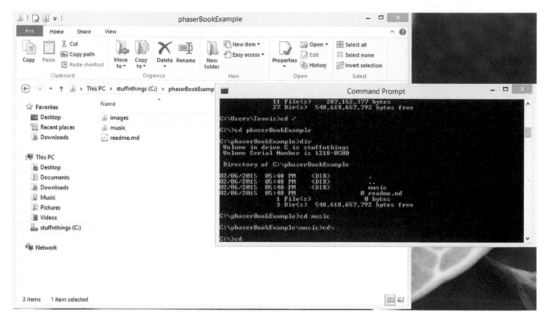

FIG 4.2 Changing directory via folder dropping.

are arguments used for specifying outputs, inputs, or other customization options that don't toggle how the command itself works.

4.2.2.7 Command Prompt Hints

For the most part, unless otherwise noted, it is expected that you will be in the root folder of whatever game project you are working. However, for the next parts of this setup chapter, you don't need to be anywhere in particular. Now that we have Node and npm installed, we can use the command line to install a number of useful tools. We'll be entering new commands into the prompt that are provided by Node and npm, but the process will remain the same. Enter the text and hit return. Sometimes, the command won't run instantaneously. Instead, you'll see that the terminal will just hang. This doesn't mean it is not working; it's just that it needs some time. Often it will be downloading files and arranging them on your filesystem. If something does go wrong, you will see an error pop up soon enough.

If you had the command prompt open, go ahead and close it and open a fresh one for these next steps to ensure that the commands for the programs you installed will be available to you.

4.3 Node Package Manager

Node package manager is a way to download JavaScript library bundles onto your computer. These libraries are developed by individuals for varying goals, ranging from creating full-featured web servers in Node to checking to see if the JavaScript that one writes adheres to best practices (a process called linting). Additionally, npm can be used to keep the packages updated, making it easy to update to new versions of the libraries that fix issues or add new features.

Another crucial feature of npm is the capability to detect and download any other packages that a library needs automatically. These other packages that are not necessarily part of the library but are required for the package being installed to run correctly are called dependencies. When installing some of the packages described in this chapter, note that a number of different packages will be installed with names that do not match the original package specified (you wanted npm to install "grunt" but it installs another package called "taskrunner"). These other packages (most likely not made by the creator of your library) are specifically configured inside of a package.json that comes along with the original library.

The next few sections of this chapter deal exclusively with npm. An important thing to keep in mind with npm is that it can install packages in two locations: locally or globally.

> *Global*: If you use the "-g" (short for "global") argument when installing a node package, it will download the files to the node directory and add the package to your computer's path. With it added to the path, the package becomes a valid command for the terminal and can be run by typing the command name and hitting enter at the prompt. This will also give other node packages access to the command, letting them run the libraries behind the scenes without you specifically having to run the command yourself in the terminal.
>
> *Local*: Conversely, if the -g command is not present, the npm will install the library where the command prompt folder is located, making a new folder named "Node_modules" to store all the downloaded files. This is typically used for packages of code that are needed for individual projects to run.

Because locally installed packages typically contain a lot of files that are hard to move or delete, node projects will often include a file called "package. json," which is a JSON file that describes all the local code packages that need to be present for the project to run. This ensures that the code can easily be transferred from place to place without all the node modules. When one needs to work on the project on a new computer, the modules that the project is dependent on can be installed via the command "npm install." In order to save a package to the local JSON file, use the flag -save-dev when running the npm install command. This flag will both add the package to the project and specify it is a required part of the project that must be present before it can run.

4.4 Installing Bower

Npm is typically used for code that is never going to be sent to the user. Some of its primary uses include production tools that help the developer as they work or actual node server development that sends data to the user but does all the processing on a remote machine. Because both of these uses don't have to deal with moving all the required files around very often, the package manager has an unfortunate tendency to download a lot of unnecessary files that bloat the file size of the project. In general, npm is not set up for dependency management for projects that will eventually be deployed to user's machines.

Bower is another package manager that was constructed with client-side deployment in mind, and will work quite nicely with Grunt, once properly configured.

In order to install bower, hop into the command prompt and enter this command.

```
npm install -g bower
```

There are two different ways to install packages via Bower—either individually from the command prompt or, if given a bower.json file, via the command "bower install" at the project root. Bower won't be used too much throughout this book—once to install Phaser and a few other times to install some plugins needed for more advanced game work. Just remember that if you want a library that will eventually be sent along with the game to the user, install it via Bower.

4.5 Installing Browserify

Browserify is a Node package that enables JavaScript developers to break up their scripts into smaller files, including the content of those smaller files in others where that code is needed. For example, a large game project might include scripts to run the different states of a game (start, game, game over), the different units within the game (player, enemy, boss), and the entire game project itself. Each of these scripts will need to reference others to make sure their code is included before it can run properly. The gameplay state will not be able to run if it can't create a player or enemy, so the code for those objects need to be available to the state somehow. Before, this would mean either writing all the code into one single file or breaking these files up into separate files and writing several script tags inside the index.html file. Either way can be cumbersome when it comes to making sure that all the scripts are included in the right order and ensuring all dependencies in the scripts are met.

One solution to this is to use Browserify, which is a tool that (with a few additions to your separate code files) will check for all those script requirements, and produce a single file that ensures all the scripts have their dependencies met. Browserify makes the assumption that there is one script that is the entry point for your application which will include all the other scripts needed (included scripts can also specify their own dependencies, so it is possible the first script won't include all the final, bundled scripts). The final output from the Browserify command will wrap all the separate files up into one final app.js file that can be linked into the html with a single script tag.

In order to get browserify into your development environment, type this command into your command prompt:

```
npm install -g browserify
```

If you want to know more about browserify, you can read about it at http://browserify.org/.

4.6 Babel and Babelify

The next versions of JavaScript (ECMAScript 6+) have proposed a number of very useful additions to the language that are yet to be fully implemented. The two most useful approaches to game development of this book are the addition of classes and modules. Working with classes, while not strictly needed for JavaScript development, helps when crafting individual objects and reduces the (somewhat) confusing prototype syntax JavaScript typically requires. In the future, ECMAScript 6 modules will be the *official* way to specify which JavaScript files are dependent on others.

Other Ways to Include Files

The problem of breaking up JavaScript files into small, manageable chunks that can be required by other files has been a thorn in the community's side for a long time. There have been a number of different attempts prior to ECMAScript 6's modules to solve the problem, each with their own advantages and disadvantages. The nature of JavaScript will keep these module managers relevant for many years to come, keeping ECMAScript 6 as only an *official* if not perhaps the ubiquitous approach.

There are two module managers you might come across the most: The first one is AMD (asynchronous module definition), which is used for frontend module requires and implemented in a library called require.js. It is most easily recognized in use by a "define()" function that wraps the rest of a module's code. The second one, perhaps currently the most commonly applied manager, is the CommonJS module syntax, which is used by Node.js to require and include other files at runtime, given away by the module.exports call at the end of module files.

The issue with using ECMAScript 6 is that while a number of browsers are getting their implementations of the specification ready, no browser is quite ready for production use. There will also be a number of people and devices that will never get around to getting a browser ECMAScript 6 support. This unfortunately means that, at least for a few years, there will be a requirement for an intermediary technology that can take this newer code and translate it into a version of JavaScript that the majority of users can run. There are a few transpilers out there that will do this, but Babel.js has become one of the more commonly used ones.

Babel will take JavaScript files and translate them from the future versions of JavaScript (ECMAScript 6+) down to ECMAScript 5. It will only do this on individual files, translating the code down to something that node can recognize and understand.

Because it will not combine all the different classes and modules into a single export file, it is reliant on other packages to finish the compilation. Browserify is a package that will take multiple files and piece them together in the correct order to get them working. The final piece of this puzzle is a package called Babelify that will allow the two (Babel and Browserify) to work together.

```
npm install -g babel
npm install -g babelify
```

You can learn more about Babel.js from https://babeljs.io/.

4.6.1 Installing Grunt

Grunt is a JavaScript task runner, which sort of sounds pretty impressive. In essence, it's a way to bundle up a number of actions that one might have to do manually on a computer, and it lets node handle them instead. Grunt has a number of useful capabilities we will be using later on such as the ability to start a small web server to test our games, automatically compiling our scripts together using Browserify and exporting our finished project in a clean format. The only potential drawback of Grunt is that every time one goes to work on the project, they will need to open a command prompt in the project root and start the development task before work can begin.

To install Grunt, type this into your command prompt:

```
npm install -g grunt-cli
```

If you want to know more about Grunt, you can read about it at http://gruntjs.com/.

4.7 Setting Up a Basic Project

With luck, those few commands went pretty quickly and you're now set up with all the tools to get a modern HTML5 workflow ready. With these packages installed, the next step is to make a project folder with the necessary parts and components to build and run the games that we will be making. This will require two parts: setting up Grunt and downloading a few more libraries to the project template itself.

4.7.1 Getting Ready

First, create a new folder for this setup. A name like "PhaserBasicSetup" for this step would describe it well. Navigate to that folder in your command prompt (remember that you can type "cd" with the space and drop the folder onto the prompt from the file system in order to quickly get to that folder).

The rest of the commands in this section will need to be run inside this project folder.

Once inside the project folder, type "npm init." This will take you through a series of configuration questions. If you're in a rush or just noncommittal, you can hit "enter" to go with the defaults (it won't hurt, and you can easily change them later). After specifying all the options, a file named "package.json" will be created inside that folder. This file is used in part to store the names of all the packages that are required for the project to work correctly. When installing the packages in this chapter, make sure to use the -save-dev flag to add the package name to the json file, which tells a developer they will need these packages before they will be able to run the project. The stored package names are also useful for easy transferability and your own personal reference, letting you move the project around without the weighty node_modules folder.

4.7.2 Getting the Grunt Packages

Grunt is going to be a major part of this book's development workflow, but there needs to be a number of Grunt tasks in the project for it to be ready to do a lot of the heavy lifting for us. During development, Grunt will do different important tasks for us including compiling code, moving files, and launching servers. The tasks come as node packages, and currently our project doesn't have any installed. To get Grunt ready to go, two steps need to be taken. First, the packages that accomplish the different tasks will need to be downloaded to the project folder, and second, we will need to set up Grunt to run the tasks as we desire (through the use of something called a gruntfile).

4.7.2.1 Local Grunt

The first thing to install is a local version of Grunt that will find and run other commands in the project. This is different from the grunt-cli and must be installed per project. Type in the command prompt the following:

```
npm install grunt --save-dev
```

4.7.2.2 Grunt Connect

Next, up to install is Grunt connect, which is a command that makes a lightweight web server to test games on. A web server is a necessity due to security restrictions in the browsers that require the files to be sent by a server before JavaScript is able to do essential things like render WebGL or load in text documents (used for tilemaps and sprite atlases). This restriction does not apply when building apps that are installed to the user's phone, but Chapter 8 will cover the pros and cons of that step in more depth.

Once properly configured, the web server will be started automatically when one starts working on the project. This lets the developer get away from needing to run an entire, full-featured web server like apache (or, even worse, uploading every little change to a remote server) just to test their changes.

```
npm install grunt-contrib-connect --save-dev
```

4.7.2.3 Grunt Watch

The next tool to be installed is watch. This is a handy task that will watch for any changes in a group of files (essentially, checking to see if the file is different from what it was before when it is saved). If there is a change to any files being watched, the watch task automatically runs other Grunt tasks for the developer. One common use case of watch is to automatically run Browserify, changing the developer's ECMAScript6 code into ECMAScript5 code automatically without any extra work. This will save you the time and annoying step of having to click a button or enter commands to actually run the transformation you want to see your code update. Another common use of the watch task is to run JSLint on all the files a developer is working on. JSLint will check to make sure the JavaScript is written in a form that is maintainable and uses "proper" JavaScript practices.

```
npm install grunt-contrib-watch --save-dev
```

4.7.2.4 Copying Bower Files to the Project

When Bower installs new libraries for the developer to use, it will download the file that the developer wants (typically a minified JavaScript file) along with everything else in that file's git repo. This means that the "bower_components" directory will include a bunch of extra files that aren't really needed while building the game. They're just there for reference at best. Since the developer only needs one file or folder, it is common to see these files manually copied into the project folder. This isn't a bad approach since it won't happen too often but can run into issues when sharing the project with others. In order to keep everything in the project automated, we're going to use a package that will automatically move Bower components over to our scripts folder.

To install this automatic copier, type this into the command prompt.

```
npm install main-bower-files --save-dev
```

4.7.2.5 Babel and Babelify

Finally, install the grunt-babel and babelify packages. These two tasks will be set up to allow Grunt to take all the smaller ECMAScript6 JavaScript files and package them up into one, neat JavaScript file that can be easily included on a page.

```
npm install grunt-browserify --save-dev
npm install babelify --save-dev
```

4.8 Writing the Grunt File

Now that the project has all of the required Grunt libraries installed, the next step is to write the file that instructs Grunt on how to use those packages when Grunt is running. This file is named gruntfile.js and should be included in the project root (alongside index.html and package.json). The gruntfile comes in three parts: configuration of tasks, loading of tasks, and registering sets of tasks to run under different names.

First, make a gruntfile.js file in your root directory and open it up in your text editor of choice. Here is the gruntfile.js in its entirety. Following this file's contents will be a discussion of what each major section does.

```javascript
module.exports = function(grunt) {

  grunt.initConfig({
    pkg: grunt.file.readJSON('package.json'),
    browserify: {
        main: {
           options: {
              browserifyOptions: {
                debug: true
              },
              transform: [["babelify", { "stage": 1 }]]
           },
           src: 'src/app.js',
           dest: 'scripts/app.js'
        }
    },
    watch: {
      files: [ 'src/**/*.js' ],
      tasks: ['browserify'],
      options: {
          spawn: false,
        },
    },
    connect: {
      target:{
            options: {
                port: 9001
            }
        }
    },
    bower: {
        flat: {
            dest: 'scripts',
            options: {
                debugging: true
            }
        }
    }

  });

  grunt.loadNpmTasks('grunt-contrib-connect');
  grunt.loadNpmTasks('grunt-contrib-watch');
  grunt.loadNpmTasks('grunt-browserify');
  grunt.loadNpmTasks('main-bower-files');

  grunt.registerTask('default', [ 'bower', 'connect',
    'watch']);

};
```

4.8.1 module.exports

The first bit of code that should go into the text editor looks like this:

```
module.exports = function(grunt) {

}
```

The purpose of module.exports is to specify what code in this file should be available to any other files that request it. For Node to properly run this file, all the configurations must come inside this anonymous function, because it is the only code that Node will be able to find within this file.

4.8.2 grunt.initConfig

The next bit of code starts with a grunt file and looks like this.

```
grunt.initConfig({

});
```

Between these two lines of code will come the configuration of all the different tasks that Grunt will run. After the first line in the configuring (which loads in some details from package.json that may be used later on in the project), there are four tasks configured: browserify, watch, bower, and connect.

4.8.2.1 Browserify Task

```
browserify: {
  main: {
    options: {
        browserifyOptions: {
          debug: true
        },
        transform: [["babelify", { "stage": 1 }]]
    },
    src: 'src/app.js',
    dest: 'scripts/app.js'
  }
}
```

This task will compile the content of the JavaScript files in the src folder into one larger file to be included on the project's HTML page. The two properties at the bottom specify the file to start looking at (src/app.js) and the file to create when all the files are compiled together (scripts/app.js). The first app file in the src folder acts as the "root" file. If there are no inclusions in that file, then this task will simply copy over src/app.js to scripts/app.js. However, if there are inclusions at the top (like in the app.js example in the next chapter), it will include those files as well. If any other files have inclusions, Browserify will continue to copy these newly included file's content into the final export file.

Note that there is a property of "transform" set to babelify. This tells Browserify to transform any of your ECMAScript6 code into ECMAScript5 code before it is placed into your export file.

In this particular config, Browserify's debug has been set to "true," which creates something called a sourcemap. This will let you easily debug your projects when something goes wrong. Without a sourcemap, if your scripts encountered an error, the error console would show you a line number in the compiled file, which can be a bit of a pain to track down first, and then you would need to go find it in the original file. With a sourcemap, JavaScript will be able to tell you where the error occurred in the original file. Instead of seeing "error on line 1134 of app.js" you will see "error on line 10 of Player.js."

4.8.2.2 Watch Task

```
watch: {
    files: [ 'src/**/*.js' ],
    tasks: ['browserify'],
    options: {
      spawn: false,
    }
}
```

A fairly simple task to configure. Watch will observe files for any changes (a modification and save of the file). When the watch task sees a change in any of the files it is watching, it will run the specified other tasks automatically.

This watch task is configured to look for a change in *any JavaScript file* inside of the src folder and its subfolders. When it sees a change, it automatically runs the Browserify task we just configured, compiling the changed code into the scripts/app.js file. Essentially, it lets a developer work with JavaScript in a faster manner, closer to the way JavaScript development used to work (make a change, and then refresh browser to see change). That said, they will need to keep an eye on the terminal during changes. The compilation step may not be instantaneous, so watching for the success message is important. Additionally, there is a chance that you wrote some code wrong, resulting in a file that cannot be compiled. If that is the case, the error will be displayed in the command prompt and will need to be fixed before returning to the web browser (see Figure 4.3).

4.8.2.3 Connect Task

```
connect: {
  target:{
      options: {
        port: 9001
      }
  }
}
```

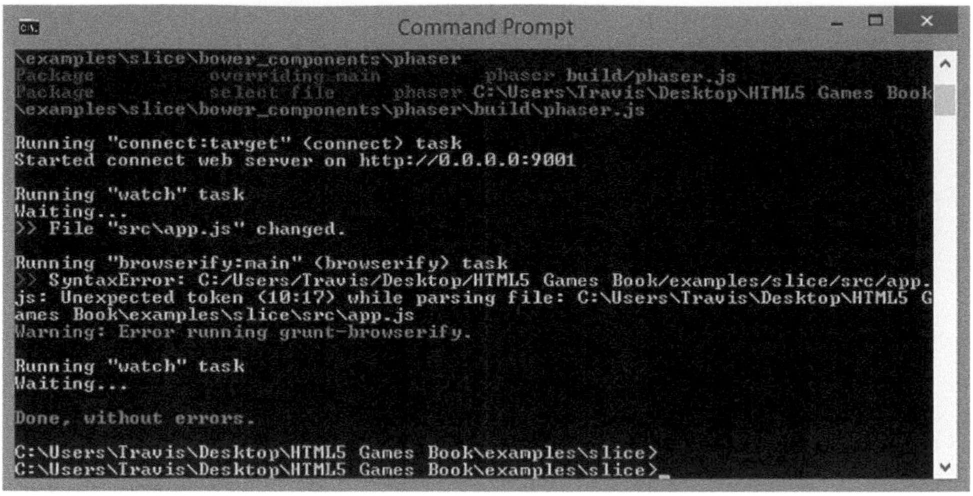

FIG 4.3 A task that has encountered an error.

Connect starts a lightweight web server that will serve files from the project root. Just in case the machine is already running a web server, the config file specifies a unique port to listen on, port 9001, instead of the default port of 80. Once the server is up and running, typing http://localhost:9001 into your browser's address bar will load up the site. Just like with other web servers, index.html will be the default html file returned if no other file is specified. When working with the projects in the book or using this workflow, remember to always go to this URL instead of opening up just the index.html file manually. If you don't, files won't load and images won't render correctly.

4.8.2.4 Bower Task

```
bower: {
    flat: {
        dest: 'scripts',
        options: {
            debugging: true
        }
    }
}
```

The last task is one that won't be run quite as often, only at the start of a development session. The bower task is set up to take all of the frontend (user facing) components from the bower_components folder and copy over the primary files to the project's primary scripts folder. Because this particular script is configured with the "flat" attribute, all of the files will be copied into simply the "scripts" folder in the root, making them easy to include. If you downloaded, say, easystar.js, then to include it later, one would only need to write a script tag that referenced "scripts/easystar.js" instead of "scripts/bin/easystar.js."

4.8.3 Loading Tasks

```
grunt.loadNpmTasks('grunt-contrib-connect');
grunt.loadNpmTasks('grunt-contrib-watch');
grunt.loadNpmTasks('grunt-browserify');
grunt.loadNpmTasks('main-bower-files');
```

With the configuration of Grunt complete, the next step is to load the tasks. This is a quick step that instructs Grunt to load the associated files needed for it to do its job. To do so, one writes `grunt.LoadNpmTasks` ("name-of-npm-task"). This config file uses connect, Browserify, main-bower-files, and watch, so all four are loaded.

4.8.4 Registering Tasks

```
grunt.registerTask('default', [ 'bower', 'connect',
   'watch']);
```

Last in the setup of Grunt is the process of registering the tasks to execute when Grunt is run. This is a fairly simple Grunt file at the moment, so there is only one task registered, the default task. A default task is one that will run when "Grunt" is typed into the command line without any other arguments.

When a command prompt is opened at the project root and the "Grunt" command is entered three operations will happen. First, the main files for any Bower packages will be copied into the output folder. Because this happens only once, make sure to install any bower packages before running this Grunt task, so they'll get into your scripts folder. Second, a web server will start up via our configured "connect" task. This server will stay open as long as Grunt is running and the terminal remains open. Finally, grunt will begin to watch for changes in the src folder, automatically compiling the changes in your source to the final scripts/app.js file via the Browserify task. The order tasks specified are important for the register task command. If the order of connect and watch is swapped in the array, the watch task will run first and grunt will never get around to starting up the web server.

After running this command, *leave your command prompt open*. Closing the terminal will stop all of the tasks, closing the server and halting Grunt from compiling your code. Additionally, if something goes wrong during the compile step of the process, the terminal will give important feedback, so don't forget to check it if something seems off.

4.9 Testing Grunt

With luck, all the files are downloaded and installed into the project directory and the Grunt file is properly configured. The time has come to test and make sure that Grunt is properly configured and ready to go. This is another command prompt step, so open it up and navigate to the folder with the Grunt file. Once there, type this command (see Figure 4.4):

```
grunt
```

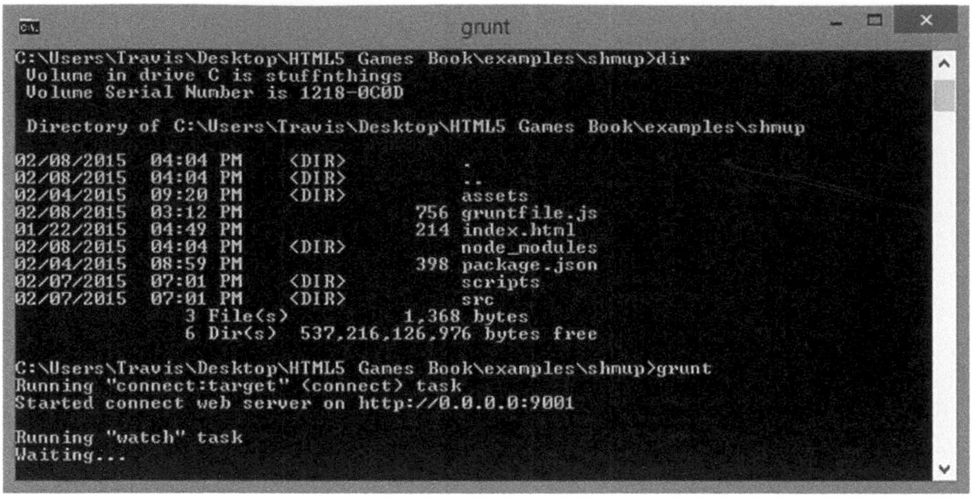

FIG 4.4 Successfully running the watch task.

If everything is in order, you will see a message in the terminal indicating that Grunt is running a server and watching your files for changes. Here are a few steps to walk through in order to verify everything is set up as needed:

1. In the root of your project, make an index.html file. Fill it with this basic page markup:

```
<html>
    <head><title>Testing grunt</title></head>
    <body>
        <h1>It works!</h1>
    </body>
</html>
```

2. Type http://localhost:9001 in your browser's address bar and make sure you see that page returned to your browser.
3. Make two directories, src and scripts, in the same folder as index.html.
4. Inside of the src folder, add an app.js script. It should contain this code:

```
import SecondScript from "./Second.js";
```

5. Inside of the src folder, create Second.js script. It should contain this code:

```
export default alert("Browserify is working as
    intended.");
```

6. Save those scripts and refresh the browser page. You should see one of those annoying alerts pop up.
7. Open up scripts/app.js to see how browserify combines your different scripts into one (optional).

4.10 Installing Yeoman

Hopefully it is becoming rather apparent that a lot of work goes into the setup of these files to get a workflow configured. When it is time to start working on a new game, the process to create a new project based on this environment is less involved. One needs to copy over the file structure (sans the node_modules and bower_components folders) and run the commands "npm install" and "bower install" from the root of the project folder.

If even this is too much work, however, or playing the configuration game just isn't something you want to do and you skipped to here from the start of this chapter, there is a simpler way to get this particular directory structure setup (and many others). This simpler way is a tool is called Yeoman, which is a command line tool that will create project directories with build scripts and Node modules from simple prompts in your terminal. Yeoman is reliant on other people to a "template" for the project type you want to make. There is one template on the Yeoman templates directory that has been developed to recreate the structure outlined in this chapter, giving you a familiar base to use throughout the rest of this book.

Before using Yeoman, you will need to install a global tool.

```
npm install -g yo
```

Then, if you ever want a basic game structure as outlined in this chapter (and the next since this generator will set up the html for you as well), these three lines will ask a few questions and scaffold out a game application for you to use.

```
yo phaser-book-simple
npm install
bower install
```

Running the first line will download all the files for an empty game, set up the Grunt file, and put the package.json and bower.json files into the root directory. Next, npm install will fetch any of the packages that are specified in the package.json file as necessary for the project and install them. Bower install will get the frontend scripts, similar to npm install. Once both of these commands have been run, you are ready to get coding a new game with a minimum amount of setup time.

Phaser Yeoman Generators

There are a number of different generators for Phaser games—all take slightly different approaches to the basics for a game. While the approach in the book-simple generator works, it is a simple base that is intended to explain and illuminate the basics. It would not be a bad idea to see what else is available to scaffold out a basic game by heading to Yeoman's generator index at http://yeoman.io/generators/.

4.11 Conclusion

Setting up a development environment is not the easiest thing to tackle in JavaScript application development, but it does pay off in terms of faster development later on, more maintainable code, and code that is easily transferred and shared with others. The primary tool that enables all of this is Node was originally developed to make server-side applications in JavaScript, but it has turned into a multipurpose tool that no one can go without. Node will let the developer easily and quickly download new libraries of code and, in tandem with Grunt.js, run a number of tasks automatically that would otherwise take time out of development and production.

The next chapters will assume that this project structure is used as the base for all of the work, so be able to recreate it via copying files or through scaffolding the project out via Yeoman.

CHAPTER 5

Phaser Project Setup

Now that we have gotten through the trials of setting up a Grunt-based workflow, the next step is to get it fully structured and tested by making a simple game. In this chapter, we're going to walk through some of the basics of Phaser games using this build method and make a quick clicker game to make sure we've got it all set and ready to go.

To start, copy the files from the setup phase into a new folder, except for the node_modules folder. Open up a command prompt at the root of this folder and run "npm install" in order to get the Grunt files installed again. Again, if you're not too worried about learning about this setup, you can also use the Yeoman generator to quickly scaffold a new project by running "yo phaser-book-simple."

5.1 Setting Up the html

This project (and all subsequent projects) will only need one html file to run, named index.html. Go ahead and edit the index to look like this:

```html
<!DOCTYPE html>
<html>
<head>
    <title>Game Name</title>
</head>
<body>
    <div id="game"></div>
    <script src="scripts/phaser.js"></script>
    <script src="scripts/app.js"></script>
</body>
</html>
```

The only major addition is the `div` element with an `id` of game. This is where Phaser will place the canvas to render our game's graphics once it loads up properly. Unlike the previous game example, where all of the codes for the game were written on the page itself, this game and future ones will be complex enough that the code for the game will be pulled out into its own script file, app.js. This script file needs to be included after the Phaser library, or it will try to run without all the Phaser capabilities loaded, and won't get very far before it tries to do something it doesn't know how to do, eventually hitting an error and halting script execution.

5.2 App.js

Next, inside of src/app.js

```javascript
var game;

import Boot from "./states/Boot.js";
import Preload from "./states/Preload.js";
import Game from "./states/Game.js";

window.onload = function () {
        //hi
    game = new Phaser.Game(800, 600, Phaser.AUTO, 'game');
    game.state.add('boot', Boot);
    game.state.add('preload', Preload);
    game.state.add('game', Game);
    game.state.start('boot');
};
```

This bit of code is a little different from the first Phaser game in this book, taking a more robust, if more complex, approach to setting up a game. `Phaser.AUTO` is a separate way to specify the mode to render to the canvas. By default, it will render in 3D (using webGL) but will fall back to canvas if the device or browser it is running in cannot do hardware acceleration.

Second, there is an id ("game") specified in the last argument of the constructor call. This will tell Phaser to put the game into the div with that id, helping one position the game in the final rendered HTML via CSS. This is especially great for games that will be deployed to the web where the "box" the user views the game in needs to be positioned. Simply tell Phaser to put the game into that box, and then the box can be positioned with traditional techniques.

Perhaps the most jarring new addition is the states. In the first game example, one state was created and passed into the Phaser constructor because it was a fairly simple game. In this template, several states are included from other files (because they can get pretty long) and passed into Phaser's state manager. The grunt file will then at runtime go and fetch these states and include them in the final, compiled app.js file. Browserify loads its modules in a weird format, so to specify a folder beneath the current file, the path needs to start with a dot and navigate down from there (unlike the approach that HTML and CSS paths take, where the path would simply forgo the dot and slash and start with the folder name). Each of these files contain unique Phaser states with their own individual preload, create, and update methods.

5.2.1 Boot State

The boot state is the first state to run in this Phaser setup. This state is used to ready and prepare the app's base configuration, so the other states don't need to deal with application-wide concerns. Common tasks here include setting up the input method (is this a mouse-only game, or will it only work with one finger, or multiple), preparing resolution of the game, and determining how Phaser handles device rotation and rescaling.

```
export default class Boot {

  preload() {
    this.load.image('preloader', 'assets/images/
      loading_bar.png');
  }
  create() {
    this.game.input.maxPointers = 1;
    this.game.state.start('preload');
  }

}
```

This is a simple boot state that can be used to scaffold more complex ones later on. A single class is exposed from this file, which contains Phaser preload and create methods. The preload gets an image ready to show as the loading screen for the next state, the preloading state. Once that bar is loaded, the create method restricts this game to one finger or mouse interaction and moves onto the preload state. If you're looking to use multitouch interaction, removing or at least upping the number on the maximum pointers line will be necessary.

5.2.2 Preload State

The preload state is the state that runs while the game loads the assets needed to play and gives the user feedback on how much longer of a load time they will have (hopefully not too long, users can tend to be impatient).

```
export default class Preload {

  constructor() {
    this.asset = null;
    this.ready = false;
  }

  preload() {
    this.load.image('loading_bg', 'assets/images/
      loading_bg.jpg');
  }

  create() {

    //background for game
    this.add.sprite(0,0, "loading_bg");

    this.asset = this.add.sprite(this.game.
      width/2,this.game.height/2, 'preloader');
    this.asset.anchor.setTo(0.5, 0.5);

    this.load.onLoadComplete.addOnce(this.
      onLoadComplete, this);
    this.load.setPreloadSprite(this.asset);

    //do all your loading here
    //this.load.image('player', 'assets/images/
      player.png'); //width and height of sprite

    //staaaart load
    this.load.start();
  }

  update() {

    if(this.ready) {
      this.game.state.start('game');
    }

  }

  onLoadComplete() {
    this.ready = true;
  }

}
```

This state comes in three parts: starting the load in the create phase, showing feedback during the update phase, and changing to a new state once the load is complete.

This state also introduces another feature of Phaser: inside of a state, most parts of the Phaser core code can be accessed by simply referencing the state itself ("this"). In this state, all of the loading and game manipulation are done from "this" (the state) instead of navigating up to the game object via "this.game." Not everything is accessible through the state, but some of the key game objects are, such as the world, the display list, input, and the loader.

This state has a few properties that will be accessed throughout its different methods and need to be initialized before the state starts running. Any of these object-level properties that need to start off at a certain value can be set in the object's constructor method, which will run the moment the object is created. This state's two key properties are its preload asset (a bar that will change in size as the files load, giving users an indication that the application is still running and how complete the load is) and ready command (a Boolean variable that will flip to "true" when the game is ready to go).

Because this is the first time we are using states, it is important to note that actions taken in previous states can affect the current state. In this current preloading state, a background is added and then a loaderbar is placed on top of the background. Nowhere in this state is there any code to load up bar graphic. The loading of the bar happened on the previous state (boot). In other words, it is possible to load assets in one state and use them in another. Phaser's asset cache is not cleared between states. In fact, that is just the purpose of the preload state. It is going to load in all the assets before moving on to the game proper.

Why Preload Assets

Everyone hates preloaders. They're a pain to write and they take up the user's time when they just want to get to gameplay. At their worst, the loaders take too long and the players leave before they can even get to the game itself. Wouldn't it just be great to start the game and load in assets as needed? Unfortunately, this would result in chugging gameplay. Imagine you are playing a game and the big boss is about to come in and the game has to halt to load up the boss. Players would not be happy at all. Essentially, everything for a section of gameplay needs to be ready the moment the game begins, or there will be slowdowns and halts as the game takes the time to fetch what it needs to play.

> **Dealing with Large Load Times**
>
> Large load times can be dealt with in two ways: asset optimization and loading in stages. When working on the web, it is that assets are optimized for the smallest size possible. Some techniques for optimization will be covered later (such as image atlases), others include understanding the different file formats and choosing the right format and image size for the right place.
>
> Another approach to loading is to not load in all the assets for the game at the very start of the game. Instead, only the assets needed to get into the first stage or menu are loaded (and maybe some of the bigger items that can be put into a first, longer load). Then, as the user moves into different parts of the game, they will encounter shorter load screens where a few more assets are loaded for specifically that stage. This gets the player into the action faster, but does put little pauses into the gameplay that the players might find jarring, depending on the game.

The Phaser load system has a number of signals that will fire throughout the loading process, but the one that the preload state most needs to respond to is the moment all of the assets have completed their loading. An `onLoadComplete` signal is set up to run a function (only once) when the assets are fully loaded. All this handler does is toggle the load ready to `true`, letting the `update` function handle the actual transition of states.

Perhaps the most important part of this state is the preload asset, which is the bar that will scale as the assets are loaded in. Phaser will handle this scaling automatically if the asset is set as a loader sprite, making it start at an x scale of zero and progress to a scale of one, based on the percentage of data currently loaded compared to how much needs to be loaded in total. For instance, if two megabytes of data needs to be loaded in this state and one megabyte has been currently loaded, this asset will have a current scale of .5, making it appear half its full width.

The next part of this state is the essential part of the state that will be edited in later games. Here, all of the assets for the game are loaded via Phaser's load object. Among the items that can be loaded are sprite sheets, audio, tilemap files, physics data, and pure text. All of these assets are queued up via the load object, and the loading is started via `this.load.start`. Once all of the assets are loaded, the load system will fire the `onLoadComplete` signal and the ready property will be set to `true`. Inside the `update` function, when the ready variable is `true`, the next state (game) is then started.

With the boot state and preload state complete, the game is ready to run. This is the end of some of the common "boilerplate" stuff that will appear in just about every game. Next is the more challenging part of actually making a game someone wants to play.

5.3 Testing the Setup with a Simple Game

To get a feel for this setup, let's take a moment to go through and make a cloud busting game (Figure 5.1). It is going to be a simple game that pops some clouds up in front of the player, which they need to tap or click to make them go away. This is a sort of whack-a-mole but with a less annoying theme. This will take us through the process of loading in images and then using the assets inside the game state.

5.3.1 Before Starting Development

The development of this game and the future games discussed in this book, which are based on the ECMAScript modules and classes, are reliant on the Grunt script to be running at all times during development. Before writing any of this code, open up a command prompt at your project root and type "grunt." This will prepare your project to automatically compile all your code changes, give feedback on any coding errors encountered, and will let you see the game in a web browser at http://localhost:90001.

5.3.2 Getting and Loading the Assets

To begin, grab the assets at https://github.com/meanderingleaf/ PhaserBookExamples/tree/master/CloudClicker2024/assets/images and move the files into the /assets/images folder of this project (make the folder if you need to, of course).

Returning to the preload state, where the state mentions to "do all your preloading here," add these two lines to load the assets for the game.

```
this.load.image('cloud', 'assets/images/cloud.png');
this.load.image('game_bg', 'assets/images/
  game_bg.jpg');
```

FIG 5.1 Screenshot of the final busting game.

5.3.3 Writing the Gameplay

Moving to the Game.js file, let's fill in some basic game code to get a fully working game out of this setup. This cloud busting game will create cloud sprites at random places on the screen. When the user taps on a cloud, it will be removed from the screen, giving the user an increase in their score. This will be the first time that object pooling will be used in one of our games as well, so a working implementation of a pool in a game will be implemented.

```
export default class Game {
    create() {
        this.add.sprite(0,0,"game_bg");
        this.clouds = this.add.group();

        this.score = 0;
        var style = { font: "24px Arial", fill:
            "#FFFFFF" };
        this.txtScore = this.add.text(10,10,this.score.
            toString(), style);
    }
    update() {
    if(Math.random() < .01) {
        var cloud = this.clouds.getFirstDead();
        if(cloud) {
            cloud.x = Math.random() * this.game.
                width;
            cloud.y = Math.random() * this.game.
                height;
            cloud.revive();
        } else {
            var cloud = this.clouds.create(Math.
                random() * this.game.width, Math.
                random() * this.game.height, "cloud");
            cloud.inputEnabled = true;
            cloud.events.onInputDown.add(this.
                onCloudClick, this);
        }

        cloud.alpha = 0;
        this.add.tween(cloud).to({ y: "-50", alpha:
            1 }, 800, Phaser.Easing.Cubic.Out, true);
      }
    }
    onCloudClick(cloud) {
        cloud.kill();
        this.score ++;
        this.txtScore.setText(this.score.toString());
    }
}
```

This game will have three state-level variables that will be used throughout the state: clouds, score, and txtScore. While there is no place to denote this in the code, keep them in mind as we work throughout the code. These state-level variables are set in the create function.

```
this.add.sprite(0,0,"game_bg");
this.clouds = this.add.group();

this.score = 0;
var style = { font: "24px Arial", fill: "#FFFFFF" };
this.txtScore = this.add.text(10,10,this.score.
  toString(), style);
```

There's not a lot new going on in the create function code. A background sprite is added to the game to give some grounding and context to the game, and the score is set up both through the numerical score and the score text field. Also, a group is added to the display list to manage all the clouds. This is the group all the clouds will be added into and will also be used to pool the clouds, so no more clouds are created than needed.

Moving onto the update method that will implement the gameplay of randomly popping up clouds.

```
update() {
    if(Math.random() < .01) {
        var cloud = this.clouds.getFirstDead();
        if(cloud) {
            cloud.x = Math.random() * this.game.
              width;
            cloud.y = Math.random() * this.game.
              height;
            cloud.revive();
    } else {
        var cloud = this.clouds.create(Math.
          random() * this.game.width, Math.
          random() * this.game.height, "cloud");
        cloud.inputEnabled = true;
        cloud.events.onInputDown.add(this.
          onCloudClick, this);
    }

    cloud.alpha = 0;
    this.add.tween(cloud).to({ y: "-50", alpha:
      1 }, 800, Phaser.Easing.Cubic.Out, true);
    }
  }
```

The gameplay starts with some simple chance-based code to run the rest of the instructions. Math.random() will return a number between zero and one, with the numbers nearer to one and zero being less likely. This if statement, checking for a Math.random() <.01, will trigger fairly infrequently. Then, using a feature of the Phaser's group, we first check to see if there is a cloud that is in the group but not alive (or currently active in the game). If there is a dead cloud, instead of making a new game object, the dead cloud is moved to a new location and revived. This saves program memory space—there will never be more clouds than needed for the game to run, and the game will not be collecting a bunch of "dead" clouds in memory that are unused.

Chance Roll

If `Math.random()` < (someChance) is too obscure or verbose for you, Phaser has a built-in feature that does about the same thing: chance roll. A line of `phaser.utils.chanceRoll(1)` will accomplish the same task as the `Math.random()` approach.

Next we'll create the update method that will create the randomly appearing clouds. Instead of using Phaser's `add.sprite` method that would add it to the display list root, the new cloud is added to the clouds group (thus putting it in a space where it can be easily recycled once it is dead). By default, sprites do not receive user input, so it is enabled for input that allows it to receive mouse events such as `onInputDown` (a tap or click depending on the context). The only important thing to note with this signal is the second part of the argument, the word "`this`." Function contexts are notoriously difficult to deal with in Javascript, and this is Phaser's way to being explicit about the context in which the function should run. Even though the function exists in the "game" state, the function itself can be run "on" any object. Oftentimes, this object is not what one wants it to be like the document root (giving one access only to very-high-level variables, like the "game" variable in app.js), or it might also run on the cloud clicked (so the developer would be able to change the clouds properties, but nothing else). It would be very hard to get access to the score or score text from the cloud object or the document object, so by passing "this" as the second argument, the context for the handler will be the game state, giving the function onCloudClick access to all the other properties that we have been working with in this file.

Finally, after the cloud is created (or revived), as an additional bit of flair, the cloud is animated into view, starting at invisible and ending up fully opaque. This is done via Phaser's tween engine. Setting its alpha to zero, the tween then fades the cloud into fully visible over the span of 800 ms (millisecond). While that would look okay, a second argument in the tween, y, is given a textual argument. If a tween receives a textual argument, it will treat those numbers as a relative value and apply the motion starting from where it currently is located. This relative animation with tween will take the cloud's current position and make it move 50 pixels upward. It is a small effect but brings a bit of motion to call attention to the new clouds and can feel quite slick to the user.

Almost always add some sort of easing to a tween for a more natural look, save for those rare instances you are trying to recreate mechanical motion. An ease out will make the motion fast at the start and slows to a stop. It is great bringing things into view, which is precisely what we needed here.

The last method needed to finish this game is the cloud click handler.

```
onCloudClick(cloud) {
    cloud.kill();
    this.score ++;
    this.txtScore.setText(this.score.toString());
}
```

When a cloud is clicked, both the numerical and textual scores need to be updated. Numerical first, and then show that amount in the text on the screen.

Additionally, this is the end of that particular cloud for now. Since the click handler knows what cloud was clicked, calling `cloud.kill()` will take it out of the game for now. When there is an object in the game that needs to go away and not be running its `update` function, colliding with other objects, or being visible, the kill method is the appropriate choice. This keeps the object around in memory, but functionally it is not in the game until it is revived again. Once this method runs, the user will get a point, the clicked cloud will disappear, and that's the code for this game.

Head over to localhost:9001 and check on the game. There should be clouds appearing at random on the page, and, when clicked, they disappear. It is not a first person shooter, but there might be a bit of fun to be had there.

CHAPTER 6

Phaser Principles

All game engines offer a set of capabilities to the developer who chooses to use it. In fact, it is often these capabilities that make someone choose to use one engine over another. One of the great things about Phaser is simply that it is so full featured, with lots of great features ready right out of the box and others available via plug-ins. The features that make up Phaser result in quite a large system what is thankfully well documented at phaser.io/examples and phaser.io/docs. The size and complexity of a framework is always a blessing and a curse. While it is great that the framework can do so much, it also means that a developer needs to understand what the framework offers, how it works, and the limits of the technology before they can delve in and start working.

The purpose of this chapter is to explain the different parts of Phaser to give an overview of how the engine works and that is, in general, possible with it. This chapter contains source code where needed to help explain the ideas or establish snippets that can be referenced for when you sit down to write your own game later on. This is not an exhaustive list of what Phaser is capable of, and it is highly encouraged that you take some time later on looking over at the very least the example area of the live Phaser site to find more capabilities and code snippets that you can work into your own games.

6.1 Game Loop

The first thing to understand about a game engine (and this will be true of nearly any game engine) is the game loop that runs the whole game. In order for a player to perceive the motion in a game as smooth and uninterrupted, a game needs to run some code ideally 30 times a second, though it can dip to around 20 and still be passable. Not only does the code that runs all of the game need to execute tens of times a second but also it needs to do it reliably each time the update runs. If something happens during a time it is executing that takes very long, then there will be less time for the next frames to run, and the number of frames rendered in that second will be reduced (often called a frame drop). To get a function that runs reliably that many times a second is a bit of an adventure.

In the early days, a game loop was beautifully simple. It would create a block of code that would run forever (a `while(true)` doing the trick of never stopping). Inside that code block, the game would run through three major concerns of a game engine: getting input from the user, updating the game state, and rendering the result of the two previous steps to the screen. The input method will get whatever the user is currently doing with their interface devices, notably mice and keyboards, but items like controllers or remotes fall into this category as well. Updating the game state is where all the gameplay itself is implemented. Images are moved around, audio is triggered to play, and collisions are processed in the update method. Finally, the render method clears the entire screen and redraws every single visible element in the game. With the following approach, all this happens as fast as possible with the goal of hitting or exceeding the 30 frames/s mark.

```
while(true) {
    getInput();
    updateLogic();
    render();
}
```

While quick and easy to create, this simple loop comes with two flaws. First, the code would slow down if too much computation was done inside it. More code, complex algorithms, or just poor programming meant a slower loop and less frames per second. The second issue with this approach was that in the past the speed of the game was dependent on the speed of the processor running it. Games that were programmed for old computers that were "state of the art" in their days quickly began speeding up on later computers that became significantly faster as Moore's law held true and processors doubled in speed every 2 years. Games quickly became unplayable as they were processing at warp speed (relatively speaking).

The solution to the problem of a very fast update was to force a game to wait until it is ready for the next update by having the computer pause processing time until a certain fraction of a second has passed. This will not address the opposite speed issue of a slow game that is taking too long per game loop. The fix to this issue is to store the time elapsed since the last update and run the logical updates as often as needed to catch up to the current time. This "catch up" process occurs in between a full loop. So the game will get input once, run several times to update just the logic, and then render once. A slow machine might need to update the game logic a few times to catch up, while faster one will have to do it less, getting closer to the ideal of just one logic update per full game loop.

It is important to remember that the rendering and logical updates do not occur at the same time, or even in lockstep. It is entirely possible to process updates for the game without rendering those updates, and this can sometimes be very useful for the game to get everything "set up and settled," such as in a physics-based game. Movements and other updates may also be different between the update and rendering. When moving an object five pixels to the right per update, that is not the same thing as moving it five pixels per frame render. It actually may move further based on the number of logic updates that occur before rendering.

6.1.1 Logic Update Step

The logic update step is where the code that implements all the gameplay is run. This method is actually two that are run in order for each update: preupdate and update. During the preupdate phase, everything is cleaned up and prepared for updating, but no actual gameplay code is run. Once everything is ready for an update, Phaser will then run the current state's update method, move positions of elements on the stage, run physics calculations, update any particle systems that are currently running, and do a few other miscellaneous tasks for the game to keep running.

The state's update method is where the developer's work comes in. This is where they will handle what to do with the input, how to move objects, when to trigger animations, and whatever else goes into the uniqueness of their game. Every game object also has the potential to run its own individual update function if the developer defines a unique function for it. Individual update functions are great for objects that need to do something more unique to itself, like AI calculations or individual state management (for instance, a door might need to close itself in a spooky game). If you want to create objects that implement their own specialized update functions, they need to extend from the Phaser classes, so Phaser can discover the update methods and work with the classes. Examples of this approach are discussed in section "Phaser Principles." The combined updates of the state and its individual objects make each game unique. The code that goes into an update for a side-scrolling platformer is going to be vastly different from the code for a match three game.

So long as the game is not paused, Phaser will run through each of these methods for each logic step update. The following is a list of all the methods that Phaser runs in order to process an update. Note the three phases (pre update, update, and post update). First, the developer's gameplay code is run (in `state.update()`) and then the Phaser system does the rest of the work of the game engine automatically. All of this happens behind the scenes and doesn't often need to be tampered with, but it is good to know the order things are happening in the game.

```
this.debug.preUpdate();
this.world.camera.preUpdate();
this.physics.preUpdate();
this.state.preUpdate(timeStep);
this.plugins.preUpdate(timeStep);
this.stage.preUpdate();

this.state.update();
this.stage.update();
this.tweens.update(timeStep);
this.sound.update();
this.input.update();
this.physics.update();
this.particles.update();
this.plugins.update();

this.stage.postUpdate();
this.plugins.postUpdate();
```

6.2 States

All of the custom game logic that makes your game unique is placed inside a state. States bundle up a series of methods that help get the program into and potentially out of a section of gameplay. A basic game that only has one section of gameplay or interaction will only have one state, but the real power of states comes when making multiple different states and transitioning between them to take the user through the sections of a game. Common uses for different states include creating title screens that transition to gameplay or different levels within a game. They are especially useful for games that have different types of gameplay on different stages, like a flying stage followed by an underwater stage. States give Phaser the ability to turn these very different sections of gameplay into separate chunks of code that can be more easily and logically managed.

Phaser states are actually an implementation of a programming structure called a "finite-state machine" (FSM). Due to their nature as FSMs, Phaser will run the methods inside the state in a specific order, starting with the preload, staying on the update method, and calling a final cleanup function if you need to transfer to another state. Phaser will call these methods automatically just like how it automatically calls the current state's update to run the unique gameplay for a game. Before delving deeper into the particularities of Phaser's states, we will discuss some background on how state machines work and their particular uses will help to trying to hook up these different states in the game.

6.2.1 Finite-State Machines

The goal of an FSM is to create a series of different unique modes that a program can be in. These states are "finite" in the sense that, at any one time, only one of the states can be currently active or running in the game. The state machine is a construct that is made to ensure that only one state is ever running and enables the smooth transitions between states. Transitions between states happen by shutting down the current state (letting it destroy things or do last-minute saves before it stops running) and turning that state off. Once the old state is shut down, a new state is started letting it go through its setup phase. Then this new state will run its update method in tandem with the game update until it is shut down for a transition.

A workday is a good example of different states and the transitions between them. Many people start off their workday at home, where they wake up and work around the house. This could be thought as a "preparation" state. Next comes the commute, often via car, which is a "driving" state. Next comes the actual work and its associated "working" state. Each of these states do not overlap, at least not in our idealized world here. When the employee is driving, they are simply driving. That said, there is clearly an amount of time between each state, such as the time the worker takes to leave the house and get into their car. Doors have to be opened, houses left, keys found. This bit of putting away the items needed for one state and getting moving to where the new state takes place can also be viewed as a *transition between states*. These transitions come in two parts: finishing the old state and starting the new one. In the case of transitioning to the commuting state, the house needs to be exited and locked, closing off the "preparation" state. Next the car needs to be opened, entered, and turned on, starting the "driving" state. The combination of the shutdown and setup methods becomes that transition between the meatier update loops of the state.

Phaser's states work in the exact same way. Once a particular state is running, its update loop will handle all of the game concerns. The game has a few methods for changing from state to state, which will automatically call the functions on the current state to wrap up the state's concerns properly and then create and set up a new state to get it running.

Other Finite-State Machines

Another great place to see FSMs in action are the animations inside of video games, where one animation needs to complete before another can begin. Fighting games are a great example of the application of FSMs. When controlling a fighting game character, only one "attack" animation of that character can be active at a given time. Once a character's attack animation has been triggered and started, it will play through its animation timeline and then transition once the attack state is over. The transition can be to an idle state, or in the case of combos, might be to another animation so long as the chain of input is valid. The restriction of potential moves based on the current state of an object is actually another great use of FSMs and can be applied to great effect in your own games with a bit of work and attention.

6.2.2 Creating a Phaser State

Phaser states are just objects with specifically named functions that the game engine will know to call. This state object below has all of the methods attached to it that Phaser will call automatically in a state's lifespan. An example of a basic state is as follows:

```
var sampleState = {
    init: function() {
        //do any setup needed before the state
            begins to run
    },
    preload: function() {
        //load in assets needed for the game
    },
    create: function() {
        //setup the state with game objects
    },
    update: function() {
        //specific game code
    },
    shutdown: function() {
        //last minute considerations before the
            state is over
    }
}
```

6.2.3 Phaser State Flow

When a new Phaser state is created, either in a transition from one to another or as the first and only state in the game (as is the case in the simple example in this book), the state will run the init, preload, and create methods before the update loop begins it cycle. In the case of update and preload, the state will actually run two functions in order to complete those parts of the state flow (see Figure 6.1).

To start with, the state will run any "init" method it has. This method can come in handy if there is some setup that needs to be done before any of the other concerns of the state are handled. The next function, "preload," is used to load in assets that this and future states may need. Because preload may take some time, Phaser actually runs a simple game loop while assets load, giving the developer access to a "load update" and "load render" functions to update the user on game loading progress (typically through the use of a loader bar or displaying the percentage of assets loaded). Once the loading is complete, the "create" method is executed, giving the developer a chance to initialize and set the stage up for gameplay.

The meat of a Phaser state comes in its implementation of the game loop. There are two methods that are called while the game loop is

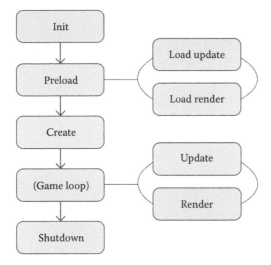

FIG 6.1 The Phaser state stages.

running: "update" and "render." The update method is run first and is the method where the majority of gameplay is implemented. The render method, contrary to the implications of the name, is actually run after the game has rendered (drawn to the screen) all the visible objects. This can be used for any post-render effects like blur and color correction.

The final part of Phaser's state flow is the "shutdown" method. This is called before the current state object is destroyed and a new one takes its place in the state transition. The shutdown method is great for saving data that need to persist from one state to the next or handling any complex destructions that need to take place before the state can be safely forgotten.

6.3 Display List

A great place to start with when it comes to any game engine is to understand how the graphics are rendered to the screen. Phaser (and most two-dimensional [2D] graphical systems) approaches the challenge of drawing graphics to the screen using a method called a "display list." The display list is essentially an array of objects to be drawn to the screen. In order to show updated positions and graphics, the screen is cleared every frame (typically around 30 times a second), and the graphics in the display list are painted into the visible screen area each time after the clearing of the frame data.

The order that the graphics in the display list are drawn to the screen is based on their position in the display list array. Graphics near the start of the array are drawn first (so a graphic at index zero will be the furthest back, great for backgrounds), and the last graphic in the array will be drawn on top of the others. If two objects would overlap visually in the display list, it is the one higher up in the list that will appear "on top" of the other object. Phaser has a basic display list built into the root of the game (see Figure 6.2).

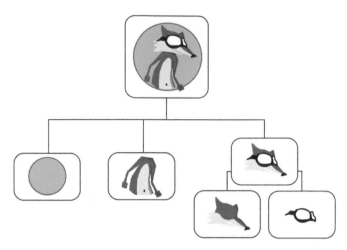

FIG 6.2 The display list.

The order that graphics are added to the display list affects their position in the backing array. Whenever you see a call to `game.add.sprite` or `game.add.group` methods, it is adding a new object to the back of the display list, putting it on top of the other graphics in the list. If something needs to be near the back of the game (like a background for a game), then it should be the first item added in your game before all the other graphics.

To make things even more complex, many objects in Phaser can have their own display lists. When Phaser encounters a group or object with a sub-display list, it will go and render all the objects in that sub-display list in the same order (first to last). The display list will render all the objects in this group before moving onto the next graphic (see Figure 6.2). The result is a sort of branching structure for the list, with many objects containing multiple graphics and lists of their own that are rendered for their bit of the display list algorithm.

6.4 The World

The game world is the space where all the game objects inhabit. This world has a width and height where objects can exist in, which is originally set mirror the visible size of the window into the game. If game objects are moved outside the size of the world, the game will stop processing them and some pretty strange bugs can occur, so it is best to make sure the world is set to a size you know is big enough for your game. If the game is set to be 800 × 600 pixels, then the world will be 800 × 600 units big, and objects can move freely about in that space.

The world does not have to just be the size of the screen. Imagine a Mario game where the entire stage was visible the moment it loaded up. Beyond the simple reaction of "but that's just Donkey Kong," it would also be a fairly boring game of Mario. Instead, the Mario stage (its "world") stretches far to the right. For many games, a world will need to be resized to fit the actual world of your game, only some of which will be visible to the player at any given point during gameplay.

If a bigger world is needed, two methods need to be called to resize your game's world space. These two methods are setBounds and resize. Resize will increase the width and height of the game, but not in the negative direction (up and left). The command setBounds is similar; however, it will allow the game (camera, physics, and thus game objects) to move negatively as well.

6.5 Camera

If the game world is now bigger than the window looking into it, there needs to be some way for Phaser to know from what position of the world it should currently be rendering objects. This object is called a camera (a term borrowed from 3D game engines where the camera does more camera-like things). Phaser's camera has x and y positions in world space that can be moved manually to look about the graphics in the world.

In lieu of manually changing the camera's position, quite often the camera is given an object in the game world to follow automatically by using the camera's follow method. By default, a camera that is following an object will mirror the x and y changes of the object it is following perfectly. A five-pixel move to the left for the target object would mean a five-pixel move to the left for the camera, letting the user see more of the world to the left (see Figure 6.3).

A one-to-one movement ratio can get pretty jumpy, moving everything around on the screen even when the player makes tiny motions. The chance

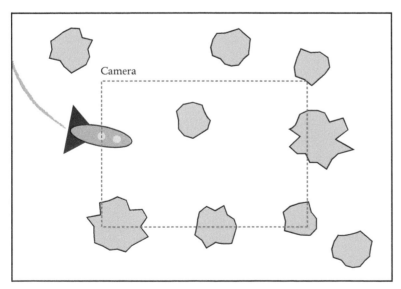

FIG 6.3 Game world.

for a bit of motion sickness to kick in for the player is can be strong because of all of these tiny little motions. In order to mitigate the amount of time the camera spends moving (and making the movements themselves less jumpy), there are other follow styles that will make the camera a little less jarring and work more naturally. There are three follow styles (topdown, topdown tight, and platformer) and they work by defining a "dead zone," or part of the screen where movement within the screen area will not cause the camera to move until the player has passed the bounds of the dead zone. Because any movement inside the dead zone doesn't move the camera, it keeps the view into the world steady for longer periods of time and gives the player some space where they can explore without having the camera follow their every little move.

6.6 Loading and the Asset Cache

When Phaser starts in the web page, it doesn't have any of the assets that it needs to run the game. All of the images, sounds, map files, physics descriptions, or other miscellaneous files needed for the game need to be loaded into the engine before gameplay can begin. Phaser has a robust loading engine that allows a game developer to load in a number of different assets and gives the game access to the asset later on via Phaser's asset cache.

Technically assets can be loaded at any point during the game, though it makes the most sense to load them before the game begins to run during the game's preload phase. There are a few instances when it might be acceptable to break the loading up across the game, notably if the game has a series of asset-heavy stages where a bit of loading time in between each level is acceptable (so long as the stages themselves provide a decent amount of gameplay).

6.6.1 Asset Cache

During loading, it is important to note the first argument which is a string name. This argument is the asset's key of asset and must be unique. When Phaser finishes loading the asset, it will place it into the asset cache with that string as the key used to access it. The asset cache will store all the objects loaded into Phaser throughout the lifetime of the game and will persist throughout the whole game session, so changing states or resetting the gameplay will not remove all the assets in the cache. Later on, when an asset is needed, the key that was specified will need to be provided to the game object creation method (technically an object factory), so it can correctly look it up. In the following code sample, note how the key ("cat," in this case) for the image loaded and the sprite displayed are the same:

```
function preload() {
    game.load.image('cat', 'img/cat.png');
}

function create() {
    game.add.sprite( 0, 0, "cat");
}
```

6.6.2 Displaying Load Progress

Because the assets that go into a game can often be quite large and may take a bit of time to load into the game, it is important to give users feedback on the status of the load time while they wait. While it won't keep everyone around, if a user knows that the system is still working and the loading is done soon, they are more likely to wait around during the preparatory time. The feedback is typically accomplished with a graphic that is scaled from an invisible 0% loaded to 100% as the percentage of loaded graphics increases (often called a "loading bar" because it is commonly of a long, bar shape).

Phaser has a built-in support for the most basic type of loading bar that was described earlier and it can be implemented with this line of code.

```
this.load.setPreloadSprite(someBarlikeImage);
```

When working in this way, one will need to know when all of the assets are loaded into the game, so the loader bar asset can be removed from display list or the current state switched to a game state. The loader class has a set of signals (discussed later in this chapter) that it will fire during different stages of the load including the start of a load, each time more data have been loaded, and when the loading is done. The following code makes use of the `onLoadComplete` signal to run a function entitled "onLoadComplete" when the loading is done. The function "onLoadComplete" can then do whatever is needed to set up the game, typically by switching to a new game state that will make use of all the assets that are now ready to be used.

```
this.load.onLoadComplete.addOnce(this.onLoadComplete,
  this);
this.load.start();
```

The final line of `load.start()` must be in if you plan to use the loading events. This line tells Phaser that the loading has begun and to start firing the other signals as the loading progresses.

6.6.3 Preloading Phase

Note that in the aforementioned code sample the loading of the image was started in a function named "preload." All of the preloading of assets must come inside of this function, and it makes good practice to keep the preload code bundled close to each other so you can easily reference the different keys of your game assets when loading them from the cache later on.

As this chapter discusses the different game objects you are able to make, some might require preloading. The code that you see in the discussion of loading these game objects should always come in the preload method.

6.7 Images

Graphics are the basis of most games and the most basic way to get a graphic into the game is through an image. In Phaser, images are static visual data that cannot have frames of animation but they can be moved around on the screen, rotated.

6.7.1 Loading an Image

Loading images couldn't be easier. All one needs to do is provide the path to the image file (preferably one of the major image files of the web: GIF, PNG, or JPG) and specify the key for the image to be accessed at later on. This bit of code loads in a duck image that can be created with the key of "ducky" via a game.add.sprite or game.add.image.

```
game.load.image('ducky', 'assets/sprites/ducky.png');
```

6.7.2 Adding an Image into the Game

The first way to get an image into the game is through the Phaser image type. This is a barebones image file. While it can still do all the things one expects an image to be able to do, such as transform its size and receive input, it cannot animate nor be added to the physics system. It is just an image. When adding images, a screen position for the image is first supplied, followed by the key of the asset to show as the sprite.

```
game.add.image(20, 10, "ducky");
```

6.8 Sprites

Sprites are the primary way to put the "video" into "video game" by adding (typically animated) graphics into the world. They can be static images like the aforementioned image type, but they can additionally be animated and added to the physics system. It is possible to load in image assets into Phaser as static images, sprite sheets, or sprite atlases. Each has their own uses and best practices.

What Image Format

When saving sprites for use in Phaser, it is important to save them as either a png or a gif image. Both of these image formats are called lossless formats, which means that no image data is lost when saving the images. Image data that is lost often results in blurry images or pixels that don't quite match the original image.

Equally important is that both of these formats have an alpha (or "see-through") channel that lets the sprites not be entirely square. When saving an image, always make sure that the transparency is also exported. An added benefit of saving to the png format is that the pixels on a sprite can have partial transparency, which can be used for effects like tinted windows or glasses.

6.8.1 Loading and Using Static Sprites

The process to load a static, non-animated sprite is the same as that for an image.

```
game.load.image('ducky', 'assets/sprites/ducky.png');
```

However, when adding the image to the game, add it as the sprite type instead. This will add a sprite at the coordinates specified, but unlike an image, these sprites can be added to the physics system.

```
var sprite = game.add.sprite(20, 10, "ducky");
```

6.8.2 Sprite Sheets

Sprite sheets are the way to get animation into a sprite. Each frame of the animation will need to be laid out in an image and then loaded in. These animation frames will then be used in animation timelines that you will need to write for each sprite. Phaser makes the assumption that the different frames of a sprite's animation are laid out in a horizontal format, and that each frame takes up the same width and height. These are the traditional sprite sheets that are common to find out on the Internet and fairly easy to make. See Figure 6.4.

6.8.2.1 Sprite Sheet Layout

Sprites in Phaser have a set width and height. By default, Phaser will make frames out of every rectangle that the height and width can fit in the image, starting from the top left corner and fitting in as many sprites as it can horizontally. If it hits the right edge of the image and there is enough space to fit in another row of frames beneath, it will return to the left and start a new row of frames, moving until there is no space either vertically or horizontally. See Figure 6.5.

FIG 6.4 Example of a sprite sheet layout with two rows.

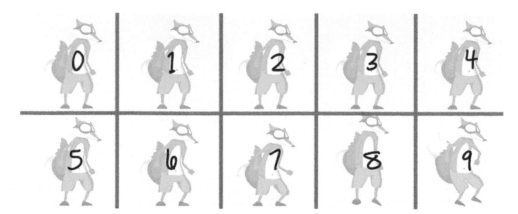

FIG 6.5 Frame numbers associated with each sprite frame.

6.8.2.2 Loading a Sprite Sheet

Once you have a sprite sheet laid out in the proper format, Phaser's load command needs to know the width height of the sprite's frames. If the image contains more white space than it has actual sprite content, the final argument can specify how many frames to load in total.

This load will create a sprite called Marella that has each frame of animation set to be 16 × 32 pixels tall, with 12 frames of animation.

```
game.load.spritesheet('Marella', 'assets/sprites/
    Marella.png', 16, 32, 12);
```

6.8.2.3 Specifying the Frames of a Sprite's Animation

Adding animations is done via the animations property of a sprite. An animation can be added with either all the fames or only specific frames. With each of the following lines of code, a new animation will be added to the sprite with the name that is specified as the first argument ("idle" and "jump"). Just like with the keys used in the asset cache, these names will be important for playing the animations later.

In order to add an animation that contains every frame in a loaded sprite sheet, add the animation with only a name and no other arguments.

```
spriteName.animations.add('idle');
```

More commonly, one will add specific frames to an animation. This is done by passing an array of the frames that compose the animation as the second argument:

```
spriteName.animations.add('jump', [0,2,4,5]);
```

6.8.2.4 Playing an Animation

After an animation has been added to any sprite, it is possible to play the animation via the play method. When calling the method, one needs to specify the name of the animation, the frame rate to play, and whether its animation loops (returns to the start and plays again once it finishes) or is a one shot (plays once and then stops). The frame rate is specified in frames per second, so higher number equals faster animation times.

This line will play the idle animation at 10 frames/s (which is a decently fast animation time). The true at the end will force it to loop, so assuming the idle animation is a little breathing clip, the sprite will breathe forever until another animation is triggered.

```
spriteName.animations.play('idle', 10, true);
```

6.8.3 Fixed to Camera

By default, when a sprite is added into the game, it is added into the game world itself. If the game camera moves, the sprite will move as if it is positioned inside the world. This means that a big enough move of the camera will result in the sprite no longer being visible on screen. Great for most objects, but not really all that preferable for user interface (UI) objects, which should not scroll away when the camera gets to moving.

For UI objects like heart bars, text, or power meters, fixing them to the camera's motion is the way to go.

```
someSprite.fixedToCamera = true;
```

6.9 Texture Atlases

Texture atlases are another approach to placing several different frames of an animation (or even different images altogether) into a single, larger image. The major difference from sprite sheets is that these images can be of different widths and heights and may be laid out in a manner that saves overall image space.

Because the frames of the images in an atlas are not a standard width and height, they will come with a second data file that describes the frames that are present in the image and how to extract that frame's data from the image. The frames are typically described via the upper left corner of a frame and the width and height of that frame. Once loaded, it is possible to use texture atlases either as frames of an animation or as static images. Either approach helps reduce the size and number of images that need to be loaded into the final game. See Figure 6.6.

6.9.1 Loading Atlases

In order to load an atlas, Phaser needs to be pointed toward an image and the data file that describe the frames inside the image. There are a number of different atlas data formats that Phaser supports, but this book will only be dealing with the JSON hash version. For your reference, here are the currently

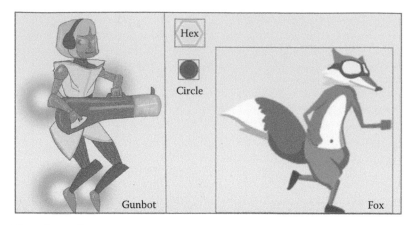

FIG 6.6 Texture atlas.

supported versions of hashes that Phaser can load and use. Take note that while the function names are different, the format of the function call is always the same. Each atlas load takes the key for the atlas, the path to the image, and the path to the atlas data.

The first format is the Starling atlas, typically used in conjunction with the Adobe Flash platform and exports from the Flash Professional animation tool.

```
game.load.atlasXML('penguins',
                    'assets/sprites/penguins.png',
                    'assets/sprites/penguins.xml'
                    );
```

A much more common export format for recent games is JSON, in part because it is a format used throughout the JavaScript world. Phaser can load in JSON atlases as arrays or as hashes. An atlas array will have different frames listed via array numbers (0, 1, 2, 3, and so on). The hash version of an atlas will have the frames listed by the string names of the different images in the hash ("red_apple," "blue_kangaroo," "buffalo"). In general, if given the choice, it is better to export and load the atlas as an array if you are planning to use it for animation and load in the atlas as a hash if you are going to use the individual images.

To load in a JSON array, use the atlasJSONArray method.

```
game.load. atlasJSONArray('penguins',
                    'assets/sprites/penguins.png',
                    'assets/sprites/penguins.json'
                    );
```

Alternatively, if the atlas has been saved as a hash, use atlasJSONHash method.

```
game.load.atlasJSONHash('penguins',
                    'assets/sprites/penguins.png',
                    'assets/sprites/penguins.json'
                    );
```

6.10 Tile Sprites

Sprites be hard to manage if you need a background to appear as it scrolls forever or wraps around the screen. Typically the solution to this problem is to create a series of sprites and move them all at the same rate as the background "scrolls." Once one of these sprites goes off screen and is no longer visible to the player, it is moved to the opposite side of the screen (just out of view), ready to move inward and appear again. Moving these chunks of background from one edge of the screen to the other can give the illusion of infinite scrolling. See Figure 6.7.

Tile sprites are a built-in object that handles the creation of all the smaller sprites and swapping. When creating a tile sprite, the first two arguments are the position and the last is the key of the image asset, just like with a normal sprite sheet. The middle two arguments are the width and height of the sprite, which make up the area that the sprite will take up and scroll across when moving its tile position.

```
game.add.tileSprite(0, 0, 500, 500, 'wasteland');
```

Because a tile sprite is still a sprite, the x and y properties will still move the position of the sprite in the world space. In order to move the scrolling position of the background of the tile sprite, one needs to change the x and y positions of a tile sprite's `tilePosition`.

For instance, this bit of code in a Phaser state will make the background of a tile sprite scroll to the left indefinitely.

```
function update() {
    gameBackground.tilePosition.x -= 5;
}
```

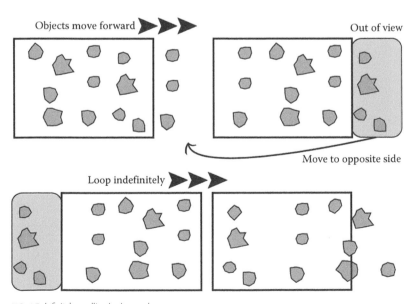

FIG 6.7 Infinitely scrolling background.

6.11 Input

Without input, a game wouldn't be all that fun to play. The player wouldn't be able to affect anything that was taking place in the simulation, which would lose that key feature of interactivity that makes games so engrossing. Phaser supports a wide array of different inputs, and if you need more, there is a chance there's a good JavaScript library out there that can help. The three types of input that Phaser supports are the keyboard, pointers (which are counted as both mice and touches), and gamepads (like XBOX controllers).

6.11.1 Keyboard

The keyboard is the most basic type of input an HTML5 game can have. It is easy to implement and everyone using a basic web browser on a desktop or laptop computer will have access to the keyboard. Using the keyboard will prevent your game from being played on mobile devices where access to the keyboard is nearly impossible when playing a game.

A key on a keyboard can either be up or down, though many game developers will also want to respond to the moment a key is pressed or released.

6.11.1.1 Testing if a Key Is Currently Depressed

Testing for a simple key down is great for games where a constantly depressed key is vital such as shooters where bullets need to be constantly flying, or a racing game where the acceleration is always on. The code for a key down test should always come inside of the update loop.

```
if (game.input.keyboard.isDown(Phaser.Keyboard.LEFT))
{
        //acceleration, fire bullets, anything else
          that needs a constant press
}
```

Why Not Use the Browser Keyboard Events?

Phaser abstracts away the keyboard events of the browser, so the game developer doesn't need to handle the built-in key repeating rate of the operating system. By default, the browser will claim the key is down when it is first depressed and then up for a few moments before kicking in the repeat of the key until the finger is finally lifted. You can test out the repeat rate on your keyboard by opening up a text document and just holding down a key. Note that there is a moment when, even though your finger is still resting on the key, no new characters are being added. This momentary "up" is a delay built into operating systems with no JavaScript API to disable it. Instead game engines create a system that listens only for the physical ups and downs, storing the state of the key for a developer to use in their game without the repeat pause.

6.11.1.2 Responding to Key Presses

A key press can be thought of as an event that occurs for the first frame when a user has pressed a key down. Since they are singular events that only repeat when a user triggers them again, they are usually used for the meat of a video game. Great examples of actions in games triggered by key presses are jumps, kicks, punches, and opening doors.

Phaser's key objects have signals that will fire on key down.

```
function create() {
        this.kickKey = game.input.keyboard.
            addKey(Phaser.Keyboard.SPACEBAR);
            this.kickKey.onDown.add(doKick, this);}
}

function doKick() {
        //this function will be called when the
            spacebar key is pressed
}
```

If you prefer to keep all your key event handling inside of an update function, it is also possible to check if a key was just pressed in a similar format to checking if it is down. The keys will need to be set up in the create function and then later checked inside the update function.

```
function create() {
        this.kickKey = game.input.keyboard.
            addKey(Phaser.Keyboard.SPACEBAR);
}

function update() {
        if (this.kickKey.justPressed(250))
        {
                //kick!
        }
}
```

Key Up Events

The key up is a lesser used key state but has its uses as well. Uses like a charge-up shot or a golfing meter that challenges the player to hold a key down until just the right time are great examples of the key up event. The cost of time tends to give these actions a bigger feeling of power to the player and can emphasize the importance of timing and patience over rapid key presses.

6.11.2 Pointers

As stated previously, the pointer input in Phaser works as either the mouse or as touch input on mobile devices. The number of pointers that Phaser can handle is limited only by the system that is running it, though Phaser has some build-in objects to get access to a few touch points quickly. Pointers have x and y positions on the world and a size of 44 pixels.

Phaser will use these values when checking for taps on buttons and other objects in the game.

Important pointer properties include the following:

- The **x** and **y** positions of the pointer on the screen
- The **movementX** and **movementY** properties that state how far the pointer moved since the last frame
- The `isDown` property that returns true if the user's finger is holding down the mouse button or is pressed to the screen

---

Don't Want Multitouch?

There is an option in the Phaser input manager named "maxPointers" that limits how many pointers Phaser will recognize. Setting this property to one will limit the number of pointers that will be followed to a single pointer. This removes the chance of multiple touch points and makes a game that can be controlled similarly by both a mouse and a single finger.

Just like keyboard keys, pointers can be either pressed or released, which can be used for watching for general input from the user. Unfortunately, currently Phaser does not have gestures built into the game system, but creative use of the down and up events can be used to implement gestures for a game (see the slicer game for an example of writing a simple gesture watcher).

If the game is set to just one pointer and the game is meant to target both mobile devices and traditional computers, always access the pointer input via `game.input.activePointer`. This will be either the mouse or the first (and only) pointer in the game.

The quickest way to access a pointer is via `game.input.activePointer`. This will work properly only on games that have a maximum of one pointer and will return the only active pointer in the game. If you need access to more than one pointer, you can get access to them via `game.input.pointer1` progressing up to `game.input.pointer10`.

6.11.3 Gamepad

At about the time that HTML5 game development was showing itself as viable the browser manufacturers started adding support for using gamepads (or video game controllers) with their browsers. Gamepad support is not fully implemented on all browsers at this time, but it can make for a fun addition for the Firefox and Chrome browsers. The gamepad API gives the browser the capability to respond to button presses on any game controllers that are connected to the computer such as the XBOX controllers or any of the other number of USB gamepads on the market.

Unlike pointers and keyboards, it is necessary to start up the gamepad API with the `game.input.gamepad.start()` command before trying to access the gamepad. After that, it is possible to access the first gamepad at `game.input.gamepad.pad1`. Phaser supports up to four total connected pads and each is accessible by changing the pad number.

Because the gamepad is something that could conceivably be attached, detached, and reattached to the computer, it is important to check to make sure the gamepad is attached and running before using any of the gamepad API calls. Failing to catch a detached controller may result in an error and the game crashing.

```
if( game.input.gamepad.active && game.input.gamepad.
  pad1.connected ) {
      //gamepad code like justPressed and isDown
         checks here
}
```

6.11.3.1 Gamepad Buttons

Once a controller is connected and the gamepad API is started, the process of working with the buttons is the same as the keyboard keys. There are ways to check to see if a button is down or has just been pressed. By default, Phaser provides some built-in mappings to the XBOX 360 controller, one of the more common gamepads that happens to have a fairly standard button layout.

To check for a button just being pressed, the following is done:

```
if( game.input.gamepad.pad1.justPressed(Phaser.
  Gamepad.XBOX360_B) ) {
  //respond to button press
}
```

To check if a button is down, the following is done:

```
if( game.input.gamepad.pad2.isDown(Phaser.Gamepad.
XBOX360_A) ) {
  //acceleration or other constant input
}
```

6.11.3.2 Gamepad Joysticks

Joysticks work differently than buttons. Instead of having discrete states of left, center, or right they have a range of values. These values are split into two axes, the up and down axes of y, and the right and left axes of x. The numerical range of these axes goes between −1 (far left or bottom) and 1 (far right or top), with 0 meaning that the stick has not been moved from its center point. See Figure 6.8.

Having a range of values means that the input can be split up into incremental values. Perhaps, if the user has only slightly moved the stick to

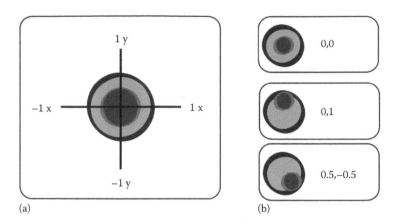

FIG **6.8** (a) Gamepad joystick axes. (b) Gamepad joystick positions.

the left, the player will move at a crawl, while if the user has pushed the stick all the way to the left, the player will sprint at a good pace. In the following example, a simple check is done to see if the user has moved the stick far enough to the right or left to be considered an intentional move. So long as they keep the joystick far enough to either direction, the player will be moved in the direction the controller stick is pressed.

```
if (game.input.gamepad.pad1.axis(Phaser.Gamepad.
  XBOX360_STICK_LEFT_X) < -0.1)
{
    player.x--;
}

if (game.input.gamepad.pad2.axis(Phaser.Gamepad.
  XBOX360_STICK_LEFT_X) > 0.1)
{
    player.x++;
}
```

6.12 Sound

Audio in the browsers (specifically WebAudio in this case) remains one of the more problematic areas for HTML5 game developers. While it will certainly get better in the future, there will remain a number of browsers and devices that will not support these newest and most advanced features for some time. The two major concerns with browser audio are the lack of a single supported audio format and the problems some browsers have with playing more than one sound file at a time. If sound is a must in your web-based game, it would be good to consider using an audio sprite and making sure to get your sound-encoding workflow properly set up.

6.12.1 Loading Sound

Loading music and sound effects works approximately the same way as loading an image. The major difference is that the audio loader's second argument takes an array of strings. The reason for this array of strings is to provide paths to versions of the audio in different formats. Phaser will then attempt to choose the audio file that will work properly in the current browser.

The following line will load in audio that can be played later on using the "music" key in the asset cache. Note that it specifies both an MP3 and an Ogg audio format as options for the sound.

```
game.load.audio('music',
                [
                  'assets/audio/gameMusic.mp3',
                  'assets/audio/gameMusic.ogg'
                ]
              );
```

6.12.2 Playing a Sound

Once a sound is loaded, playing it is as simple as creating an audio element and using its play method. Sounds can be played either as a one-off or a looping sound. For the most part, looping sounds are used for music (and maybe engine noise sound effects). The other sounds, like the clangs and bloops in the game, will be one shots.

```
levelUp = game.add.audio('levelUp');
levelUp.play(); //plays once

gameMusic = game.add.audio('music');
gameMusic.play('', 0, 1, true); //plays forever
```

6.12.3 Changing Audio Loudness

The second argument to the play method will control how loud to play the sound. Zero will be inaudible, one is its basic volume, and a value of .5 being half of its original loudness.

```
levelUp.play('', .5);
```

6.12.4 Audio Formats

It is proving difficult for the different browser manufactures to decide on a single audio format that is acceptable for everyone to use. Here are the major three audio formats a web developer may consider using, along with their advantages and disadvantages.

MP3 is a very common audio format. One of the reasons for its popularity is that the format does good job of compressing sound without losing too much quality. The final compressed file is small enough that they can be easily stored and transported, making it a great choice for games where space and download times are important. Unfortunately, due to patent concerns, many builds of Firefox and Opera do not support MP3 playback. While it is true that Mozilla is working its way forward with MP3 support as best it can, it still would much prefer people to be using the open-source Ogg format encoding instead.

The WAV format is also quite common. It is an uncompressed file format that stores the exact samples for every moment of sound, giving it the best audio fidelity of the three audio options. This great sound often comes with a very high file size that might still be passable for sound effects, but would be too large for music of any type. The format is supported by a wide range of browsers save for some builds of Internet Explorer.

Ogg: A final file type that is perhaps more rare than the previous two. It is also a compressed audio file that grants sounds and sizes comparable to MP3 (though not always as efficient), but with less of a concern of patent enforcement.

At least two audio formats will need to be included with any web game that wants to have sound reliably play in all browsers. With file size being a large concern (faster downloads being preferable), it would be wise to choose the two that are compressed. When building for the web, try to include MP3 and OGG files as those two combined should give you the biggest browser range with the smallest sizes.

6.12.5 Decompressing Audio

While the smaller file sizes of the compressed MP3 and OGG formats are great for download times, they come with a cost of decompression time. Another word for compression is "packing," so just like when you're moving and you pack everything up, once the boxes are moved, everything needs to be unpacked again and put into place. This unpacking process happens on the user's device that decodes and readies the audio to play, and it can take some time to get through all of the audio files. Lower-powered devices like mobile phones will typically take longer than others. It is important to keep in mind that even if an audio file is loaded, it may not be ready to play. The Phaser method "setDecodedCallback" can be used to tell when a set of sounds have all been decoded. This method takes an array of sounds and calls a function when all the files have been decoded. The callback needs an array of sounds because, even though the sounds may be added to the game in a certain order, it is not assured they will be decoded in that same order. Additionally, like many other Phaser calls throughout this book, the final argument to the method call is "this," specifying the context in which the function will run when the callback fires.

```
var poof,jumpSound,levelUp;

function create() {

    poof = game.add.audio('poof');
    jumpSound = game.add.audio('jumpSound');
    levelUp = game.add.audio('levelUp');

    game.sound.setDecodedCallback([ poof, jumpSound,
      levelUp ], audioReady, this);

}
```

```
function audioReady() {
 //sounds have been decoded
 }
```

6.12.6 Audio Sprite

In addition to the lack of support of a single audio format, some current browsers have issues loading and playing more than one audio file at a time. If you are looking to support the most devices and browsers and you want to play multiple sound effects at the same time, the best solution is to create an audio sprite. Just like a sprite sheet that contains several different images in one file, an audio sprite has multiple different sounds and music packaged into one audio file. For the sprite to work, a second file is created that describes the sounds, when they start, and their duration.

Once you have the sprite audio and descriptor files generated, loading the sprite is done via the audio sprite method. Note that audio sprites still require multiple sound formats to support all browsers.

```
game.load.audiosprite('sfx',
                       [
                       'assets/audio/sfx.mp3',
                       'assets/audio/sfx.ogg'
                       ],
                       'assets/audio/sfxJSON.json'
                       );
```

6.12.7 Generating Audio Sprites

While it is possible to manually create an audio file that is a combination of multiple sounds and add a series of markers in code that specify the start of the individual sounds in that audio file, it is much easier to use a program that can make an audio sprite automatically. An audio sprite generator will put a series of audio files together into one, transform the combined file into different formats (ogg, mp3, and wav), and create the JSON file that will tell Phaser what sound is where in the sprite.

One tool that generates a file that works with Phaser perfectly is tonistiigi's audiosprite generator. It is yet another node tool, so the next few commands will be in your command prompt or terminal.

To install audio sprite globally, enter this command into the prompt.

```
npm install -g audiosprite
```

6.12.7.1 Installing Codecs
This will only install the command-line utilities to make the audio sprite, but it will not install the codecs required to make the audio files. The process of installing the codecs varies based on the operating system.

To install the codecs on MacOS:

Installing the codes on a Mac is done via brew. If you don't have brew on your computer yet, head to http://brew.sh/ and follow the instructions to get it installed (it is as simple as pasting some text into the terminal).

Once brew is installed, you can use the terminal to install the required codecs with this line:

```
brew install ffmpeg --with-theora --with-libogg
   --with-libvorbis
```

To install the codecs on Windows, follow these steps:

Download ffmpeg from http://ffmpeg.zeranoe.com/builds/. Extract the files to a permanent (unchangeable) directory on your computer (some people are happy with C:/dev/ffmpeg). Once extracted, edit your Windows path to include the ffmpeg's bin directory inside of the ffmpeg root. In the case of the example directory applied, the folder you would add to Window's path would be C:/dev/ffmpeg/bin.

Adding to Your Path on Windows

The Windows path is a listing of a number of directories that contain programs one may want to run from the command prompt. It can be edited by going to system -> advanced system settings -> environment variables. Select the path in the system variables list and click edit. Add a semicolon (;) to the end of the list and then append path to ffmpeg. Clicking "ok" will update the path, but you will need to close and reopen any command prompts you have opened for the change to effect them.

6.12.7.2 Using the Audiosprite Tool

The audiosprite tool is fairly easy to use once it is downloaded and set up. In the command prompt, navigate to a folder that has a collection of audio files you want to include in the sprite. They do not need to be in the same format. For example, if you had a file called "sound.wav" and "somemusic.mp3" (or as many sounds as you need), you could type in this command:

```
audiosprite --output audioSpriteName sound.wav
   somemusic.mp3
```

This will take the different sounds and combine them, putting this combined sound in the same folder with the name "audioSpriteName" in four different formats: MP3, M4A, AC3, and Ogg. After running this command, there will be four new files in that directory along with an audioSpriteName.json file that contains the data for the duration and start time of each sound in the combined file. These four audio files and the JSON file are what you will need to put into your assets folder to load into a Phaser game.

6.12.8 Adding Markers and Playing Audio Sprites

Audiosprites are really just markers that specify when to start and how long to play. It is also possible to add markers to audio inside of the game code itself, and then use that marker to play the sound from the marker's start point and duration.

The add marker method needs at least three arguments: the name of the marker to use when playing the sound later, when the sound starts (in seconds), and how long that particular sound lasts (also in seconds). The following code adds a marker manually and then plays the sound from that marker. Later, when calling play, simply pass in the string name of the marker in order to play that sound from the list of the markers.

```
sounds = game.add.audio('sounds');
sounds.allowMultiple = true;
sounds.addMarker('gameMusic', 2, 1.2);
sounds.play('gameMusic');
```

The only other important item to note when using audio sprites is to set the audio's allowMultiple property to true, which helps the sound to be played multiple times (good for a single sound that may be triggered multiple times to play many different instances of the same sound, like overlapping bullet sound effects).

If the audio has been loaded in as an audio sprite, then the markers are added for you automatically. The previous code can be simplified by the removal of the add marker method.

```
sounds = game.add.audio('sounds');
sounds.allowMultiple = true;
sounds.play('gameMusic');
```

6.13 Maps

Many people, when they think about the possibility of making games, dream of creating the lush worlds and environments that the players will eventually inhabit and run around in. Laying out all these areas via code can become quite a time-consuming task. To compound the problems of game world creation, if each individual part of the world that was displayed in game was a unique graphic, the game would have so many assets to download, the wait would stop players from ever wanting to give it a try. Equally bad, the artist for the game would have to work forever to make all those little pieces of the game, resulting in an extremely long development time. Asset reuse and GUI-based map creation solve these problems, and each will be explored throughout this book (examples shown in Figures 6.9 through 6.12).

The two major approaches to creating maps for games are scenes and graphs. Scenes are a form of map where the objects don't need to be placed

FIG 6.9 A map used to create a platformer environment.

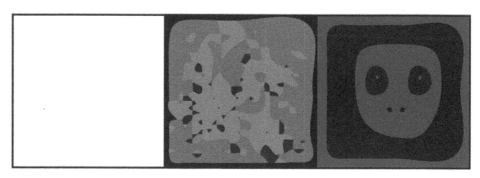

FIG 6.10 Tiles that are repeated to build a map.

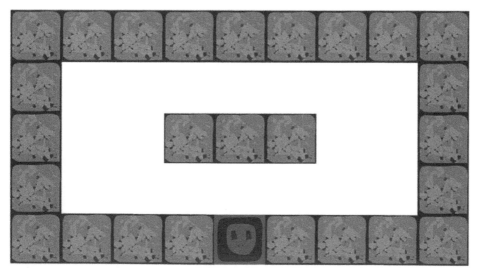

FIG 6.11 Visual representation of the numerical map.

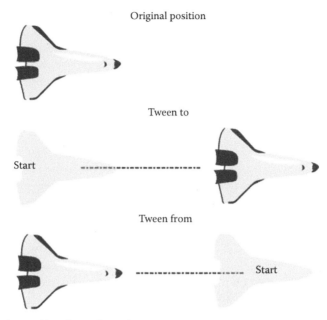

Original position

Tween to

Start

Tween from

Start

FIG 6.12 Difference in start and stop positions of a ween from and tween to.

in particular areas and can take up as much or little space as they want. Graphs are much more rigid, with spaces parceled out to different objects that can only take up a set width and height on the screen. Each has their advantages and disadvantages, discussed throughout this chapter, though currently the Tiled map editor is the only clear winner for the most robust mapping system in Phaser.

What about Other Map Editors?

Although Tiled is the strongest map editor while this book is being written, it may not always be the best tool for creating maps for Phaser. Keep your eyes on the Phaser discussion boards as the community seems to be moving quickly on making more Phaser-specific tools. There is a good chance that there will be at least one if not more map editors built just for Phaser that are nearly as good as Tiled when it comes to creating maps for your games.

6.13.1 Scenes

The easiest way to begin to envision a scene-type map is to think about everything in the map floating in space. It helps to even imagine the objects as spacefaring objects to begin with. While, technically, all the planets in space are moving quickly, for simple games, they can be imagined as simply fixed in place. A scene is a similar great vastness with objects floating in their locations throughout it. In fact, one of the best uses of scene levels is for space games, where physicality might not be best represented through graphs or rigid positioning. However, it can also be great for more organic games (such as underwater systems or advanced platformers), where a grid system would appear too out of place and unnatural. This is also the type of system that 3D games use to represent the positions and locations of all the objects in their game maps.

When using a scene system for games that need to work like 2D platformers, the platforms will need to have their gravity turned off and their physics body type set to static. Since there is no good editor for this type of Phaser game yet, each world object in a scene will need to be created and placed into the scene in the game state's create method. Here is an example of this basic approach, seen before in some of the more simple examples in this book. In this example, a group is set as ground and any object added to that group will work as if it were ground. Essentially the world created in this example will be made up of a series of floating platforms (or walls) that will not budge a single pixel when a player hits them.

```
function setup() {
        game.physics.startSystem(Phaser.Physics.
          ARCADE);
        game.physics.arcade.gravity.y = 250;

        player = game.add.sprite(200, 100, "player");
        player.anchor.setTo(.5,1);
        game.physics.enable(player, Phaser.Physics.
          ARCADE);
        player.body.drag.x = 1000;

        ground = game.add.group();
        ground.enableBody = true;
        ground.create( 100, 500, "ground");
        ground.create( -100, 400, "ground");
        ground.create( 300, 400, "rockyGround");
        ground.setAll("body.immovable", true);
        ground.setAll("body.allowGravity", false);
}
```

This process of creating each individual bit of a level and adding it to the game inside the create function manually can get a bit out of hand quickly when there are large levels that may need to be loaded in and set up. Another approach that helps mitigate the need of hardcoding the level data in the setup function would be to create a level dataset. This dataset can provide the objects in the scene and where those graphics should be placed. The best data format to use if one needs a bit of extra data to drive their game is the JSON format. Here is a very small example of what a JSON-level description might look like.

```
{
    "ground": [
      { "x": 100, "y": 500, "key": "ground" },
      { "x": -100, "y": 400, "key": "ground" },
      { "x": 300, "y": 400, "key": "rockyGround" }
    ]
}
```

The JSON format specifies the key of an asset to be used, which references the asset in Phaser's asset cache. It also gives the position to place the asset once created. This particular example is only for ground, but other objects could be created and specified in other arrays named "collectables," "enemies," or "traps" as needed. The next steps in the process are to load in the data and then use that data to create the objects in the scene, making them fixed ground objects in the game just as before.

```
function preload() {
    game.load.json('scene_data', 'data/scene_data.
      json');
}

function setup() {
    var sceneData = game.cache.
      getJSON('scene_data');

    ground = game.add.group();
    ground.enableBody = true;
    var currentObject;
    for(var i=0; i<sceneData.ground.length; i++){
        currentObject = sceneData.objects[i];
        ground.create(
            currentObject.x,
            currentObject.y,
            currentObject.key
        );
    }
    ground.setAll("body.immovable", true);
    ground.setAll("body.allowGravity", false);
}
```

Assuming the other assets have been loaded in before, we then add a new line to the preload method that loads in the scene data JSON file. Any JSON file that has been loaded in can be accessed from the Phaser cache via "game.cache.getData." When accessed, it returns a JavaScript object that can be navigated via the dot operator just like any other JavaScript object.

Using this approach to scene layout, it becomes easy to separate the objects that are in the scene from the code that actually does all the game-state setup. One potential advantage of this method is the increased chance that the actual layout of the game world could take place in another application that simply exported the JSON for use in the Phaser engine.

6.13.2 Tilemaps

A major goal of a level layout system is to enable the creation of levels that are small in total file size. This is done by creating level systems that do not need lots of unique assets to still look varied and interesting. Tile engines are a common solution because they give a structured way to create large worlds with a very small amount of graphic assets. They encourage asset reuse by breaking the world up into a grid that can have tiles placed into each grid cell. The tiles come in one image file and are typically small in size. A game developer benefits in two ways if they choose to create a world based on a tilemap. Firstly, grid code is very simple to write. Everything can only take up one space on the grid, and each grid space is defined by just its x and y locations. Second, any game logic that takes place on that grid is easy to calculate. Algorithms like A*, Conway's game of life, and even simple fluid dynamics are typically implemented and represented with grids. If a game world can be broken up into small manageable chunks, then the game can take advantage of these techniques and will generally be easier for a programmer to work with.

A tilemap works by placing a series of (typically square) images into the game in a grid layout. These images will work as the "game world," with certain tiles being platforms and walls, and others being parts of the world the player can walk through. The end result is rather like a series of tiles put onto a bathroom floor to create a graphic (thus the name "tile map"). The images that make up these tiles are not loaded in individually, but rather they are brought in as one large file. The different tiles are laid out side-by-side in the single image, a similar manner to a sprite sheet. The tile engine then copies the tiles to the game map piece-by-piece based on their index number provided by a map file.

Because the images are loaded in a single file, the computer needs to know how these tiles should be copied into the world to create the full map. Much like the animation frames for a sprite sheet, behind the scenes the computer stores an array of numbers that specify which tile it should be drawing to the world in what location. When the game starts up, before anything is drawn to the stage, the world map is rendered by looping through this map and copying the frames to its full map image file.

Here is a computer's representation of a map. This would be a map with a little platform in the middle, assuming zeroes are navigable area and ones are ground or platforms.

```
var tileMap = [
     [1,1,1,1,1,1,1,1,1],
     [1,0,0,0,0,0,0,0,1],
     [1,0,0,1,1,1,0,0,1],
     [1,0,0,0,0,0,0,0,1],
     [1,1,1,1,2,1,1,1,1]
];
```

The next step for a tile engine after getting the numerical map data is to use those numbers to draw the visual map. A tile set image will need to be created with tiles that can be used for each number. Figure 6.10 is an example of a tile set imageaforementioned. Each tile needs to be the same size, and note that there are three tiles in total, one for each of the numbers in the numerical map. The white tile is tile zero, stone is tile one, and skull is tile two.

If the tileset image and the tilemap were provided to Phaser in a format it understood, Phaser would then go through and place the tiles into a bigger map, putting the white tiles where a zero appears, ground tiles where a one appears, and the skull where a two appears. The final result of the combination of map and tileset looks like Figure 6.11.

Once the map is drawn, the next step is getting the player and other game objects into the world that the map represents. Tile collisions become the next consideration for a tilemap to work correctly. If all of the tiles are not collidable, the map would be just about worthless. The player would either fall through or walk through all the tiles with ease. Conversely, if all the tiles were set to collide with the player and other objects, the world would pin everything down into its solid state and nothing would ever move.

Tile engines typically have a way to setting which tiles are "open" and which ones should count as solid objects that the player cannot get past. For the this tile map, setting tile zero (the white tile) to open would give the player a nice space to navigate around while not being able to fly beyond the edge of the world.

Tile Metadata

More advanced tile engines (and the editors that come with them) might add more attributes to each tile beyond walkability. Items like wind, death zones, or poison areas are all completely valid attributes that a tile may have that can be calculated inside of a tile engine as it runs its collision code for the player and other game objects.

6.13.2.1 Loading Tilemaps

Here is the base way to load a tilemap, with the format that will be used later on in this book (the Tiled format).

```
game.load.tilemap('map',
                 'assets/tilemaps/maps/tilemap.
                   json', null,
                 Phaser.Tilemap.TILED_JSON
                 );
```

Similar to sprite atlases, there are several different tilemap formats that can be saved. There are two different tilemap formats that can be loaded into Phaser. The first is Phaser.Tilemap.CSV, which is simply an array of numbers separated by commas. It is very similar to the 2D example map array explained earlier. The second format (`Phaser.Tilemap.TILED_JSON`) is a tilemap from the program Tiled, which can be used as a type of full-featured level editor for Phaser. This format comes with a number of extras including multiple layers to the map and additional zones that can be used to place objects with the right additions.

6.13.2.2 Tiled

While writing a comma-separated list of indices isn't a bad way to go about making a game world, it lacks a bit of visual feedback that is useful for making sure that the world is coming out the way the designer is expecting it to. Some may go through esoteric routes of creating editors, like using the pixels in an image to represent tiles in a game (red means lava), but in general, a full-featured tile map editor really speeds up the workflow for a game designer who wants to make a game with a large tile-based world.

There are many tilemap editors available free usage. Some good examples include Mappy, Tiled, and DAME, which all have good communities and are feature-rich choices. In fact, making a tilemap editor is easy enough that many programmers (for better or worse) take it upon themselves to write their own editor instead of using a prebuilt solution. If you'd rather get to using an editor and not making one, Tiled is the program of choice for Phaser game developers.

It actually includes a number of extra features beyond simply laying out tiles that can turn it into a nearly full-featured level editor if used correctly. Additional features of Tiled (which Phaser supports) are its ability to do several layers of tiles and to lay out other assets where they would appear in the game world itself. While Phaser doesn't automatically recognize non-tile assets placed throughout the world, it is able to access the data that can be used later on to do things like placing doorways, enemies, or collectables for the player to find.

Tiled has installers for Windows, Linux, and Mac and can be found at the (wonderfully named) website http://www.mapeditor.org/.

6.14 Tweens

Tweens are a way to animate properties of an object from one value to another over a specific amount of time. For most games, the animations will be controlled via the game's physics and a few simple rules programmed into the game objects like user input and AI responses. These animations are great, but they can be a bit unpredictable. Oftentimes a developer will have a need for an animation where the duration, start, and end points of the motion are all fixed and known. UI animations commonly need to have these sorts of predictable animations to have things like title graphics fade it and buttons bounce and respond to user input. Cutscenes in games also may need these predictable animations to ensure an object reaches a specific location before reaction animations occur. If a developer needs a reliable animation for these or other reasons, tweens are their best option to get the motion they are looking for.

> **What Does the Word "Tween" Mean?**
>
> The term "tween" is taken from the world of traditional 2D animation. When working on an animation, the lead animator would draw two (or more) key poses for a figure that described positions at critical parts of the animation. These poses were chosen for their ability to define what the motion between them would look like. Good choices for two poses might be the "ready to swing" frame and the "hitting the ball" frame of a golfer. Once the two poses were defined, timing notations would be added to the frames and the work would be passed on to an assistant who would draw all the frames in between (or "tweens" as they were called). Today, the computer can do the tweens for the programmer or animator, but the term persists.

6.14.1 Writing Tweens

When writing a programmatic tween, the computer needs to know three things. First, it needs to know the starting property values of the object being tweened (position or other properties such as its alpha or visibility). Second, it needs to know the final values of those same properties. Third, it expects the time or duration that the tween will play over.

Because the game objects being tweened on the screen already have visual properties for the current position, rotation, and alpha, it can be assumed the start or stop points of the animation are those properties that the object currently has. The animation methods from and to are different ways to specify how to use the current properties of an object as values in an animation. From will start from the current position and move to the specified one. Conversely, to will start at the values provided and move back to where the sprite currently is.

6.14.1.1 Tween Syntax

The general syntax for tweening an object in Phaser appears a bit odd since it is added to the game via `game.add`. The tween is actually an object that can be created, stored, and replayed as necessary. The basic syntax starts a tween on an object and tells it to move either to or from the properties specified in the first argument's object. The duration comes in milliseconds and an easing object can be specified (covered later). Finally, if you want the tween to play automatically (which is typically the case), set `autoStart` to true.

```
game.add.tween(object).to({property: value},
    duration, easing, autoStart);
```

For example, here is a tween that will move the player to an x position of 400 pixels over the span of 0.7 s. The animation starts right away and will ease out based on the cubic easing model.

```
game.add.tween(player).to({x: 400}, 700, Phaser.
    Easing.Cubic.Out, true);
```

A great use of the "from" animation method (and relative animation positions) is for UI transitions. This will start the logo 400 pixels higher than it currently is, and then tween the logo back to where it was before the tween began. The power of this technique comes from the developer's ability to get the UI laid out correctly first, and then add in the transitions as a final effect.

```
game.add.tween(logo).from({y: "-400"}, 700, Phaser.
    Easing.Cubic.Out, true);
```

6.14.1.2 Tweenable Properties

While it is possible to tween any property, when it comes to animating visual elements, there are a few that are the most commonly tweened.

- **X, Y** are the most commonly tweened properties, as they can be used to move objects into, out, and around the screen.
- **scale.x, scale.y** are used lesser, but still common. Changing an object's scale is a good way to fake 3D space without having all the complicated calculations that come with it. A bit of scaling of UI elements can go a long way to provide a visually appealing experience. Tweening scale is somewhat different from tweening other properties. The scale tween has to be a separate tween targeting the object.scale property.

```
this.game.add.tween(bar.scale).to({ x: .8 }, 350);
```

- **Alpha** is used for fading in or out. Starting from an alpha of zero and progressing toward one will fade an object in. Going toward zero is an easy way to fade it out. Fade outs are an easy way to cheat in enemy death animations or other transitions.

6.14.1.3 Easing

Most motion in real life does not move at a set pace from start to finish. Anything that starts at full speed and moves at that speed until it suddenly stops looks very strange and robotic to a human observer (or terrifying, if the motion is applied to humanlike figures). Instead, most motion naturally starts slow, speeds up to its fastest pace, and slows down to a stop. This applies to a wide range of cases, including the swing of a clock pendulum (or human arm), the acceleration and deceleration of cars in between lights, and sliding an object across a table not made of ice. Tweening engines will typically include a series of different functions that ease the tweens so that they look natural to the viewer. Following is a list of the built-in easing functions, with a brief explanation of the general use cases for each.

Each of these easing functions comes in three different forms: in, out, and inOut. These refer to when the ease is applied to the animation. An ease "in" will start slow and speed up, ending the animation at full speed. Great for moving things off screen or for an animation with a very sudden collision. An ease "out" will start the animation at full speed and slow the motion to a stop. Ease outs are great animating things into view from off screen, or having characters skid to a stop in a cutscene. Finally, the ease inOut will start slow and end slow. It is typically used for motions where the object will both start and stop on the screen. Great examples of an inOut-type motion would include avatar motions or sliding pieces around on a game board.

Easing is a subtle thing that really makes animations shine, but it does take a bit of fiddling with to truly understand. Take some time to play around with them and get a sense for what does and does not feel good. When in doubt, exponential or quadratic are great default easing functions.

- **Linear** is first on the list because it is technically not an ease. Instead, a linear tween is just the interpolation without any slowing near the start or the stop. Instead of writing in or out for the easing, the easing command is "`Phaser.Easing.Linear.None`."
- **Back** eases will provide some "anticipation" of the motion by briefly moving in the opposite direction of the ease, effectively overshooting or winding up the motion.
- **Bounce** eases will hit their intended destination early and then bounce three times as if someone had dropped a basketball onto a floor. Can be a bit too animated, use with caution.
- **Circular** eases have a particularly long application time, taking until near the end of the animation to get to full speed. Great for very subtle motion that still looks organic.
- **Elastic** is similar to a back ease. The animation will overshoot its final destination and have to correct back on the last few frames. If used sparingly, it can be a nice effect.
- **Exponential** easing is a very quick motion into or out of the full speed of the animation.
- **Cubic, Quadratic, Quartic,** and **Quintic** are placed together because they are all technically the same idea, just more powerful versions of each. They're less extreme versions of exponential but still provide a strong ease into or out of the motion.
- **Sinusoidal** is one of the "smoother" eases, like circular. Very subtle, though it can feel a bit slow.

6.14.1.4 Chaining Tweens

Many animations will contain multiple different transitions that need to occur in a certain sequence. In a cutscene, a character might be scripted to walk up to a computer terminal, wait, and then walk over to a motorcycle to speed off on a few moments later. This is a chain of animations that can be implemented in Phaser with a chained tween. Unlike the previous tween examples that play automatically, these animations are queued up and set in motion by the start command at the end of the chain.

```
game.add.tween(robot)
    .to({ x: 600 }, 1000, Phaser.Easing.Linear.None)
    .to( {rotation: 90 }, 500, Phaser.Easing.
       Linear.None)
    .to({ y: 300 }, 700, Phaser.Easing.Linear.None)
    .to( {rotation: 0 }, 500, Phaser.Easing.
       Linear.None)
    .to({ x: 100 }, 1000, Phaser.Easing.Linear.None)
    .start();
```

Game engines often need to simulate physical interactions along with the messiness that comes along with it. Racing games need the ability to accelerate, turn, and slow to a stop. Destruction games like Angry Birds needs objects to have velocity, gravity, and to accurately apply collision forces when those balls-become-birds hit their targets. Built into Phaser are two primary physics systems, arcade and P2, which give a developer all the tools they need to make many of these games. The physics systems have different purposes and take up different amounts of computational resources, so the next portion of this book will explore that.

Other Physics Systems

Currently, there are two other physics systems in Phaser. The first, Ninja, is similar to the arcade system save for the fact that it introduces sloped tiles and wall running capabilities. The second system, Box2D, is a very robust physics system that is worth looking into if you need polygonal collisions between items and very realistic physics. Box2D is a paid add-on to Phaser with great documentation, which is why it is not covered in this book.

The easiest system to delve into is the arcade physics system that provides a fairly simple approach to the necessary elements like collision, gravity, and velocity. A major downside to arcade physics is that it uses squares for its collisions, making it hard to implement things like slopes or polygonal (non-square) collision shapes. Due to the simplifications, the physics will run significantly faster but they can be a bit less than realistic (thus the "arcade" nomenclature).

The second physics system, P2, is a more robust and "realistic" engine. This system can have complex shapes (potentially made in other programs) for the objects in it and implements a more realistic physics model. P2 is the engine one may wish to use if they are looking to make a game with vehicles that have shocks and thrust provided by the contact of the wheels on the ground. This power comes with a price. P2 will typically take up more computational resources than the arcade system, and it will take a bit of study to really understand and master everything P2 has to offer.

6.15 Physics Primer

Before getting into the particularities of the different physics systems that can be used in Phaser, it would be helpful to know a little bit about the terms that will be used in those systems and how those factors affect the motion and interaction of objects on the screen. In this section, we're going to talk about these factors and explain in simple terms what they are and how they work. It is by no means a replacement for a real study of physics, but should be enough to get one grounded in the use of the systems in game engines.

6.15.1 Velocity

Velocity (or, in simpler terms, speed) is the rate at which a game object is moving in a direction. This is a critical component of an object's physics properties. Without a velocity, there would be no change in location on the screen and players would be staring at static objects.

In Phaser, all objects have their velocity split into the rate of movement on the x and y axes. Large velocities in either the positive or negative direction mean that the object is moving quickly. Smaller numbers represent a slower speed. Zero is the slowest an object can be going, or not going since zero represent no motion at all (examples are shown in Figures 6.13 through 6.29).

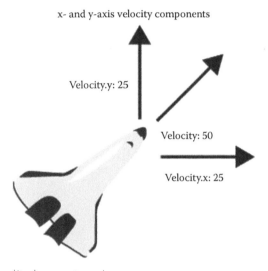

FIG **6.13** Velocity and its subcomponents per axis.

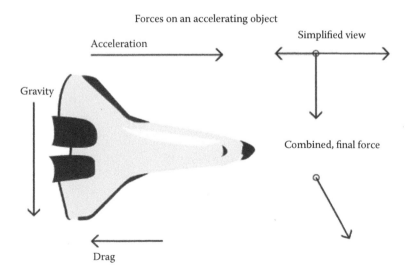

FIG **6.14** Component forces and final combined force.

Change in position each frame (with acceleration)

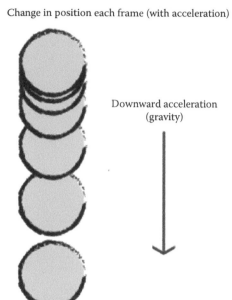

Downward acceleration
(gravity)

FIG 6.15 Effect of acceleration on object positioning.

Distance traveled with different drags

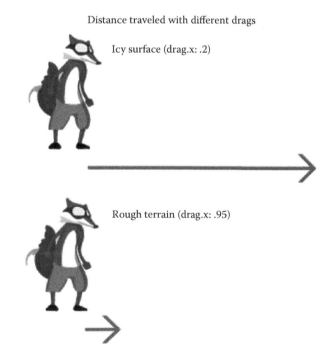

Icy surface (drag.x: .2)

Rough terrain (drag.x: .95)

FIG 6.16 Slide difference based on drag values.

Total speed with different drags

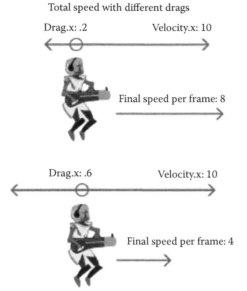

Drag.x: .2   Velocity.x: 10

Final speed per frame: 8

Drag.x: .6   Velocity.x: 10

Final speed per frame: 4

FIG 6.17 Maximum speed with different drag values.

Difference in bounce height at different restitutions

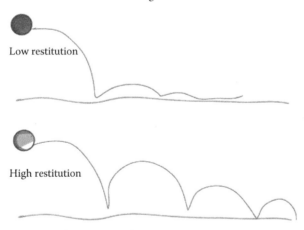

Low restitution

High restitution

FIG 6.18 Bounce height at different restitution values.

Moment of impact

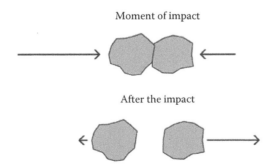

After the impact

FIG 6.19 Transferring motion from a physics impact.

Sprite bounding box

FIG 6.20 Bounding boxes used for collisions.

Adjusted bounding box

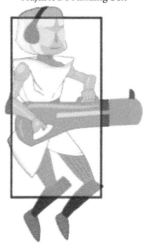

FIG 6.21 Decreased bounding box size for less collision chance.

A quad tree with sub-quads

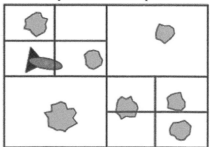

FIG 6.22 Division of game space into smaller quad trees.

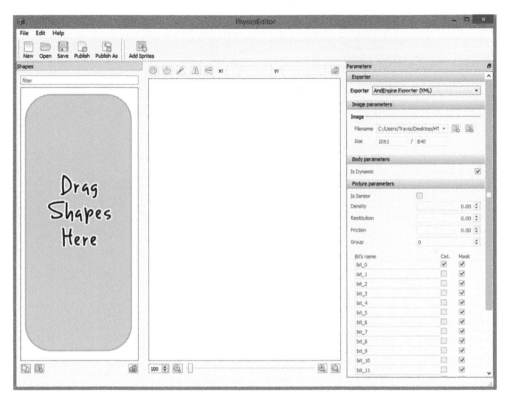

FIG 6.23 Physics editor shape space on the left.

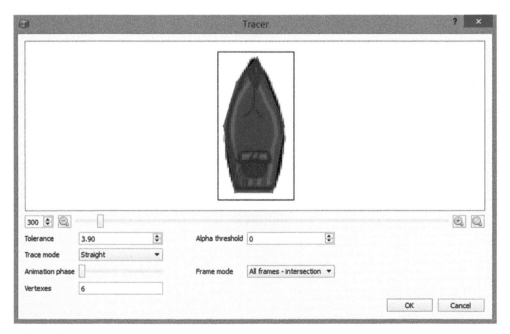

FIG 6.24 Physics editor tracer and resulting polygonal shape.

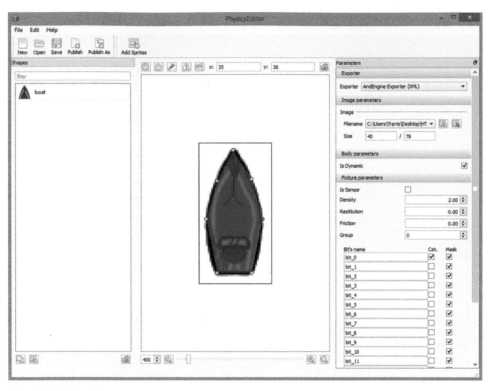

FIG 6.25 Manually adjusting a polygon.

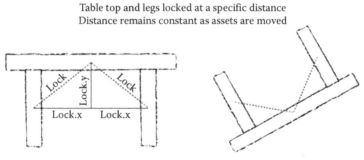

FIG 6.26 Lock constraints.

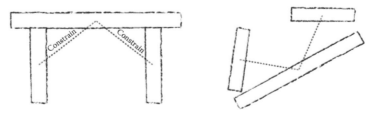

FIG 6.27 Distance constraints.

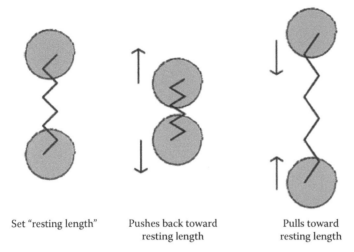

Set "resting length"   Pushes back toward   Pulls toward
                          resting length   resting length

FIG 6.28 Spring constraints.

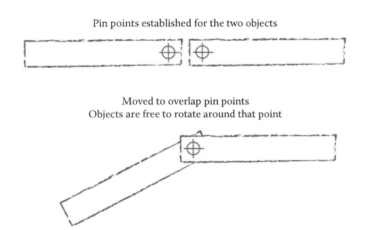

FIG 6.29 Revolute constraints.

6.15.2 Forces

When it comes down to it, most physics in games is about forces. Forces are the things that ultimately change an object's velocity, with bigger forces having more of an effect. Forces can come in two forms: impulse and constant. Impulse forces happen just once. Some examples of impulse forces include kicking a soccer ball or throwing an object into the air. These forces transfer some energy to the game object and are done. Constant forces are continuously applying a force to an object and always pushing on that object. A constant force we need to live with every day is gravity, though there are many others like the acceleration of a car or the ground pushing back on our feet as we stand.

6.15.2.1 Acceleration

Acceleration is a constant force that is pushing an object in a direction. It is also the change in a velocity over time. It can be used to speed objects up or slow them down. It is great for a natural motion effect because nothing ever goes instantaneously from not moving to full speed in real life (though in games that's not always the case). Perhaps the most important acceleration in many games is gravity, which is a constant downward force on the characters and objects in a game (see Figure 6.15).

An object with no velocity that is given a positive acceleration will begin moving in a positive direction, faster and faster, until that acceleration is turned off. If that object needs to be slowed, giving it a negative acceleration will begin to decrease that object's velocity, though it is possible to decrease the velocity to a negative amount and the object will begin moving in the opposite direction.

6.15.2.2 Friction (Drag)

Friction is a critical force that pushes in the opposite direction an object is moving. In a frictionless world, everything would be sliding around, nearly incapable of coming to a complete stop. Games without friction would appear as if everything were sliding on ice, or the players were in space. While there are games where that is the intent, many games will rely on drag to bring their objects to a resting position.

Different surfaces and areas can have different amounts of drag. A rocky road will have a sufficiently large amount of drag and quickly stop people or vehicles. Conversely, an icy road won't do much to slow down anything on it and the smallest inputs can have huge effects on motion (see Figure 6.16).

Friction is applied during all motion, not just when something has stopped accelerating. This is why it is easier to get going faster (and reach a higher speed) in plain air compared to walking underwater. The water is going to push back on all your motions, slowing both the acceleration and reducing the fastest speed you can reach. Higher amounts of drag on an object can make it seem significantly slower, because it is going to take longer for that object to get moving and will effectively reduce its maximum speed (see Figure 6.17).

6.15.2.3 Restitution (Bounciness)

Everything in the world pushes back on an object hitting it. Some will push back more than others. Restitution is the term that defines the amount of a force returned to an object when it hits something. The difference is easy to see between a bouncy ball and a stone. Throwing the ball at the ground will cause it to rebound to a great height, while the stone will just thud to the ground once and be done with its adventures.

While the restitution of an object is technically a very complex calculation, game engines commonly represent it as a number between one and zero. A restitution value of one means the object is perfectly bouncy. This "perfect" object is dropped from a certain height on the screen it will return without fail to the original height it was dropped from. The opposite restitution, zero, will not bounce the object at all. If an object with a bounciness of zero hits something, it will have no recoil and simply stop dead in place (see Figure 6.18).

6.15.2.4 Collisions

When objects collide, they transfer energy to each other. Hitting a baseball with a bat, the bat will transfer its velocity energy to the baseball, sending it flying away. At the same time, the baseball will transfer some of its energy to the bat. This is how batters can feel the hit, or why bats may shatter. The actual energy transferred is a factor of the current velocity of each object, their mass, and their restitution. If the objects are equally matched, they will transfer their energy perfectly. Two boxes flying in perfectly opposite directions will collide, transfer their energies, and come to a dead stop. Heavier objects will take more energy to get moving, and objects with larger restitution will tend to have much bouncier responses (see Figure 6.19).

6.15.2.5 Putting the Physics Properties Together

When creating your game objects, make sure to take some time to play with their velocities, acceleration (including gravity), and drag to get the right "feel" for the game you are trying to make. They will most likely be different numbers for your different objects and it is important to get them all right. A heavy car is most likely going to have a slow acceleration with some very strong drag working on it. That car also wouldn't bounce around too much, so a bounciness closer to zero would be preferable. A paper airplane won't have much drag on the x-axis but may have a huge drag on the y-axis to cause it to fall very slowly.

6.16 Phases of a Physics System

Most physics systems follow a general pattern of setup and execution flow. While the point of this book is not to go into detail of how to construct all the parts of a physics engine, it will be helpful to know in general how they work to be able to make sense of later code examples and debug future problems.

In general, physics engines execute three major steps: first they check for potential collisions between objects (the broad phase), second they look for actual collisions between objects (the narrow phase), and finally they attempt to separate the objects so they are not overlapping. When working in a basic system like the arcade physics engine in phaser, the bounding boxes are easy enough to calculate and separate that these actions can take place quickly without a lot of hassle. More advanced systems take a lot more factors of the colliding bodies into account (such as restitution, mass, and friction) and can have some odd shapes for engine that require longer and more advanced calculations.

The broad phase of the physics engine is important for cutting down on processing time. Once a game gets a significant number of different entities into it, calculating if any of them are colliding (and running the resulting collision separation code) with any others can take a significant amount of time. During the broad phase, the physics engine will do a series of quick calculations to figure out which collisions even have a chance of happening and store a list of potential game object collisions it needs to check more closely. This can often take out a large number of collisions right off the bat.

In the narrow phase, the engines check all of the lines that make up the parts of the body of the object and see if they are inside of any of the areas of a potentially colliding object. If they are, then the engine will separate the objects, moving them backward until they do not overlap anymore. In an arcade system, this is done automatically, and any of the properties of the collision are also applied (momentum transfer based on mass, friction between the two objects, any bounciness). In other systems, the engine will attempt to push the object backward based on how fast it was moving inward toward the object it collided with. When these advanced systems start pushing objects away from each other, they have to consider all the other objects in the system. In order to mitigate the effect of causing another collision by pushing the object all the way back, the systems may not completely separate an object right away so the other objects in the world can have a chance to collide with resulting, backward movement from the collision. The other physics components like friction and bounciness are also applied over these steps. Over a few iterations the system tends to become a reasonable "solved" version of the world with no collisions.

> **Fixed Time Steps**
>
> Many physics systems work on a fixed time step. This means that the physics calculations won't be run for every frame, but only on a fixed time interval. Knowing how much time will pass in between each physics step lets the engine be predictable about how to move items during the frames it is not running physics calculations. It can also predict where objects may be in the future with a certain degree of certainty (barring user input). Many of these systems will actually run the physics calculations a few frames in advance of the rendering of object positions to give the system a chance to catch up on unexpected changes in the model, such as users taking a sharp left turn into a wall and creating a 10-car pileup.

6.17 Bodies

In order for physics systems to work, it needs to have objects inside of the physics "world" that can collide against each other. These objects are termed "bodies." A body is something that has a certain shape like a box, circle, or complex shape made up of points and lines and exists in the world.

These bodies are not visual elements and are only used by the physics system to calculate things like change in position and collisions. Since they are not visible objects, they are often associated with a visible element that will reflect the position and rotation of the physics body In a visible way on screen.

By default, Phaser sprites do not have bodies associated with them. The bodies need to be activated for the physics system you will be using. Once activated, the sprites will be controlled by the body in the physics system. For instance, to create a body for a sprite and add it to the physics system in arcade physics, this is the general approach.

```
var meteor = game.add.sprite(200, 0, 'meteor');
game.physics.enable(meteor, Phaser.Physics.ARCADE);
```

6.18 Arcade Physics

As stated previously, the arcade physics system in Phaser uses exclusively boxes and rectangles for its physics bodies. The technical term for the boxes the arcade system uses is "axes-aligned bounding boxes." This is a fancy way to say the boxes can never rotate but always remain fixed, so the width of a box will always be how much space the box takes up on the x-axis and the height of a box will be how much space it takes up on the y-axis.

Before using any of the arcade physics in Phaser, it needs to be initialized with this call:

```
game.physics.startSystem(Phaser.Physics.ARCADE);
```

6.18.1 Bounding Boxes

By default, these bounding boxes equal the width and height of the sprite's graphics, but they can be adjusted to be smaller or larger as necessary (see Figure 6.20).

6.18.1.1 Changing Bounding Box Size

While most of the time a bounding box that takes up the width and height of a sprite makes sense and works well, there are instances where it can become frustrating to the player when a bounding box is larger (or smaller) than expected. One use case for adjusting bounding boxes includes making smaller bounds for an enemy, so the player can more easily dodge them on the screen. Alternative, another use case might be making the player's attack bounds bigger, making it easier to hit objects in the game. Keep in mind that this does not change the size of the sprite, just what counts as the body for the physics system collisions (see Figure 6.21).

Changing collision box size is part art and part science. Here is the general form to adjust the bounding box.

```
sprite1.body.setSize(300, 200, 20, 20);
```

6.18.1.2 Debugging the Bounding Boxes

When changing the size of a bounding box, it can be helpful to have the game draw the actual bounds of a sprite. It is possible to have Phaser draw the bounding boxes, so you can verify exactly how much "space" an object takes up in the physics system. For the arcade physics system, debug drawing is done in the render method of a Phaser state.

```
var phaserState = {
    render: function() {
        game.debug.body(spriteName);
    }
}
```

6.18.2 Quad Trees

Collision detection can quickly become a very expensive process in a game with a lot of objects that need to check if they are overlapping. When a game has 100 objects that all may be hitting each other, that's a 10,000 different calls to check for a collision between any one of them. The method Phaser uses to reduce those numbers of checks is called a quad tree.

A quad tree stores references to objects in different (increasingly smaller) quadrants in world space. If enough objects are in any particular quadrant, it will break that rectangle into four smaller quads and continue to store locations in these smaller rectangles. With these quad trees, it becomes quick and easy to rule out groups of sprites that couldn't possibly be colliding with others based on how far away one quad is from another. With even a basic quartering of the world space, it is possible to cut out sprites on the three quads that a sprite does not exist in, potentially removing a lot of collision checks in the process (see Figure 6.22).

6.18.3 Collision

A physics system would certainly be incomplete without some way for different entities to collide with it each other. The arcade physics system can check for collisions between: a sprite and another sprite, a sprite and a group of sprites, and a group of sprites against another group of sprites. Each of these has a callback that contains references to the two objects that have collided against each other. The key to checking for collision between any of these three different types of objects is the collide method.

```
game.physics.arcade.collide(itemOne, itemTwo,
                    collisionCallback,
                      processCallback,
                      context
                    );
```

⊙ Note

Collisions will also separate the two objects that collided, pushing them back to a state where they do not overlap visually on the screen. There will be some times when separation isn't needed or gets in the way of the final game. Phaser has another method, overlap, that only checks to see if objects are overlapping.

6.18.3.1 Sprite versus Sprite

The most basic way to do collisions in Phaser is check for collisions between two single sprites. In the following example, a raindrop is created and given a downward velocity. The collision check is called in the update function to verify when it hits the ground. When the raindrop does hit the ground, it will destroy itself.

Take note in this example and further examples that it is necessary to create the bodies on the sprites (via the game.physics.enable call). After enabling the physics bodies on the sprites, it will be possible to access all of the properties and methods of a sprite's body, such as acceleration and velocity.

```
var ground, rain;

function create() {
    game.physics.startSystem(Phaser.Physics.ARCADE);

    ground = game.add.sprite(200, 400, 'ground');
    rain = game.add.sprite(200, 10, 'rain');

    game.physics.enable( [ ground, rain ], Phaser.
       Physics.ARCADE);
    rain.body.velocity.y = 100;
}

function update() {
    game.physics.arcade.collide(ground, rain,
       collisionHandler, null, this);
}

function collisionHandler (obj1, obj2) {
    obj2.kill();
}
```

Collision checks in the arcade physics system need to be done in the update function. The first two arguments to the collide function are the objects to check to see if they are colliding. The third argument is a function that will be called if the two do collide.

The arguments to the collision handler function are always passed in the order they were specified in the collide method call. Because rain was the second argument to the collide method call in the update function, it will be the obj2 variable in the handler. In this example, we kill the rain sprite, though we could also play sound effects or whatever else that needs to happen when rain hits ground.

6.18.3.2 Sprite versus Group

Colliding a sprite against a group isn't much different from colliding a sprite against a sprite; the only change is that the process creates a group and enables all the bodies in that group to be part of the physics system. Here is some code that creates a minefield and sends a poor spaceship off to almost certain doom.

```
var ship;
var group;

function create() {

    game.physics.startSystem(Phaser.Physics.ARCADE);

    ship = game.add.sprite(10, 10, 'ship');

    game.physics.enable(ship, Phaser.Physics.
      ARCADE);
    group = game.add.group();
    group.enableBody = true;
    group.physicsBodyType = Phaser.Physics.ARCADE;

    for (var i = 0; i < 50; i++)
    {
        var mine = group.create(
                    game.rnd.integerInRange(20, 780),
                    game.rnd.integerInRange(20, 580),
                    'mine');
    }

    ship.body.velocity.x = 20;
    ship.body.velocity.y = 20;
}

function update() {

    game.physics.arcade.collide(ship, group,
      collisionHandler, null, this);

}
function collisionHandler (player, mine) {
    player.kill();
}
```

The major changes here are the creation of a group and the enabling of all the physics bodies on that group via group.enableBody and group.physicsBodyType. This will create bodies for all the sprites in the group without having to go through each sprite individually and run game.physics.enable to create the body. Otherwise, the update function should look pretty similar, though now the second argument to collide becomes a group instead of a single sprite. This will check for collisions between the player and any mine, running the collision handler for each collision it finds (though in this case, after the first collision, the player will be dead, so future collisions will not occur).

6.18.3.3 Group versus Group

Now that we know how to collide groups against single sprites, the process to do a group versus a group should be pretty easy to understand: create two groups, enable the physics for them, and collide them.

Here is a variation of the last example, but with several ships. Let the carnage begin.

```
var ships;
var mines;
function create() {

    game.physics.startSystem(Phaser.Physics.ARCADE);

    ships = game.add.group();
    ships.enableBody = true;
    ships.physicsBodyType = Phaser.Physics.ARCADE;

    mines = game.add.group();
    mines.enableBody = true;
    mines.physicsBodyType = Phaser.Physics.ARCADE;

    for (var i = 0; i < 50; i++)
    {
        var mine = mines.create(game.rnd.
          integerInRange(20, 780),
                    game.rnd.integerInRange(20, 580),
                    'mine');
        var ship = ships.create(game.rnd.
          integerInRange(20, 780),
                    game.rnd.integerInRange(20, 580),
                    'ship');
        ship.body.velocity.x = 20;
        ship.body.velocity.y = 20;

    }

}

function update() {
    game.physics.arcade.collide(ships, mines,
      collisionHandler, null, this);
}
function collisionHandler (ship, mine) {
    ship.kill();
    mine.kill();
}
```

6.18.4 Gravity and Immovable Objects

Gravity is a downward acceleration applied to sprites in the game world. It is easy to put a bunch of objects on the stage and add gravity, but if we want them to stay visible and not just fall past the bottom of the screen, there needs to be something for the objects to collide with to stop them. Because the collide method is a standard physics call that will transfer forces when two objects hit, if we put some ground on the stage that was not affected by gravity and had a player collide with, the ground would begin to move from the force of impact. If you have objects, like ground, that should not be moved by a collision they should be set to immovable.

This example is a quick sample of how to get a player controlled by left and right arrows on the screen, an island for them to fall into. The island is not affected by gravity nor can a collision transfer an impulse to its body.

```
var player, ground, cursors;
function create() {

    //setup game
    game.physics.startSystem(Phaser.Physics.ARCADE);

    game.physics.arcade.gravity.y = 300;

    player = game.add.sprite(200, 100, "player");
    player.anchor.setTo(.5,1);
    game.physics.enable(player, Phaser.Physics.
        ARCADE);

    ground = game.add.sprite( 100, 500, "ground");
    game.physics.enable(ground, Phaser.Physics.
        ARCADE);
    ground.body.immovable = true;
    ground.body.allowGravity = false;

    //controls
    cursors = game.input.keyboard.createCursorKeys();
}

function update() {
    //run game loop code

    if(cursors.left.isDown) {
        player.body.velocity.x = -200;
        player.scale.x = 1;
    }

    if(cursors.right.isDown) {
        player.body.velocity.x = 200;
        player.scale.x = -1;
    }
    game.physics.arcade.collide(player, ground);
}
```

The important lines in this snippet are the inclusion of gravity via `game. physics.arcade.gravity.y`, which will give all the arcade bodies a downward acceleration of 300. The ground has gravity explicitly turned off (`ground.body.allowGravity = false`) and is immovable, so when the player hits the platform, it stays where it is. Next, now that physics is enabled, it is preferable to use the body's velocity over modifying x positions directly for movement. This will let the sprite work nicely with the physics system. Finally, in this example, it is not important to write a handler for collision between the player and the ground. Instead we just need the collision to happen between the player and the ground so that they are separated correctly when they do collide.

6.18.5 Drag and World Bounds

One thing you may have noticed with the last example is that the character will seem to slide forever in one direction or another without fail and eventually will fall off the screen. This is because currently the character exists in a world without friction. While a world without friction can be cool for a while, at some point it would be good to introduce drag into the game so the player doesn't have to constantly be adjusting for overshooting goals. Then, just in case the player does jump off the edge of the platform, we can keep the player avatar on the screen using a built-in command, collideWorldBounds. This command automatically collides the player against the four edges of the screen.

If you want to add friction to the previous game example, right after the player is enabled for the physics system in the create function, add these two lines of code:

```
player.body.collideWorldBounds = true;
player.body.drag.x = 1000;
```

6.18.6 Angular Velocity and Bounce

There is one last way to move arcade bodies on the screen which is via their angular velocity or angular acceleration. Both of these properties change the "rotation speed" of the game object the body is attached to. These are lesser used properties but can find some use in top-down driving games or similar sorts of games with a top-down view.

This final example puts the player in control of a ship that can be driven around on the screen. Additionally, because most ships will absorb most of the recoil of an impact and float at least a little away, the bounciness of the ship and the asteroids has been adjusted to get a good feel for the game.

```
function create() {
    game.physics.startSystem(Phaser.Physics.ARCADE);

    player = game.add.sprite(200, 100, "player");
    player.anchor.setTo(.5,.5);
    game.physics.enable(player, Phaser.Physics.
      ARCADE);
    player.body.collideWorldBounds = true;
    player.body.drag = { x: 1000, y: 1000 };
    player.body.angularDrag = 750;
```

```
asteroids = game.add.group();
asteroids.enableBody = true;
asteroids.physicsBodyType = Phaser.Physics.
  ARCADE;

for (var i = 0; i < 10; i++) {
    var asteroid = asteroids.create(game.rnd.
      integerInRange(20, 780),
game.rnd.integerInRange(20, 580), 'roid');

    asteroid.body.bounce = .9;
}

//controls
cursors = game.input.keyboard.reateCursorKeys();
}

function update() {
    //run game loop code

    if(cursors.left.isDown) {
        player.body.angularVelocity = -200;
    }

    if(cursors.right.isDown) {
        player.body.angularVelocity = 200;
    }

    if(cursors.up.isDown) {
        game.physics.arcade.velocityFromAngle(player.
          angle, 200, player.body.velocity);
    }

    game.physics.arcade.collide(player, asteroids);
}
```

6.19 P2

The second major physics system that comes with Phaser is P2. Developed by Stefan Hedman, it is a full-featured physics system that includes colliders (another term for parts of a body that can hit other parts) that come in more shapes than just square. Some of the major colliders it may have include circles, planes, rectangles, capsules, and convex polygons. All of these colliders don't need to be aligned to the axis, so rotation of an object affects collisions in a natural way.

These colliders are often used to create fun and interesting physics simulation games. Common types of games that P2 could be used for include building-destruction style games like Angry Birds, landing or vehicle games with rough 2D terrain to be navigated, or advanced 2D platformers with rickety bridges that wobble as the player runs across it. Unlike the arcade physics engine, this system processes collisions by default. Once a body is added to the world, it will always collide with the other bodies around it.

6.19.1 Setting Up the P2 World

Like every physics system in Phaser, P2 needs to be started before adding bodies to the world.

```
game.physics.startSystem(Phaser.Physics.P2JS);
```

Once started, sprites can have their bodies enabled. Just like the arcade bodies, by default the collider will be box shape around the width and height of the sprite.

```
brick = game.add.sprite(300, 400, 'brick');
game.physics.p2.enable(brick);
```

6.19.2 Debugging Bodies

When working with the P2 system, quite often it can be handy to see visually what the body of a sprite is. Adding a "true" as the second argument when enabling the sprite will cause Phaser to shade the body of the sprite differently.

```
game.physics.p2.enable(brick, true);
```

6.19.3 Adding Basic Objects

The default body for a sprite is a box that matches the width and height of the sprite. To add a different shape, the default body will need to be removed and replaced with the new body shape. Phaser has functions to create and replace simple bodies automatically. The primary replacement methods are setCircle and setRectangle.

In the following code, the original box of the pill sprite will be replaced by a circle. Then that circle body will be again replaced with another box of a size different from the original.

```
game.physics.startSystem(Phaser.Physics.P2JS);

pill = game.add.sprite(300, 400, 'pill');
game.physics.p2.enable(pill);

pill.body.setCircle(40);
pill.body.setRectangle(50, 100);
```

6.19.4 Building Compound Objects

Not all bodies in the real world are perfect circles or boxes. Most are very complex, though games will often simplify them down to a compound of primitive shapes. For instance, a 2D chair has at least four boxes that make it up (the seat, back, and two legs). The shapes that can be used to make these compounds are boxes, circles, and capsules (a pill shape). Lesser used options include lines and planes, which take up entire areas of the game world (great for bounds, or ground).

When creating compound bodies, the old body shapes will first need to be removed from the sprites via `body.clearShapes()`.

In the following case, a baton sprite with circular weights on each side of the bar is loaded into the game. A box wouldn't represent this baton well. It would either be too large for the middle or too small for the circles. A capsule would at least have rounded ends, but still would be affected by the same problems of the box. The best solution would be to create a box for the midsection and two circles for the weights.

```
game.physics.startSystem(Phaser.Physics.P2JS);

baton = game.add.sprite(300, 400, 'phaser');
game.physics.p2.enable(baton, true);

baton.body.clearShapes();
baton.body.addRectangle(35, 10);
baton.body.addCircle(10, -20, 0);
baton.body.addCircle(10, 20, 0);
```

When adding shapes, the arguments after the ones that size the shapes (width, height, and radius) are the offsets. By default, all shapes are placed over the center point of the sprite they are being added to. If offsets are specified, they are offset from the center of the sprite but that much. In the earlier code, note that the x offset for the two circles is set to 20 and −20. This will place the circles at the edges of the baton where they should be.

6.19.5 Adding Complex Objects

Some shapes are just impossible to represent as a combination of rectangles, circles, and pills. These shapes are often represented as a polygon, which is a collection of line segments that define the outer regions of the shape. While it is possible to write the code that would create these lines, it is much easier to create the shapes and load in the shape data into Phaser.

6.19.5.1 PhysicsEditor

One program supported by Phaser that is made to create and export shape data is PhysicsEditor. This program, made by the CodeAndWeb can trace sprites to create fairly accurate polygon outlines that can also be manually edited by the player. To follow along, find the download at https://www.codeandweb.com/physicseditor.

For the quick and easy way to add a shape to a sprite, drag the sprite into the left-hand "shapes" area (see Figure 6.23). It is possible to trace and outline many different shapes in this program before exporting all the bodies, so when your project has many custom shapes you can do all your work by moving between the different entries in the shapes panel.

Once you have a shape into your working area, find the magic wand tool over the picture and click that tool. You'll be presented with a screen that will automatically trace the sprite object for you, based on the alpha transparency of the object, using the border between visible and transparent for the base of the shape (so make sure to be saving your images as a png). Adjusting the tolerance upward will make the shape calculation more lenient, typically reducing the number of points in the final shape. A reduced number of points will create a faster-to-calculate shape for the physics system. Adjusting downward toward zero will add more points creating a more accurate shape with more points that requires more processing (see Figure 6.24).

Once you are happy with the shape, click okay and you can fine-tune the shape by grabbing and moving the points around manually. It is also possible to remove points by right-clicking on them, or add new points by right-clicking on a blank part of the polygon's lines.

6.19.5.2 Exporting from PhysicsEditor

When you have all your shapes traced to your liking and you are ready to bring your work into a Phaser game, the data needs to be exported into a readable format. Before exporting, make that Lime + Corona (JSON) is selected in the right hand of the screen under exporter (see Figure 6.25). The publish button will then prompt for a name and location to save the physics data. Because this file will hold the data for multiple objects, it is common to name it something pluralized like "sandwiches" or "vehicleBodies." Here is the output from the export of just a boat.

```
{
    "boat": [
        {
            "density": 2, "friction": 0, "bounce": 0,
            "filter": { "categoryBits": 1,
              "maskBits": 65535 },
            "shape": [29, 18, 35, 42, 29, 72, 10,
              72, 4, 42, 10, 18, 19, 4]
        }
    ]
}
```

Note that the JSON data contain a key for the boat physics info. Much like the keys used in Phaser's asset cache, this name will be used later on to associate this particular boat shape with the sprite when creating the sprite body.

6.19.5.3 Importing and Using a Complex Shape

The Phaser loader method to preload physics body data is called "physics". This loader method takes a key name for the physics data and a URL to the asset. Physics data that have been loaded can be used to create a complex body shape for a sprite. Before adding the new body, the old one needs to be removed. Then the `loadPolygon` method can be used to load in a shape from a physics data file. The two arguments are the key to the physics data in the asset cache and the key to the actual shape in the physics data. If you're looking for the shape key, as mentioned earlier, it can be found in the physics data JSON file. In the previous example, the shape key was "boat," which is used to load in a boat shape for this example. After this particular loadPolygon line, the boat sprite will have a body shape that fairly accurately mirrors the visible boat.

```
function preload() {
    this.game.load.image("boat", "assests/sprites/
        boat.png");
    this.game.load.physics("vehicleBodies", "assets/
        bodies/vehicleBodies.json");
}

function setup() {
    game.physics.startSystem(Phaser.Physics.P2JS);
    var boat = game.add.sprite(300, 300, "boat");

    game.physics.p2.enable(boat, true);

    boat.body.clearShapes();
    boat.body.loadPolygon("vehicleBodies", "boat");
}
```

6.19.6 Responding to Collisions

Unlike the arcade physics system, P2 processes collisions automatically. If code needs to be run when certain objects collide (to play sounds, destroy objects, or anything else), there are two ways to create collision handlers. The first approach is to respond to a contact signal and the second method is to create a collision callback.

6.19.6.1 Contact Signal

Contact signals fire whenever one object comes into contact with another. It doesn't matter what the other object is, the signal will always fire. It is up to the developer to figure out what the other object is and what should happen based on that collision. The handler function does have one input which is the body that collided with the object. Using this input, it is possible to get access to the other sprite that hits the object and manipulate it. In the following example, the colliding sprite is destroyed and the bullet continues on its path.

```
var target, bullet;

game.physics.startSystem(Phaser.Physics.P2JS);

target = game.add.sprite(300, 400, 'target');
bullet = game.add.sprite(400, 400, 'bullet');

game.physics.p2.enable([target, bullet], true);
bullet.body.velocity.x = -40;

bullet.body.onBeginContact.add( function(otherBody)
{
    otherBody.sprite.kill();
});
```

6.19.6.2 Collision Callback

Collision callbacks added with the method `createBodyCallback` are more specific event handlers that will only fire if two specific objects collide. Phaser will not recognize and run them automatically. To turn collision callbacks on, P2 must have `setImpactEvents` set to true. Turning on impact events can get very process intense, so try to restrict this code to small worlds or only when absolutely needed.

```
var target, bullet;

game.physics.startSystem(Phaser.Physics.P2JS);

target = game.add.sprite(300, 400, 'phaser');
bullet = game.add.sprite(400, 400, 'phaser');

game.physics.p2.enable([target, bullet], true);
bullet.body.velocity.x = -40;

game.physics.p2.setImpactEvents(true);

bullet.body.createBodyCallback(
    target,
    function(myBody, otherBody) {
        otherBody.sprite.kill();
    },
    this
);
```

6.19.7 Collision Groups

Collision groups are the P2 physics system's way to specify what objects should collide with others. Using a collision group, it is possible to have objects only collide with another specific group. Perhaps like "friendly fire," one could use groups to only have player bullets hit enemies and not allies by creating different groups for the player bullets and enemies. It is also possible to set a group of objects to not collide with anything. Laser beams, snow, or ghosts all might fall into this category.

> **Maximum Number of Groups**
>
> Groups are calculated using bitmasks for quick logical checks. These bitmasks are limited to the number of bits that make up a single value, which is currently 31 in JavaScript. The maximum number of collision groups in Phaser is limited to 31, so plan your groups ahead of time.

In the following example, two collision groups are created, apples and oranges. Later on, when sprites are created and added to the game, they are set to be in their respective collision groups and to only collide with the opposite one. When the game is run, the apples will hit oranges, but sail past their other, apple friends.

```
function create() {

    game.physics.startSystem(Phaser.Physics.P2JS);

    var applesCollisionGroup = game.physics.
        p2.createCollisionGroup();
    var orangesCollisionGroup = game.physics.
        p2.createCollisionGroup();

    var apples = game.add.group();
    apples.enableBody = true;
    apples.physicsBodyType = Phaser.Physics.P2JS;
    var oranges = game.add.group();
    oranges.enableBody = true;
    oranges.physicsBodyType = Phaser.Physics.P2JS;

    for (var i = 0; i < 20; i++)
    {
        var apple = apples.create(game.world.
            randomX, game.world.randomY, 'apple');
        apple.body.velocity.x = Math.random() * 60;
        apple.body.velocity.y = Math.random() * 60;
        apple.body.setCollisionGroup(applesCollision
            Group);
        apple.body.collides([orangesCollisionGroup]);

        var orange = oranges.create(game.world.
            randomX, game.world.randomY, 'orange');
        orange.body.setCollisionGroup(orangesCollis
            ionGroup);
        orange.body.collides([applesCollisionGroup]);
    }
}
```

6.19.8 Constraints

Most advanced physics engines attempt to recreate more than just
complex bodies. Typically they also simulate the different ways a
body could be connected to other bodies. By creating and managing
these connections, constructs like vehicles, bridges, or buildings can be created.

The general approach to creating machines and structures in a game engine
is to define connections and the properties of those connections between
two bodies. These connections are called constraints in the engine, and there
are a number of different types of constraints that interact differently on the
connected objects. Some common constraints include distance (this object will
always stay a certain distance away from another), spring (great for shocks on
cars), or gears (the rotational motion of one object will transfer to the other).

6.19.8.1 Lock
The most basic and approachable of the constraints is the lock constraint.
Once two bodies are locked, they will move as if they had been

superglued together. This essentially makes them move like one body, with any movement and rotation on one of the objects being applied to the other. Great for very rigid structures like desks or chairs.

A lock constraint is created by specifying which objects should be locked together and the distances to keep them locked at. This distance is broken up into distances they should be separated on the x and y axes. In this example, the tabletop and legs are locked together, with the legs locked 30 pixels lower than the top. If the tabletop rotates, the legs will rotate with it, so while they won't be 30 pixels down visually anymore, they will still be attached "beneath" the tabletop.

```
var tabletop = game.add.sprite(300, 300, 'top');
var tablelegs = game.add.sprite(300, 400, 'legs');
game.physics.p2.enable([tabletop, tablelegs]);
game.physics.p2.createLockConstraint(tabletop,
    tablelegs, [0, 30], 0);
```

6.19.8.2 Distance
A distance constraint attaches two objects together with an invisible "pipe" that drags one object along with the other as they move. The total distance between two objects cannot change, but they are free otherwise to move in the x and y directions in an orbit so long as that doesn't change the distance between the two. Distance is a bit easier than locking. After passing in the two objects to constrain, the last argument is the distance to maintain between the two objects. See Figure 6.26.

```
car = game.add.sprite(200, 300, 'car');
trailer = game.add.sprite(200, 360, 'trailer');
game.physics.p2.enable([car, trailer]);
game.physics.p2.createDistanceConstraint(car,
    trailer, 70);
```

6.19.8.3 Spring
Springs attach two objects together in a rather bouncy way. Similar to a distance constraint, they have a preferred distance to keep the attached objects apart by. Unlike a distance constraint, a spring allows for a little "give" in the distance the two objects can separate. The further away the spring is from its desired size, the more force it exerts on the objects to bring them back to this preferred length. Thus, if the objects move too far away from each other, the spring will begin to pull them back. See Figure 6.27.

The parameters that control this generated force for a spring are resting length, stiffness, and damping. Resting length is the desired length of the spring. Stiffness controls how strongly it will try to pull back to its resting length. A higher stiffness means the spring will stretch and compress less. Damping reduces how "bouncy" the spring is. A damping of zero means that the spring, once stretched out, will continue to bounce to that length forever. Higher numbers reduce its bounciness. The following snippet creates a paddle and ball and attaches them via a spring, making a rather easy game of paddle ball. The parameters for the spring, seen after the two object's names, are a resting length of 15 between the two, with a stiffness of 5, and damping of 1. See Figure 6.28.

```
game.physics.startSystem(Phaser.Physics.P2JS);

ball = game.add.sprite(200, 100, 'ball');
paddle = game.add.sprite(200, 200, 'paddle');

game.physics.p2.enable([ball, paddle]);

var spring = game.physics.p2.createSpring(ball,
    paddle, 15, 5, 1);
```

6.19.8.4 Revolute

Revolute constraints put a "pin" into two objects and affix those objects together at the point of the pin. While they cannot move freely, they both can rotate freely around that point. A great example of this would be a chain or one of those wobbly wood-plank bridges. The planks or chains are linked together at an individual point for each. Tugging on the chain will pull all of the links, but they can still be "whipped" around as they revolve around their link points. See Figure 6.29.

When creating a revolute constraint, each object needs to have a point specified where the "pin" is placed into that object. In the following example, the first plank has its pin placed to down and right, and the second plank is pinned to the upper left. Once the constraint is made, the two sprites will be moved, so their pins overlap visually.

```
var plank1 = game.add.sprite(400, 300, 'plank');
var plank2 = game.add.sprite(400, 300, 'plank');
game.physics.p2.enable([plank1, plank2]);
game.physics.p2.createRevoluteConstraint(plank1,
    [ 50, 100 ], plank2, [ 0, 0 ]);
```

6.19.9 Contact Materials

In real life, not all surfaces are made equal. Some will be more slippery, others rough, and others might be more bouncy. There's along a number of different physical properties that can change the interaction of an object colliding and moving along another. If a different reaction from contact is desired in a game, a contact material can be created in P2 to define specific properties of an interaction between two objects.

When creating a contact material, it is possible to modify the physical effects of contact between two bodies. The major properties of interest are a contact material's friction, restitution, and surface velocity. Friction is how much the objects will push against any motion on their surface and restitution is essentially "bounciness." Surface velocity is a velocity that will be applied to any object hitting the surface of this object. It is sort of like a moving walkway or current. Numbers above zero will push toward the right of the contact point and velocity below zero will push toward the left.

The slightly more obscure stiffness and relaxation properties are generally set to their defaults. Playing with these can result in some fun, sometimes giving a body more of a "squishy" appearance than normal. Stiffness is the term that defines how insistent the physics system is on pushing objects away from each other so they are not overlapping. A very high number ensures that objects never appear as if they "overlap" when colliding. Lower numbers will still separate the two objects, but not all the way, letting it appear as if the two objects are almost merging together (like a boat into water, never quite sinking but not entirely on top of the waves). Relaxation is a term for how many frames it takes to get the objects fully separated. Typically set to a number between three and five, this reduces "jumpiness" in the simulation. Larger numbers will make the simulation feel a bit slower, but again make everything move smoother in total.

In the following example, when the player collides with the ground, the resulting friction force will be quite low between them, and there will be a decent amount of bounce from the collision. A bit of an impulse will be applied to the player, sending them off and to the right with each bounce. Essentially this creates a slippery, bouncy, conveyor belt. Note that contact materials are actually the combination of two object materials, so it is a multistep process.

```
var player = game.add.sprite(200, 200, 'player');
var ground = game.add.sprite(200, 500, 'ground');

var playerMaterial = game.physics.p2.createMaterial
  ('playerMaterial', player.body);
var groundMaterial = game.physics.p2.createMaterial
  ('groundMaterial', ground.body);

var contactMaterial = game.physics.p2.createContactM
aterial(spriteMaterial, groundMaterial);

contactMaterial.friction = 0.2;
contactMaterial.restitution = 0.5;
contactMaterial.surfaceVelocity = 1;
```

Just for fun, here's a variation of the code earlier that creates a bit of ground that lets a sprite bob atop it like it was water.

```
var player = game.add.sprite(200, 200, 'player');
var ground = game.add.sprite(200, 500, 'ground');

var playerMaterial = game.physics.p2.createMaterial
  ('playerMaterial', player.body);
var groundMaterial = game.physics.p2.createMaterial
  ('groundMaterial', ground.body);
```

```
var contactMaterial = game.physics.p2.createContact
    Material(spriteMaterial, groundMaterial);
contactMaterial.stiffness = 10;
contactMaterial.restitution = 0.5;
```

6.20 Particles

Particle systems are a game developer's method for getting flashy and visually appealing effects into their game. They are used particularly when those effects require a lot of small, moving objects (or particles) to accurately represent the effect. Some great examples of particle systems include fire, smoke, rain, and the common explosion with its resulting debris. In order to create these effects, a particle system will create a collection of sprites that will be animated and moved according to the rules of the system.

The History of Particle Systems

The term particle system was coined in 1982 with the release of Star Trek II: The Wrath of Kahn. In that movie, a system of particles was used to simulate the progression of "fire" along a planet. Before 1982, animators accomplished similar effects with hand drawn animation methods. In these cartoons, someone would need to manually animate those little pieces of debris, the snowflakes, or that water splashing off a character getting doused.

6.20.1 Particle Engine Components

Particle engines are built to efficiently create and manage a lot of sprites and their motions. They are essentially display list groups with some extra features for generating particles and updating the states of each individual particle as quickly as possible. They come in two pieces—the particle that is the visible objects on the screen and the emitter that controls the properties of the particles and how they are spawned.

6.20.1.1 Particle

Without the individual particles that are displayed on the screen, there wouldn't be much of interest to a particle system. The particles are single images that are generated by the particle system and animated for the duration of their lifespan. Once their lifespan is reached, the particle will be killed and potentially reused if the system needs a new particle. The particle has several properties that will affect how it lives and changes during its lifespan and the following are the major ones:

- **Sprite** is the graphical asset associated with the particle. The sprite could be puffs for smoke, little blue dots for rain, or little sparks for a "clashing swords" effect. The sprite asset can be a single image or a set of images that will be randomly selected for the sprite.

- **Acceleration** is for particles that are affected by gravity like rain, snow, and debris.
- **Rotation** will spin the particle as it flies. Makes for a very frantic effect.
- **Life** controls how long a particle will live. Short lives are good for bursts, while longer lives are needed for ambient effects like snow.
- **Scale** controls the size of the particle over its lifespan. Increasing a particle's scale works very nicely as a dissipation effect that smoke or similar systems may need.
- **Alpha** is often used to fade a particle away as it nears the end of its life. This makes the particle system feel a bit less jarring and more "natural."

6.20.1.2 Emitter

The other half of a particle system is the emitter. The emitter creates the particles, sets up their initial properties, animates them through their lives, and handles the destruction and reuse of the particles once their visible life is over. Emitters are similar to a group inside of Phaser's display list. While technically the particles of the emitter are children of the emitter's display list, they will not change position when the emitter is moved around on the screen unless it is set to not use world coordinates for its particles.

Just like other display objects, emitters can have a width and a height. The size of the emitter is used as the "area" that a particle might potentially be generated within. A wide emitter at the top of the screen would make a great setup for rain, and a square-shaped emitter (down to nearly a point even) might work better for a smokestack or hit explosion.

Particle systems can generate particles continuously or in a burst. A looping particle emitter will run forever and generate new particles on a set interval. These looping systems are great for atmospheric effects like rain or fireflies. A burst emitter is used for moments when some visual spectacle is needed in a game. Some common uses for a burst emitter include explosions, dust rising from a player's footsteps, or nice little visual rewards when something is done right in the game.

6.20.2 Setting Up a Burst Emitter

Burst emitters are used for one-shot "explosions" of particles. Before creating a burst of particles, the emitter should be placed at the center point of the explosion and then the "explode" method can be used. The explode method first takes the lifespan of the particles to be generated (in milliseconds) and then the numbers of particles to be made.

In the following example, a particle system is set up to explode wherever the user clicks on the screen. The emitter will generate poof cloud particles and is set up to scale those particles up and fade them away during their lifespan. The scaling is set on the emitter in the "setScale" method. This particular configuration of the scaling will start all the particles emitted at a scale of one and increase the scale to three times bigger over the period of 2 s. There are four numbers because the first two are for the x scale and the second two

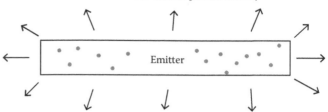

FIG 6.30 Particle area emitter with possible particle velocities.

are for the y scale. The alpha works in a similar way to scaling, taking the start and end values that every particle should be at.

```
var emitter;

function create() {
    emitter = game.add.emitter(0, 0, 100);
    emitter.makeParticles('poof');
    emitter.setAlpha(1, .2, 2000);
    emitter.setScale(1,3,1,3, 2000);
    game.input.onDown.add(makeExplosion, this);
}

function makeExplosion(pointer) {
    emitter.x = pointer.x;
    emitter.y = pointer.y;

    emitter.explode(2400, 15);
}
```

6.20.3 Setting Up an Area Emitter

Area emitters are a great choice for large atmospheric effects. To make an area emitter, the size of the emitter needs to be adjusted to take up the width (or height) of the area where a particle might spawn. Here is a simple example of an emitter that simulates some basic rain in a game scene (see Figure 6.30).

```
var emitter = game.add.emitter(game.world.centerX,
    0, 400);
emitter.width = game.world.width;

emitter.makeParticles('rain');

emitter.minParticleScale = 0.1;
emitter.maxParticleScale = 0.5;
emitter.setYSpeed(300, 500);
emitter.start(false, 1600, 5, 0);
```

6.21 Signals

Signals are a form of event-driven programming. They are a way to defer calling a function until something notable has happened that requires a response. In other words, they are functions can be defined that will handle important events throughout an application's lifetime. Some common events in Phaser include mouse clicks, sound events like complete and restart, and collision events.

Signals come in two parts. The first part is the signal object itself. This is the object that will inform others that something has happened that needs to be responded to. In order to inform other objects that the event has happened, the signal needs to be "fired." The signal object also has methods to register functions that should be run when the signal fires. Methods that respond to a signal firing are often called event handlers.

Listener Memory

Signals in Phaser take up memory and also reference count in JavaScript's garbage collector. It is important to clean away any unneeded signals so that the JavaScript engine can remove objects that are the reference of a signal. If you only need to respond to an event once, use the `addOnce()` signal listener, and, when you're done with a signal, make sure to remove all its event listeners with the `removeAll` method.

6.21.1 Using a Signal

Just about anywhere the *add* or *addOnce* methods are used in Phaser and a function is provided as an input a signal is being used. Here is a very common signal used throughout this book:

```
create() {
    this.load.onLoadComplete.addOnce(this.
      onLoadComplete, this);
}
onLoadComplete() {
    //handler
}
```

The two parts of adding the handler is specifying the function to be run (`onLoadComplete`) and the context that function should be run in (`this`). The difference between `add` and `addOnce` is that `addOnce` will respond to the signal only once. After the `onLoadComplete` function runs, the listener will be removed and the function will not respond to the signal in the future.

6.22 Making a Custom Signal

Sometimes a developer might have some events that their own objects will need to dispatch. Perhaps, it will fire an event when a player dies or when an AI has made a decision that needs to be communicated to other objects. Whatever the need, the process of creating and using a custom signal is quite easy.

```
this.countdownStarted = new Phaser.Signal();
this.countdownStarted.addOnce(this.swapBackground,
  this);
```

6.23 Removing a Listener from a Signal

Sometimes one needs to get rid of a listener from a signal, either because the event no longer needs to be handled or it is time to clean up the object and get rid of it safely. In the following example, a listener is added, and then remove once it is called, simulating the way the "addOnce" listener works. Note that when removing a listener, both the handler function and the context have to be the same (making it look like a mirror of the add code).

```
function create() {
        this.nukeWorld = new Phaser.Signal();
        this.nukeWorld.add (delayNuke, this);
}
function delayNuke() {
        this.nukeWorld.remove(delayNuke, this);
}
```

6.24 Prefabs

Games have a lot of moving parts that a developer needs to track. Even in a simple shoot 'em up game, a player is tasked with making a character to avoid enemies and attacks that are flying at them from the opposite side of the screen. Different parts of this game would include the player character, the objects being flung, a timer, a score box, and perhaps even a health bar for the player. Already for this rather simple game, there is a lot of lines of code needed to set up, manage, and update these different components in the game.

Writing the code for all the different parts of a game in one large file can quickly get out of hand. The file gets huge, the different phases of the object's lifecycle are strewn about this huge file, and editing can become a mess. A good solution to this problem is to break the code up into small, self-managing files and components. Breaking these files down into these "classes" or "components" makes the game state's code more readable and helps with the maintainability of the project in total. In the game development world, another term for these self-managing components is "prefabs," short for "prefabricated." These prefabs are typically objects that will be used in multiple scenes and in multiple projects.

The best approach to making a prefab in ECMAScript 6 is to extend a Phaser object and add on the properties and methods that make this extended Phaser object unique. Any methods that are called automatically on the base class (like update) will still be called automatically within a prefab as well. The prefab's update methods will be called when the state runs its update methods, so it is a great way to remove code from the game state and put it into a separate container. There are two common types of prefabs: UI (that usually extend a group) and game object (typically extend a sprite).

The process of making a prefab starts with creating a new JavaScript file to store the object's code. Throughout this book, the prefabs will be placed into the src/prefabs folder and will have the same name as the object in the file. If it is an angry enemy, the file name will be "AngryEnemy.js".

6.24.1 Making a Game Object Prefab

A game object prefab nearly always extends a Phaser sprite. When extending a sprite, the constructor arguments need to be passed onto Phaser's sprite prototype via the super method in the constructor. In a prefab the update method is often overridden with custom movement, input, or AI code. In later chapters, it will also be very common for new signals to be added to a sprite, so it can fire signals when the game needs to know something significant has happened internally in the prefab. Following is the boilerplate for making a game object prefab.

```
export default class PrefabExample extends Phaser.
  Sprite {

    constructor(game, x, y, frame) {
      super(game, x, y, 'spriteAssetKey', frame);

      // initialize your prefab here

      //here is a simple, speed variable
      this.speed = 2;
    }

    //simple usage of the update function
    //along with the class properties
    update() {
          this.x += this.speed;
    }
}
```

6.24.2 Making a User Interface Prefab

UI objects are typically collections of graphics and text that need to stay together in fix positions compared to each other, but the group of all the assets may be moved around based on the size of the display viewing the game. A group is great at being able to be repositioned while keeping the position of all the objects inside of it the same relative to each other, making it an optimal choice for a UI prefab. In the following example, some text is added to show a common setup for a UI prefab, but images and even particles are all acceptable items to add as well.

```
export default class UIComponent extends Phaser.
  Group {

    constructor(game, parent) {
          super(game, parent);
```

125

```
        // initialize your components here
        //add hearts, text, or whatever else is
            needed.

        //for instance, here's some text
        var style = { font: "30px Arial", align:
          "center", fill: "#fff" };
        this.txtValue = new Phaser.Text(this.
          game, 55, 55, "Hello World", style);
        this.add(this.txtValue);
    }

    update() {

    }
}
```

6.24.3 Using Prefabs

When working with prefabs like this, there is no built-in constructor in Phaser to generate the prefabs as there are for tilemaps, sprites, or text fields. Instead, the object will need to be created and added into the scene manually. Phaser supports adding new objects to the display list (including our custom objects) via the "game.add.existing" method.

Just like creating and setting up the states for the game, these prefabs need to be imported into the current script before they can be used. When creating these prefabs, the first argument must be a reference to the active Phaser game. If the game is not passed into the prefab, it will break and not work with the rest of your application.

```
//require our other computers
import PrefabExample from "../prefabs/PrefabExample.js";
import UIComponent from "../prefabs/UIComponent.js";

export default class Game extends Phaser.State {
  constructor() {
    //object level properties
    super();
  }

  create() {
      //add a prefab
      this.prefab = new PrefabExample (this.game,0,0);
      this.game.add.existing(this.prefab);

      //add a UIComponent
      this.component = new UIComponent (this.game);
      this.game.add.existing(this.component);

  }
}
```

6.25 Exists Flag

Video games remain an interesting field for many programmers because they need good performance at a high speed to be acceptable to the player. Spikes in processing time for individual frames can ruin the game, as can eventual slowdown for the entire game due to memory leaks. For small and simple games, especially ones where nothing new is being created and added into the game after setup, these memory issues are not a huge problem. A good example of these "limited memory" games would be a game of checkers. Though some pieces might change form, new pieces are never actually added to the board. The amount of stuff in the game (the "memory" it takes up) is preloaded before the game begins and thankfully never gets out of control with more and more checkers as the gameplay progresses.

Modern games sadly are not often like checkers. Games like shoot 'em ups will create and destroy assets quite often, especially if the shmup is one of the "bullet hell" variants where hundreds of bullets will be on the screen at a time. All of those bullets need to be generated and destroyed and are quite often done so very quickly. Creating, destroying, and managing those objects quickly is where the management of objects becomes tricky due to the time it takes to create and clean up objects.

6.25.1 Game Memory and the Garbage Collector

The two things it takes to make a new game object is time and memory. When constructing an object, the computer has to find space for that object in the computer memory. Once the computer has found the space for the object, it still will need to run through the object's constructor and hook up all the pieces of the object and get the values of its properties set, which will take up a bit more time on the computer.

The number of objects or variables that an application can take up is limited by the computer's free memory and the memory the computer will give to this particular JavaScript application. If the application keeps running and needs more memory, it might get a bit more memory to work with, but the JavaScript engine will also attempt to clear out unused variables, in order to get your game some new free space to work with. This attempt to clear out the unused memory is called "garbage collection," and it can happen at just about any time during your program execution. When the JavaScript engine does its garbage collection, the rest of your scripts will slow down until the collection pass finishes. The slowdown will be especially apparent if you have a lot of objects that need to be deleted from the game.

The way a garbage collector knows when to delete an object from memory is through a technique called reference counting. A reference count for an object is started at one when the variable is created. It is incremented upward for other references that refer to it. For instance, you might create a variable called "player" in the game state and then make another reference to that player in an enemy prefab (so it knows to chase the player); the final reference count would be two. If the enemy is deleted, but the player is kept in the state, the reference would return to one. Once the state is exited and destroyed (taking with it the player variable in it), there will be no variables that still reference the player instance, dropping its reference count to zero. During the next garbage collection pass, the JavaScript engine will remove the player object from the application memory, freeing the memory space up for something else.

Because it takes time to create objects, making a multitude of objects in a single frame will slow an application down for that frame. While this slowdown wouldn't be bad in backend applications, it is a killer in a user-facing game where the stutter can bother a player and make them mistime a jump or shot. If all these objects that are being created are needed for only a short time before being abandoned (such as the particles in a particle effect), the game will quickly start taking up a lot of memory space and eventually slow down from the memory load. If the developer doesn't do something to clean up an object when they're done with it (usually by clearing any references to it and setting the object to null), JavaScript's garbage collector will never mark it for deletion and it will never get properly cleaned up. Instead, more and more objects of the same type are created, taking increasing computation time that leads to an application slowdown.

The takeaway from this discussion is that all those bullets that have flown off screen and the enemies that have been destroyed in the game don't really need their physics updated, or positioned changed, or even to be rendered. The first solution to this problem of running a bunch of unnecessary computation on items that really don't need to be updated is to have a flag on the object to tell the game engine not to run the update methods on that object. The exists property that every Phaser display object has can be set to false to cause the game to stop rendering and processing the logic (physics and update) of the object. Flagging the object as not currently existing is great for removing an object from the game when it would otherwise be wasting processing time, or getting in the way of other objects in the game.

Quickly Removing Objects

Phaser game objects have a `kill()` method that will also remove the object from the game and set it to not existing. It is best to use this method in your code over simply toggling the exists flag to false because it will make sure that the loss of the object won't hurt the game and is a more readable method.

6.26 Object Pooling

Simply setting the "exists" flag to false does not remove the object from memory, just from the game state's updates. The object is still there taking up memory, but most likely it has lived out its usefulness in the game. The bullet has hit something or the enemy is dead, and their "exists" flag has been toggled off so they're not wasting time. The object is most likely ready to have the final references to it removed, so the garbage collector can pick it up and free the memory space. Until the garbage collector gets to it through, it is just a waste of space, unused and unneeded. Some smart developers quickly realized that there are two problems than can be solved here. It takes time to create a new object in memory, and there is a perfectly fine (if slightly used) version of the object that will also take time to clean up. Their solution to these time-wasting processes was to reuse those "dead" items instead of creating new ones all of the time. This winds up in the game creating and destroying a lot less assets throughout its lifespan. This approach to reusing similar objects is called an "object pool" and is something that Phaser supports (to a certain degree) via the group object. A group object that will be used as a pool needs to be used as a collection of all the similar objects like all enemies or all bullets. The group has a method that will find the first object in the group that is currently "dead," which can be presumed to be ready to be revived and brought back into the game as a "new" object.

There are a few approaches to pooling objects in a video game. The first approach is to create the maximum number of objects that could ever be needed in the game and turn off their existing property right when they are created. Then, when the game needs a new object, revive the first dead object in the group as needed throughout the game. You can rely on this approach never taking up more memory and never slowing down due to object creation. Unfortunately, if the maximum number of game objects that were prewarmed into the group is reached, no more objects will be made. In a game, the player firing the bullets would just suddenly run out of ammo.

The second approach to object pooling is to reuse old objects when they are available and create new ones if there are no old objects free. The end result is a much more "elastic" pool that grows to the size it is needed but tends to grow slowly and not get too large. This approach takes a bit more code to accomplish and will incur hits near the start of the game most likely as the pool generates the first objects. For both approaches, if the game objects are still not properly managed and toggled to "dead" when they have done their work, a memory usage buildup will continue.

Groups in Phaser can be used to collect similar objects together and find any dead ones that can be brought back to life. The most important parts of an object pool is being able to mark an object as "dead," knowing if there are any "dead" objects that can be revived, and being able to find those objects to revive them when needed. These tasks can be accomplished in Phaser with the "alive" attribute of Phaser sprites and the `countDead` and `getFirstDead` methods of a Phaser group. Following is a short code example that shows an implementation of a pool using a Phaser group.

```
var poolGroup;

function create() {
        game.physics.startSystem(Phaser.Physics.ARCADE);
        game.physics.arcade.gravity.y = 100;
        poolGroup = game.add.group();
        poolGroup.enableBody = true;
        poolGroup.createMultiple(40, "particle");
}

function update() {
    if(poolGroup.countDead()) {
            var particle = poolGroup.getFirstDead();
            particle.reset();
            particle.x = Math.random() * game.width;
            particle.y = 0;
            particle.lifespan = 1000;
        }
    }
```

This example is the first type of pool that creates all the objects before the game begins. This particular pool and example will act like a particle system, placing new particles at the top of the screen and having them live out their life falling downward. The objects will be flagged as dead after a second. Each update, if the group has at least one dead object it will be reset to its starting state and placed at a random point at the top of the screen. This object is given 1 s (1000 ms) to "live" and sent on its way, with the world gravity quickly taking its effect and pulling it down. Once the object "dies" after that second, it is open again for the group to find it with another `getFirstDead` method call, recycling it once again.

Difference between Revive and Reset

There are two ways to bring an object "back from the dead": revive and reset. For the most part, the `.revive()` method will work just fine. This simply sets the object back to existing and makes it visible again, without changing any of its other properties (things like position and physics body properties remain unchanged).

If properties from the object's old "life" get in the way (for instance, a dead object might have an unwanted velocity due to gravity), then the `reset()` method is the best way to revive the object. The reset method will clear out old positions and physics attributes on the object, essentially making it a "clean slate" version of the object. In the aforementioned example, replacing the reset with a revive would fail to reset the particle's downward velocity. They would begin to fall faster and faster, until they become almost untraceable by the human eye.

6.26.1 Life

Sometimes an object only needs to live for a short while in a game scene. A bullet will only be on screen for so long, a particle will slowly putter out, or a collectable may only need to be on the screen briefly before it disappears and stops tempting the player. The property "lifespan" is a built-in system to automatically kill objects after a set amount of time. This property can be set on various game objects, such as sprites, and is set in milliseconds (1000 to every 1 s). Phaser will automatically decrement the life of any object that has a lifespan set. Once the life hits zero, the game object will be killed. In the previous example, there is a 1 s lifespan set on the particles. When reviving them, it is important to set their life once again, so they can live out a life instead of simply existing forever.

6.27 Animation

Animation can be a key feature of many games, and it is not always feasible to rely on others to create and implement all the animations in your game, especially if it is a small game. For a small developer, it is important to know how animations are made, what formats to export, and what tools are available for the game developer to create these animations. In general, there are two different ways to create animations, each with their own toolsets and approaches. The first approach is called frame by frame, which gives the animator more control over each frame of animation. The second animation technique that gives a bit less control over the animation but is typically faster is keyframed animation.

Frame by frame is the more "traditional" way to work. When working frame by frame, an animator creates the art for each frame of movement individually. A skillful animator working per frame can create something that is quite engaging and beautiful, usually producing work that simply cannot be recreated by keyframed animations due to complex changes in positions and forms of the sprite. Traditional sprites in classic 8-bit or 16-bit video games are a great example of frame by frame animation. During this period of game development, each frame of animation was handcrafted by the animator, sometimes on a per pixel basis to get the most out of every pixel. It took a great amount of care and skill, but the result was often very powerful imagery in a very small amount of space (examples are given in Figures 6.31 through 6.36).

Keyframed animation is a second way to create animation for a game. The resulting animations are often smoother and the process of creating the animations is much faster than frame-by-frame movement. When creating a keyframed animation, the artist or animator will work with static graphics pieces that transformed from one position to another over the duration of the animation. The static assets for a humanoid character then might include individual assets for the arms, legs, head, and torso. Before doing the animation, each of the assets is arranged in the animation program, so a full human is formed. The animator then creates different positions, rotations, and scales of the assets at set moments in time (called keyframes), and the program will calculate where they should appear in between the keyframes (the tweens). See Figures 6.31 and 6.32.

Exporting keyframed animations to a sprite sheet can prove problematic for video games. In order to get the benefits of the "fluid" animation, even at the 12 frames/s for a human to perceive motion, a lot of frames of animation will need to be rendered to the sprite sheet. The number of frames required would be huge. Some programs will forego rendering out individual frames by simply

Frame one   Frame two

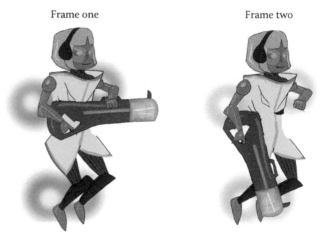

FIG 6.31 Two keyframed positions for animation.

Tween frames (at low opacity)

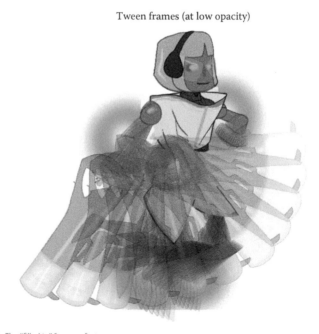

FIG 6.32 The "filled in" frames of a tween.

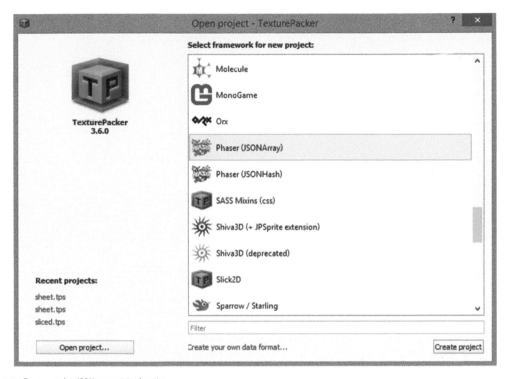

FIG 6.33 Texture packer JSON array option location.

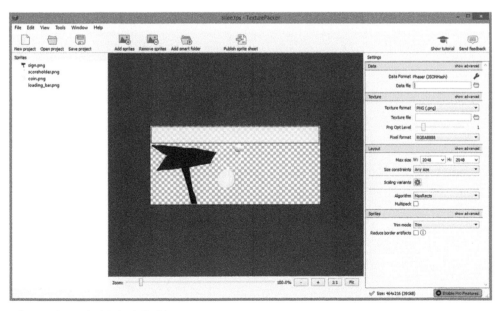

FIG 6.34 Export settings on the right-hand side of the program.

Different ratios and set widths

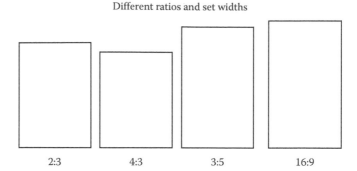

2:3   4:3   3:5   16:9

FIG 6.35 Comparison of ratio sizes.

Original and scaled sprite

FIG 6.36 Loss of visual detail from upscaling.

exporting the animation data and relying on the game to render the animations of the individual pieces at runtime. This approach takes up less disc space but will incur a hit to processor load during gameplay because the animations will have to be interpreted and performed for each individual sprite.

6.27.1 Rigs

Phaser has begun to support one type of keyframed animation called skeletal animation. This type of animation is commonly used by game developers working on character animations for their 3D game assets and has also been applied to 2D animations. In a skeletal animation, a series of bones are defined for a character. In general, each bone controls the rotation of one sprite that makes up the character, and each bone is connected to others via joints. These bones affect the bones they are attached to through a something called a kinematic chain and will drag neighbors along when they move. In a fully rigged skeleton, pulling up on a finger will drag the hand, lower, and upper arm along with it, quickly moving all the pieces into place without the need of adjusting the positions of all the individual elements. A complete set of bones is called a rig, which is animated via keyframes. Positions are specified for the rig at distinct parts of the animation and the computer will generate the in-betweens for the poses automatically.

6.27.2 Animation Software

There is a wide selection of different programs that are capable of creating animations for Phaser, especially if one is focused on creating simple pixel art for their games. The following is a curated selection of tools that tend to be popular among game developers for creating animations. It is possible to create wonderful art assets with free software and this list will attempt to indicate where a paid application brings extra power or capabilities to developers.

6.27.2.1 For Creating Pixel Art

- Photoshop is the clear winner in the professional space, but it comes at a professional's price. Many tutorials will make an assumption that you are using Photoshop or are well versed in it. It can handle everything from complex painting (and photo editing) all the way down to pixel drawing. It does a lot more than just pixel editing though and may be too bloated for some.
- Gimp and paint.net are free programs that can easily do all the things that one would need Photoshop to accomplish when creating art for games and sprites.

6.27.2.2 For Creating 2D Animations

- Creature is a relative newcomer. It is an animation system that gives an animator access to bones and the ability to deform the pixels of the sprites around the bones in a believable way. Phaser supports the exports from Creature's skeletal animations, but not the pixel deformations at this time.
- Spine is one of the leading sprite animation packages. It is a paid program that supports creating rigs for animating 2D puppets as well as mesh deformation of sprites. Spine has a large amount of support among game developers, but it does not have the best integration with Phaser at this time.
- Spriter is another puppet animation tool. It is a bit less full featured than the previous two, but it remains a good and approachable program that has a great community for support.

6.27.3 For Both Art and Animations

- Aseprite is a free program for frame-by-frame pixel animations. It has a robust feature set like a zoom view for pixel creation, a timeline view, and onion skins to see previous frames of an animation.

- Adobe Flash is one of the older animation software packages on this list. Unlike the other two programs in this section that create both art and animations, Flash is a vector animation package, meaning it doesn't edit pixels directly. Instead, it stores lines and colors between lines. The drawing tools tend to impart a more cartoony look to the final animations that can be done either frame by frame or keyframed. It is a paid application, but will worth it for complex cartoony animations.
- Graphics Gale is another sprite editing system that is similar to Aseprite. It supports the creation and animation of pixel sprites, along with the necessary tools to animate quickly like looping test animations and zooming in on the animation.

6.28 Making Atlases

Texture atlases are ways to put many different sprites into a single image. This saves some space on the computer and allows for spites to be packed as tightly as possible into an image's space. Because there are multiple sprites in an atlas, there will also be a need for a file that describes the locations of those sprites in the image. For JavaScript games, this file is typically a JSON file that needs to be loaded and associated with the packed image.

There are a lot of programs on the web that can produce sprite atlases. A search engine query for "texture packer" or "sprite atlas" will return a good selection of programs that can get the job done for you. One good choice due to its ease of use and the ability to export to formats that Phaser can use is "Texture Packer," made by CodeAndWeb. The basic features of this program are free, and you can find a download for the program at its website https://www.codeandweb.com/texturepacker.

6.28.1 Using Texture Packer

When you launch "texture packer", you will be presented with a new project screen. If you scroll down, you will see that there are two options defined for Phaser already: JSON array and JSON hash. If this atlas is meant to be used for an animation, use JSON array. Otherwise you should select JSON hash when creating a packed set of unrelated objects.

Once you create a new project, you can then drag and drop as many sprites as you want into the center area of the screen. Texture Packer will automatically lay these sprites out for you whenever you add a new one.

Once you have all the sprites you want in your texture atlas, you will need to export the project into the files that Phaser can read. So long as you started the project as one of the two of the Phaser defaults, you can go to file → export to create these files. You will be prompted twice to input file names and locations. The first prompt is for the JSON file that contains the information about what sprites are in the atlas and how big they are. The second prompt is to name the image that contains all the sprites itself. A pluralized name that fits both files is a good way to name these two, such as "`gameAssets.json`" and "`gameAssets.png`". It is best to save these assets into your game project assets folder. Once the atlas and image have been made, they can be loaded into Phaser via the `load.atlasJSONHash` or `load.atlasJSONArray` methods.

6.29 Viewport Scaling

For many games, the width and height of the screen will vary based on the size of the user's screen, such as when the game is in full screen on a mobile device. This will result in different rectangular views into the game world because devices are not made with the same resolutions (number of pixels in the display) nor do they all have the same display aspect ratio. The display aspect ratio (commonly just shorted to "aspect ratio" or even just "ratio") is the proportion of width-wise pixel to height-wise pixel expressed with two numbers. Common ratios include 4:3 (or "square TV shape"), 5:4, 16:9 (which is monitor standard), and 16:10. These ratios are only the most common ones, and there are others that may be encountered on devices and display targets for your game (see Figure 6.35).

The difference in resolution and ratio means that different resolutions will require different scales of sprites. The second issue a mobile developer needs to address is the different sizes of their canvas. Phaser has some built-in features to handle changes in canvas size that instructs Phaser on how to automatically scale the entire game scene and how to handle overflow. If not properly handled, the game can either display too small, too large, or may render assets in unexpected places with large gaps on the edge of the screen.

The base resolution of your sprites is important. If your game is too large and your sprites were built for a smaller display, your sprites will look somewhat blurry when they are upscaled. When making your games, decide on a specific resolution first, and create your graphics to match that resolution. This may necessitate making different builds of your game for different targets if you want the highest resolution graphics on each (one version for mobile, another for the web). When targeting mobile, stick to smaller graphics, even if you may want to deploy to devices with high resolutions.

When working with mobile devices you should choose a device orientation and aspect ratio as your target and scale from that ratio. When developing for mobile devices, the ratio can be swapped into two different directions: portrait and landscape. A device in portrait mode is held in one hand like a phone and will be taller and not wider. In landscape mode, a device is wider and not taller and is typically held in two hands.

For a further discussion of resizing UIs and game worlds, read through the slicer game example chapter 7.9 that implements some of the more common resizing techniques for mobile applications.

Game Examples

The previous chapters (4,5, and 6) in this book were like a box of Legos. There were a lot of pieces and potentials, but they were strewn about with no real direction on how they all might fit together. The next section of this book is going to give you a few projects to begin to show you the way these pieces can be fit together. The goal is to give you a good base to start a game and to show you some techniques that are commonly used when crafting games. Each project is described in a similar manner to online tutorials in order to keep them approachable and help you understand any other Phaser tutorials you may come across when looking for more inspiration. When finished with a project, don't just leave in its final state. Like any good Lego model, half of the project is breaking it apart and remixing the model. I will leave you with a few ideas on how to remix the games, but I hope you have a few ideas of your own by the end.

Project one is a shoot 'em up (or "shmup" for short) that will bring together the concepts of states and transpiling into the classic introduction to game development. In this game, a player will be tasked with flying around the screen and shooting as many of the enemies hurtling at the player character as possible. Collisions, prefabs, user interface (UI), and showing scores are concepts that will be explored in this game. Basic functionality like "start" and "game over" screens will also be covered in this chapter.

Project two is a platformer that builds upon the concepts in project one with the addition of tilemaps, map creation, and level object placement. Some simple artificial intelligence (AI) will be covered in this game, along with a closer look at the Tiled map editor on how it can be used to generate all the parts of a level including enemy and collectable placement.

Project three is an isometric tower defense game that explores how two-dimensional (2D) space can be manipulated to give the impression of a third dimension. While some of the math and concepts will be explored for both pathfinding and isometric engines, plugins will be used for the actual final build of the game, and there will be a brief discussion of finding and integrating external plugins into your game.

Project four is an object slicing game that tasks the user with cutting objects on the screen via swipe gestures. Because this is a game intended for play on mobile devices, resizing the game and implementation of a fluid UI will be discussed in order to handle the wide variance in screen resolutions. Implementation of basic gestures will also be covered due to Phaser lacking a gesture library of its own.

Project five is a take on the catapult destruction sim that will fall in a similar vein as games like Angry Birds. The development and layout of the objects in these types of games can be tricky to correctly implement, so this chapter will delve more deeply into the P2 physics system in Phaser.

Each game will have unique assets that will be used for the gameplay. It is outside the scope of this book to walk you through the process of creating all the assets you need, and many of the projects are reliant on the code matching the assets (so animations match up, or hitboxes are the correct size). If you want to follow along with these tutorials you will need to download the assets for the games. They all have been hosted at https://github.com/meanderingleaf/PhaserBookExamples. You should be able to find a *download zip* link on the first page that will let you download all the assets without a lot of hassle.

Each of these games will be stepped through in as much detail as possible. If, however, you just want to see the final result in order to get a better picture of how it all fits together or to check out the code for yourself and make modifications, you can find the git repo that hosts all the examples at https://github.com/meanderingleaf/PhaserBookExamples.

7.1 Shoot 'em Up

Common advice to any beginning game developer, who has a game idea with a huge scope, is to "program a shoot 'em up first." While it may sound condescending at first, it actually remains a great advice. The shoot 'em up game genre, which contains many classics like Galaga, Gradius, and Defender, contains all of the basics one needs to master in order to make games while still remaining quite simple and approachable for a beginner. Like games that claim to be "easy to play, hard to master," a shoot 'em up has a ton of room to evolve and grow and can potentially keep the novice engaged for a long time after their first shooter game. Dual-stick shooters like Geometry Wars (which doesn't restrict the player to just shooting forward), or the bullet hell–type games like Ikaruga (where the number of projectiles to dodge on the screen is just staggering), all come from the exact same template as the base shmup (examples are shown in Figures 7.1 through 7.5).

The concepts behind a shoot 'em up game are fairly simple. The player is given control of a ship (or whatever it may be). Sometimes they are restricted to one axis of movement, being only able to move horizontally or vertically. Space Invaders is a great example of a game with single-axis movement. Most shmups, however, give the player the capability to navigate in both the x- and y-axes. Objects are then spawned into the game that the player must avoid or destroy. At its very simplest as in the case of Asteroids, the enemies are dumb rocks, and the player has a very basic single shot projectiles to destroy its obstacles. More advanced versions give the player the capability to upgrade weapons, waves of opponents, and AIs to deal with. In short, the shoot 'em up provides a nice canvas that can be used as the base for a lot of engaging gameplay.

The shoot 'em up in this chapter is meant to be a simpler version of the genre that will demonstrate many of the common elements of the genre and can then be used as a base that can be built upon to make something more engaging later. Common gameplay elements that will be explored in this game include enemies, wave spawning, projectiles, collisions, and score keeping. The end result will be a game with start and end screens, a player character controlled via the arrow keys on the keyboard, enemies that shoot projects, and the capability to shoot at and destroy those enemies.

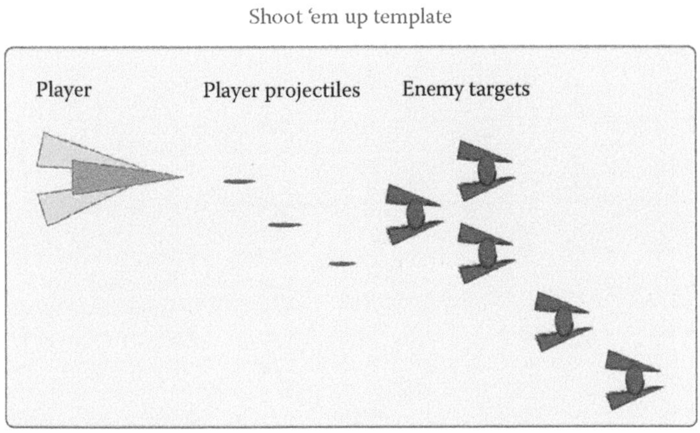

Shoot 'em up template

FIG 7.1 Basic design of a shmup.

FIG 7.2 Player character sprite sheet.

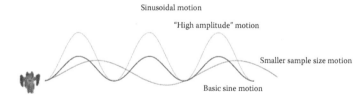

FIG 7.3 Variations on sinusoidal motion.

Score text with "framing" image

FIG 7.4 UI image frame.

Healthbar at 80% full

FIG 7.5 Scaled down healthbar.

To begin with, create the basic project structure described in chapter five. We will be adding to that base throughout this exercise. Should you need to see the finished code or to get the assets for the game, you can find the full source at https://github.com/meanderingleaf/PhaserBookExamples/tree/master/shmup.

7.1.1 Preload Phase

Here the assets for the game will be loaded in. In this case, the focus is on learning how all the pieces fit together in a game, so only images and sprite sheets will be loaded in for this game. Most of the images are self-explanatory, with nearly every asset in this game being a simple image. Future games will be including sounds, tilemaps, and a number of other sorts of extra information, so take this as an opportunity to get used to the style and syntax of loading.

In the preload.js state file, where the template mentions to do all the preloading, add these lines to load in the assets for this game.

```
this.load.image('enemy', 'assets/images/enemy.png');
this.load.image('explosion', 'assets/images/
  explosion.png');

this.load.spritesheet('player', 'assets/images/
  gunbot.png', 214, 269);
this.load.image('hexagon', 'assets/images/
  hexagon_particle.png');
this.load.image('bullet', 'assets/images/bullet.png');
this.load.image('enemyBullet', 'assets/images/
  enemyBullet.png');
this.load.image('bg', 'assets/images/bg.jpg');

this.load.image('health_bar', 'assets/images/
  health_bar.png');
this.load.image('health_holder', 'assets/images/
  health_holder.png');
this.load.image('circle', 'assets/images/circle.png');
```

The only animation in this game is for the player, who will have two different animations: an idle "flying" animation that will play when she's not doing anything else and a shooting animation. Note in Figure 7.2 how the frames can be laid out both vertically and horizontally and how Phaser will still be able to compute the frames.

7.1.2 "Start" and "Game Over" States

Before hopping into the action of the gameplay, most games have some form of home or start screen. This is the screen that is used for imparting the flavor of the game like the game name, giving a chance for the player to choose options or see instructions, and make sure the player is actually ready with their hands on the right buttons and keys before the game starts.

In a similar vein, a "game over" screen gives a developer a chance to let the player cool down from a play session, and maybe show stats and feedback from the round they just played. Or just give the player a bit of encouragement, such as in the game over screen for Earthbound.

The start and end screens for this shmup are going to fall on the simple side, simply displaying a graphic and waiting for user input. The following is a basic form for the start screen, which can easily be cloned for the game over screen as well by changing the class name and file name.

```
export default class StartScreen {

    create() {

    }

    update() {
        if(this.game.input.keyboard.isDown(Phaser.
          Keyboard.SPACEBAR)) {
            this.game.state.start('game');
        }

    }

}
```

7.2 Game Prefabs

Remember that prefabs are little reusable components where it makes sense to separate the code for that game object from the rest of the game. Usually these are things that will be operating as their own, distinct entities in the game. These could be enemy that can control its own paths and decisions, or a door that needs to manage its internal open and closed states. In this game, there are two game objects that immediately come to mind as good candidates for prefabs—the player and the enemies. Both of these are sprite objects that do a bit more than just a normal sprite and can easily manage all of their workings internally without needing help from the game application or the game state. What makes them exceptionally great candidates to be turned into prefabs is that each needs a custom update method. While it is possible to write all the update code for the player and the enemies in the game state's update method, pulling those lines of code out into a new file will keep everything clean and readable.

7.2.1 Player Prefab

The player character is our first concern in this game. Without an object in the game that the player can control, it quickly becomes less a game and more a simulation. Getting the player in will help when testing the other parts of the application and generally gives the developer a good sense of the "feel" of a game if they have access to their character right away. In a shoot 'em up game, common things a player may need to do are move freely on both axes and shoot bullets. Additionally, it makes sense for the player object to be managing other information about its state, such as the current player health, active power-ups, or player shielding (for advanced games, of course).

Because the player character is flying around with what appears to be little jet packs, we're going to add a bit of extra play in her movement by having her slow out of her movements when the player stops inputting motion. This will be done by adding some vertical drag to her motion, and moving her via a velocity instead of via pure pixel dimensions. She'll be a bit more "slippery" because when the player releases a key, she will continue moving in the same direction for a few moments, until her drag takes over and brings her to a halt.

7.2.1.1 Player Motion

The motion of the player is a combination of the drag and speed. The drag, set in the constructor, is the amount of force that pushes work against a sprite's body when it moves via velocity.

```
this.speed = 100;
this.game.physics.enable(this, Phaser.Physics.ARCADE);
this.body.drag.x = 35;
this.body.drag.y = 35;
```

When arrow keys are held down, a force is applied to the player, overriding the majority of the drag, but not all of it. The drag will continue to pull back on the player, meaning that even if the speed is set to 100 like it is in the constructor, the drag will pull back on the player when it is moving, so she'll never actually hit a speed of 100. Increasing the drag will affect the maximum speed the player can reach and how quickly the player will slow to a stop. Larger drags mean lower max speeds and faster stopping times. Changing the speed property in the constructor will affect how quickly the player moves in general. In general, when raising the speed of an object, if you want it to stop at about the same rate as it was before, raise the drag an equal percentage.

```
if(this.cursors.left.isDown) {
        this.body.velocity.x = -this.speed;
}

if(this.cursors.right.isDown) {
        this.body.velocity.x = this.speed;
}
```

```
if(this.cursors.up.isDown) {
        this.body.velocity.y = -this.speed;
}

if(this.cursors.down.isDown) {
        this.body.velocity.y = this.speed;
}

if(this.fireButton.isDown) {
        this.fire();
}
```

7.2.1.2 Firing

The next step in getting this player ready to blast her way through anything she sees is to set her up to fire bullets. The bullets will need to be on their own group in the game state's display list to be able to take advantage of Phaser's physics.overlap method to check to see if they have "hit" anything later on. This group will be passed into the player object through its object constructor. A few other setup actions related to the firing mechanic take place in the constructor, including setting up the fire button, initializing a variable that will be used to control how often the player will actually be able to fire, and setting up the animation that will play when the user fires a shot. Finally, there is a playFly event handler that triggers when the fire animation has completed.

The following is the firing-specific code in the create method:

```
this.bulletGate = 0;
this.shotInterval = 500;
this.bullets = bullets;
this.fireButton = this.game.input.keyboard.addKey(
                Phaser.Keyboard.SPACEBAR
            );
this.fireposition = { x: 160, y: 100 };
this.fireAnimation = this.animations.add("fire",
  [11,12,13]);
this.fireAnimation.onComplete.add(this.playFly,
  this);
```

The update function checks every frame to see if the fire button (in this case, the spacebar) is down. If it is, it calls the fire function, discussed next.

The following is the fire code in the update function:

```
if(this.fireButton.isDown) {
        this.fire();
}
```

The fire function does a number of interesting things and is worth a close look, especially considering the number of games that may rely on this mechanic or a variation of it.

Here is an example of the player fire method:

```
fire() {

    if(this.game.time.now > this.bulletGate) {

        var bullet = this.bullets.getFirstDead();
        if(bullet) {
            bullet.x = this.x + this.
                fireposition.x;
            bullet.y = this.y + this.
                fireposition.y;
            bullet.revive();
        } else {
            bullet = this.bullets.create(
                            this.x + this.
                                fireposition.x,
                            this.y+this.
                                fireposition.y,
                            "bullet"
                            );
            this.game.physics.enable(bullet,
                Phaser.Physics.ARCADE);
            bullet.outOfBoundsKill = true;
            bullet.checkWorldBounds = true;
            bullet.body.velocity.x = 250;
        }

        this.bulletGate = this.game.time.now +
            this.shotInterval;

        this.animations.play("fire");

    }

}
```

The first bit of code in the fire function checks to make sure that enough time has elapsed between the last shot and the current frame for a new shot to be generated. This is based on the bullet gate (which stores the next time a shot is allowed). If the time is greater than this number, a new bullet is generated, and, at the end of the *if* statement, the gate is updated to an amount of time in the future, as specified by the shot interval (set in the constructor function). By default, the shot interval is set to 500 ms, so every shot can only take place every half second. With this function, if the current time the shot is fired at is 1200 ms, the next time one can be generated is at 1700 (1200 + 500) ms, making the player wait that half a second before they can shoot again, even if they're mashing the button or holding it down.

This particular fire method uses the "elastic" form of object pooling. Because it is not prewarmed like other pools with all the bullets it could possibly need, the code looks a little bit more complex. First, it starts checking if a "dead" bullet already exists. If it does, then that means that the bullet is already set up with a velocity and everything it needs, and it simply needs to be repositioned and brought back to life. If a bullet is not available already, a new one is generated and added to the bullet layer. The bullet is enabled for physics, so it can collide against other things and be affected by velocity. Its velocity is set to a positive value making it move right nonstop because it has no drag. Additionally, the bullet is set to kill itself once it flies off screen, setting itself to "dead" and readying it for reuse later on in the game (it will be returned by the getFirstDead method when a new shot needs to be generated in this block).

When the bullet is placed onto the screen, it is placed based on the player's current x- and y-coordinates. Putting it at just the player's registration point would be a problem, however, because that point is not likely to be exactly where the gun is. In fact, in this game the registration point is near the heroine's head. While it is cool to think of her having some weird sort of hair beam, these shots are repositioned based on the final bit of configuration in the constructor: the firePosition. Adjusting the numbers in that object in the constructor will move the starting point of the bullet around on the player, but it is currently pretty close to the gun's position.

The last bit of the fire method plays the "shooting" animation. This is a quick animation, and another animation (the idle animation) needs to play once that animation is complete. In order to accomplish this, the animation has an event that was attached to it in the create method that will run the "playFly" method when the firing animation completes.

PlayFly Method

All this method does is play the flying animation. When used as the onComplete handler of the fire animation, it will bring the player back to her default, "flying" state when the shooting is over. It is actually a small detail and is barely noticeable if the player is just holding down the "shoot" button for the duration of the game because the shooting animation takes up most of the interval in between shots. If this method is not here, however, the flying animation would never been seen after the start of the game

```
playFly() {
        this.animations.play("fly", 14, true);
}
```

7.2.1.3 Player Health

Unless one wants to make a game with a pretty wicked difficulty state where the player can only take one shot before they are blown into tiny pieces, a player will need some sort of health value. Giving the player a number that be slowly decremented from (or added to, with power-ups perhaps) is the way to begin implementing player life. There are different ways to show to the player how much life they have left, with either a Zelda-style row of bars or a simple numerical value. This game is going to be using a healthbar that works similarly to the loading bar in the preload phase. When the player is at full health, they will see the full bar, while at low health, they will only see a small percentage of the bar. In order to calculate the percentage to show to the player, two numbers are needed: current health and the maximum it could be.

The numbers are set up in the player's constructor.

```
this.health = { current: 10, max: 10 };
```

Next, there needs to be some way to actually hurt the player. While it certainly is possible to just change the current health, writing a function gives opportunity to later on add signals to fire when the player dies or does checks to make sure the player's health doesn't fall beneath a certain amount.

```
damage(amt) {
        this.health.current -= amt;
}
```

Full Source of the Player class

```
export default class Player extends Phaser.Sprite {
    constructor(game, x, y, bullets) {
        super(game, x, y, 'player', 0);
        this.game.physics.enable(this, Phaser.
          Physics.ARCADE);
        this.body.drag.x = 35;
        this.body.drag.y = 35;
        this.body.collideWorldBounds = true;

        // initialize your prefab herea
        this.speed = 100;
        this.bulletGate = 0;
        this.bullets = bullets;
        this.cursors = this.game.input.keyboard.
          createCursorKeys();
        this.fireButton = this.game.input.keyboard.
          addKey(Phaser.Keyboard.SPACEBAR);

        this.health = { current: 10, max: 10 };
        this.fireposition = { x: 160, y: 100 };

        this.animations.add("fly", [0,0,1,1,2,2,3,4,
          5,6,7,8,9,10,10]);
        this.fireAnimation = this.animations.
          add("fire", [11,12,13]);
        this.fireAnimation.onComplete.add(this.
          playFly, this);
        this.animations.play("fly", 14, true);

    }
```

```
update() {

    // write your prefab's specific update
      code here
    if(this.cursors.left.isDown) {
        this.body.velocity.x = -this.speed;
    }

    if(this.cursors.right.isDown) {
        this.body.velocity.x = this.speed;
    }

    if(this.cursors.up.isDown) {
        this.body.velocity.y = -this.speed;
    }

    if(this.cursors.down.isDown) {
        this.body.velocity.y = this.speed;
    }

    if(this.fireButton.isDown) {
        this.fire();
    }
}

fire() {

    if(this.game.time.now > this.bulletGate) {

        var bullet = this.bullets.
          getFirstDead();
        if(bullet) {
            bullet.x = this.x + this.
              fireposition.x;
            bullet.y = this.y + this.
              fireposition.y;
            bullet.revive();
        } else {
            bullet = this.bullets.
              create(this.x + this.
              fireposition.x, this.y+this.
              fireposition.y, "bullet");
            this.game.physics.
              enable(bullet, Phaser.
              Physics.ARCADE);
            bullet.outOfBoundsKill = true;
            bullet.checkWorldBounds = true;
            bullet.body.velocity.x = 250;
        }

        this.animations.play("fire");

        this.bulletGate = this.game.time.now
          + 500;

    }
```

```
        }

        damage(amt) {
                this.health.current -= amt;
        }

        playFly() {
        this.animations.play("fly", 14, true);
        }
    }
```

7.2.2 Enemy Prefab

The enemy is the next consideration in our game. They are thankfully not as intricate as our player, but they still have a number of special considerations. In this particular game, we'll be making only one specific enemy that will move in a sine-wave pattern and maybe shoot back at the player. It is entirely possible to build other enemies on this base, perhaps even using the Phaser tween engine to create different paths for different enemies.

The first order of business for the enemy is movement. After enabling the body, a quick and easy way to get the enemies moving is to set their velocity to move them consistently in one direction. In the constructor, note the "this.body.velocity = -175". That will get the enemy moving to the left. Higher numbers mean faster movement, so adjust upward or downward based on the pace of the game. Setting the velocity only gets the enemies moving in a straight line. Not a challenge for the player at all to hit and sort of a dumb strategy on the opposing team's side as well. At the very least, they should be attempting to confound their opponent, perhaps by juking up and down as they approach. One way to get the enemies some vertical motion is to write some code that will make them move in a sinusoidal pattern. Let's examine how to implement sinusoidal movement in this game.

7.2.2.1 Creating a Sinusoidal Motion

Built into JavaScript is a series of math functions that come in handy from time to time. Of particular interest when it comes to making something move in a smooth, wavelike pattern is the trigonometry function of "Math.sin." This method will take a number, treat it as an angle, and calculate a ratio of the two sides of a right triangle based on that angle. The ratio will progress from zero, up to one, back down to zero, falls down to negative one, and returns to the zero once it hits the full circle. If one were to chart the path of a sine wave using an x-coordinate as the input for the sin function and the y-coordinate as the output value, one would see a wave pattern emerge, as shown in Figure 7.3.

Now, look at the sine-wave chart and imagine that the x-axis depicted time instead of position. This is how one can simulate a bouncing wave pattern on an object. By changing an input value over time and getting the sin value from it, one will get a way to create a "bouncing" value that shifts between a positive and negative extreme. If that value is used to offset a sprite's y position every frame by the value calculated, then the sprite would appear to move up and down, as if bobbing on a wave. In the update function, these two lines do just that:

```
this.bounceTick += .02;
this.y += Math.sin(this.bounceTick) * 1;
```

Note that there are two "magic numbers" left in this code, or numbers that seem to be there with no real reason for their existence. One of them is even a multiplication by one, which is technically a worthless calculation. Each of these numbers is there for a reason.

The first number (.02) you can think of is the "sample rate" or frequency of the sine curve. It lets one specify how much detail they want of the curve and also how quickly to move through it. The bigger that number gets, the further in the x-direction of the sine curve will it sample each frame. If you choose a large value, the jumps will be significant, and it will appear as if your enemy is warping about the screen. Imagine if you have a big number, say 0.5, and you're currently at the "top" of a curve. The next update happens, and you ask for a value 0.5 further down. This will "jump" from the top of the curve hallway down the hill to zero. This could be a big jump for an enemy, especially in combination with the second magic number. A smaller value will take forever to change for zero to one, and most likely your enemy will be long gone before that happens. Still, this is one of those magic values that can be toyed with, and I encourage you to do so to see how it changes your enemy's motion.

The second magic number, that useless multiplication by one, is a scalar. It works as an amplitude modifier and changes how "tall" the enemy arcs can get. Bigger numbers will make the enemy move in bigger arcs, taking up more y space on the screen and making them harder to hit. Smaller will do the opposite and have them move in more minute arcs.

The last bit of code that is associated with this wave pattern movement is in the constructor, "`this.bounceTick = Math.random() * 2;`". This is just a little trick to start each enemy off at a random point on the sine curve, so they're not moving in identical patterns each time. One might be headed up, while another is headed down on the same location on the screen.

7.2.2.2 Enemy Shooting
The approach this game takes to enemies "fighting back" is to decide randomly when an enemy is created if it will fire a shot or not. This is a slightly uncommon approach, as most shmups will include different enemy types, some of which are "dumb" and seem to exist to just soak up bullets, while others are more intelligent and will actually fire back at the player. In this game, intelligence is brought down to a simple chance roll. This constructor will, on a 50% chance, set the enemy to one of the types that will fire back at the player. If the enemy

is set to fire, it will then create a countdown timer to shoot back in 3½ s. The fire shot, similar to the player's version, will generate a new enemy attack and send it hurtling toward the left side of the screen.

The last thing to note is that the enemy constructor expects to get a reference to a group in the game used for the enemy bullets. This reference will be used in the object later on to create and set the bullets up, so it is stored in the enemy object as "bulletLayer."

Here is the firing code in the constructor:

```
this.bulletLayer = bulletLayer;
this.willFire = Phaser.Utils.chanceRoll(50);

if(this.willFire) {
    this.fireTimer = this.game.time.
      create(false);
    this.fireTimer.add(3500, this.fireShot,
      this);
    this.fireTimer.start();
}
```

The following uses the fire shot method:

```
fireShot() {
    var bullet = this.bulletLayer.create(this.x,
                                         this.y,
                                         "enemyBullet"
                                         );
    this.game.physics.enable(bullet, Phaser.
      Physics.ARCADE);
    bullet.outOfBoundsKill = true;
    bullet.checkWorldBounds = true;
    bullet.body.velocity.x = -250;
}
```

The following is the full source of the enemy object:

```
export default class Enemy extends Phaser.Sprite {

    constructor(game, x, y, bulletLayer, frame) {
        super(game, x, y, 'enemy', frame);

        // initialize your prefab here
        this.game.physics.enable(this, Phaser.
          Physics.ARCADE);

        this.body.velocity.x = -175;
        this.bounceTick = Math.random() * 2;

        this.outOfBoundsKill = true;

        this.bulletLayer = bulletLayer;
        this.willFire = Phaser.Utils.chanceRoll(50);

        if(this.willFire) {
```

```
        this.fireTimer = this.game.time.
          create(false);
        this.fireTimer.add(3500, this.fireShot,
          this);
        this.fireTimer.start();
      }
    }

    fireShot() {

        var bullet = this.bulletLayer.
          create(this.x, this.y, "enemyBullet");
        this.game.physics.enable(bullet, Phaser.
          Physics.ARCADE);
        bullet.outOfBoundsKill = true;
        bullet.checkWorldBounds = true;
        bullet.body.velocity.x = -250;
    }

    update() {

        this.bounceTick += .02;
        this.y += Math.sin(this.bounceTick) * 1;

    }

  }
```

7.2.3 User Interface Prefabs

With the primary objects in the game out of the way, the next parts of
the game to tackle are the UI elements. Our final game is going to have a
score field and a healthbar to display the current health ratio of the player.
While these objects could easily be added into the game as just parts of the
gameplay state itself, one could argue that they are self-sufficient parts of the
application that could easily be "componentized" and transferred from one
game to another if needed as well (and we'll be doing just that with them).
This lets us pull their code out of the game state and hide it in their own
objects, so the gameplay state code stays relatively clean and readable.

7.2.3.1 Score Field
Technically the score field is just going to be a graphic with a text field
overlaid on top of it, which isn't too complex to set up in the startup method
of the game state. However, pulling it out into its own object makes sense
partially because it is a unique object on the screen. Making an object
called "scoreBox" and adding it to the display list read a lot easier than six
lines of code with a comment about it setting up a score box beforehand.
Additionally, this score field will also introduce us to the process of creating
reusable objects on the screen with their own groups and layers. Note that
this score field is named generically as "NumberBox." It is named this way
so it could be used to store any number, not just a score, and it set up for

a decent amount of configurability for the background asset to be used to frame or ground the text it displays (See Figure 7.4). Its constructor makes a group and adds the "bgAsset" image to the back of the group and a text field on top of it. Calling the *setValue* method of the NumberBox object will update the text shown in this number box.

```
export default class NumberBox extends Phaser.Group {

    constructor(game, bgasset, val, parent) {
        super(game, parent);

        this.create(0,0, bgasset);

        var style = {
            font: "30px Arial",
            align: "center",
            fill: "#fff"
        };

        this.txtValue = new Phaser.Text(
          this.game, 55, 55,
                        val.toString(), style
                                      );
        this.txtValue.anchor.setTo(.5, .5);
        this.add(this.txtValue);

    }
    setValue(val) {
        this.txtValue.text = val.toString();
    }
}
```

7.2.3.2 Healthbar

The healthbar, or any sort of scaling bar, is a very common asset to make in games. It is a bar that either fills in a region, or slowly drains from a region based on player actions. Sometimes I like to think of the healthbars as sodas in a bottle, slowly draining as the sugar water gets imbibed. Much like the NumberBox, the healthbar has a number of interior concerns that make sense to pull away into its own little component. Common parts of a healthbar include a holder or asset that works as the visual "grounding" for the filling that can be drained (See Figure 7.5). The filling is a second asset and is scaled in the horizontal direction (though the same principle works for vertical bars). A scale of one will be a "full" bar, and scales progressing from one to zero will decrease down to an empty bar. These two assets are placed into a group so they can be easily placed and positioned together (moving the group's position will move all the assets inside of it automatically).

A method is placed on this object to allow setting the scale of the bar easily at runtime. The easiest way to modify the width of the filling is to simply set the bar's scale. Sometimes it is nice to add a bit of flare into a UI, and tweened transitions are a great example of this. Whenever the `setValue` method is called, the bar is tweened to its new value for a subtle but hopefully enjoyable bit of polish to this game. Take care with animations like this. They're there to add flair, but if they take too long, they will keep the player from seeing the actual values of their life during the gameplay, which may prove frustrating to them later on.

```javascript
export default class HealthBar extends Phaser.Group {
    constructor(game, xpos, ypos, barGraphic,
        holderGraphic) {
            super(game);

            this.x = xpos;
            this.y = ypos;

            this.bar = this.create(0,0, barGraphic);
            this.holder = this.create(0,0,
                holderGraphic);
    }

    setValue(val) {
            if(this.tween) this.tween.stop();
            this.tween = this.game.add.tween(
                            this.bar.scale
                );
            this.tween.to({ x: val }, 350);
            this.tween.start();
    }

}
```

7.2.4 Game State

With the prefabs and components all ready, it is time to place them into the game itself. The game will manage the creation of all the enemies, check for collision between all the different game objects, update the UI as needed, check for the game to be over, and add some bits of flair in when possible.

Some threads that will be followed throughout the game state include

- Spawning enemies on a chance, in different locations
- A wave spawn timer that makes it more likely that enemies will spawn as time progresses
- Players colliding with enemy bullets and taking damage
- Enemies colliding with player bullets, getting destroyed, and incrementing the score
- Management of particles and UI elements

7.2.4.1 Imports

```javascript
import Player from "../prefabs/Player.js";
import Enemy from "../prefabs/Enemy.js";
```

```
import NumberBox from "../prefabs/NumberBox.js";
import HealthBar from "../prefabs/HealthBar.js";
```

Add these lines of code at the top of the Game.js file, before any other code. These are the lines of code that lets the game state make use of all of the prefabs that are already done.

7.2.4.2 Create Method

This method is where the game gets set up. Any objects that need to exist at the start of the game are made here. It is important with the create method of any gameplay state to reset objects that need to be reset as well, as there is a strong chance that this state is never deleted if Phaser returns to this state from a different one. If you don't reset scores or timers or anything else that needs to start with specific settings or configurations, they may wind up having those increased values even when returning after a "game over."

Much of the work of this method is getting objects onto the display list. Since the order items added to the display list affect the render order of the objects, we're going to step through this function in the order the different display objects are added starting with the background tile sprite. This tile sprite is going to be scrolled to the left infinitely, working as a quick "cheat" to make it appear as if the player is flying through a large world when, in actuality, they are in front of one of those old time set props that scrolls a paper background behind the actors forever. This technique works best if the background doesn't have too many unique areas that a player will see repeating.

```
this.bg = this.add.tileSprite(0, 0, 1024, 768, 'bg');
```

The next step is to add the groups to be used in this game. The bullet groups won't be used until a shot is fired, but the enemies will be preloaded with a few baddies, so the game isn't reliant on the spawner to create the first enemies on the screen, which could result in a delay until the first one is randomly generated.

The preloading of enemies follows a simple loop, set to create five new enemies at the start of the game. These enemies are placed to the right of the screen, at a random y position within the bounds of the world's height and with a bit of randomness on the x-axis, so they don't all come at the same time. In case the enemies will fire a projectile, each enemy will need to know where the bullet layer is, so that layer is passed into their constructor as the final argument.

```
this.bullets = this.add.group();
this.enemyBullets = this.add.group();
this.enemies = this.add.group();

for(var i = 0; i < 5; i++) {
        var enemy = new Enemy(this.game,
```

```
                        this.game.width + 100 +
                          (Math.random() * 400),
                        Math.random() * this.
                          game.height,
                        this.enemyBullets
                      );

          this.enemies.add(enemy);

        }
```

The next step is to put in a particle system that will be used for some visual feedback when the enemies get annihilated. This needs to come after the enemy layer is added so the particles will appear atop the enemies and other objects. This particular particle system will spew out hexagon particles whenever it is active. The final line of this setup sets the particles to fade from a full visible to 20% visible over the span of 2 s starting from the moment the particle is made visible.

```
        this.explosions = this.game.add.emitter(0,0, 200);
        this.explosions.makeParticles("hexagon");
        this.explosions.setAlpha(1, .2, 2000);
```

After the explosions are configured and ready to go, the UI needs to be added. It is done as the last of the additions to the display list, so the UI elements will always appear atop the other objects in the game. This has been broken down into its own method and is called right beneath the explosion code.

The UI section creates its own layer for the UI elements to exist on, partially for organization, though this approach will be useful in later games that scroll through the world. After that, the two UI elements coded before are instantiated and added to the group. The number box is positioned to the far left and configured to use a simple circle to ground the number that will appear inside of it. The healthbar is positioned further to the right of the number box and is set up with the assets to show a simple green bar inside of a basic holder to ground that bar.

```
      setupUI() {
          this.UILayer = this.add.group();

          this.scoreField = new NumberBox(this.game,
            "circle", 0);
          this.UILayer.add(this.scoreField);

          this.healthBar = new HealthBar(this.game, 120,
            40, "health_bar", "health_holder");
          this.UILayer.add(this.healthBar);
      }
```

The last bit of setup to be done in the create method is to make and start a timer that will increase the difficulty of the game as time progresses. This timer is created and set to run the method "incrementWave" once every 20 s, which is a method that will be explored later on.

```
this.waveTimer = this.game.time.create(false);
this.waveTimer.loop(20000, this.incrementWave,
    this);
this.waveTimer.start();
```

7.2.4.3 Update Method

The next method that is critical for a Phaser state, especially one that implements gameplay, is the update method. This is the method that is responsible for the majority of the game's interactivity such as checking for collisions, moving objects about on the screen, and getting input. Much of the movement and input of the objects has already been covered in the previous sections, with the player and enemies handling their own movement in their individual update methods. All this section will need to do is move the background, check to see if objects are overlapping, and spawn new enemies.

The first step in the update function, move the background, is as simple as decrementing its tile x position. Because it is a tile sprite, this will make it appear as if the half pixel on the left of the tilesprite had been pushed over to the right. Overtime, it will scroll the background to the left, repeating itself indefinitely.

```
this.bg.tilePosition.x -= .5;
```

The next step is to attempt to spawn and place an enemy on the screen. There are numerous ways to approach this task, but this is a fairly simple chance roll. The spawn chance (defined in the create function) starts at a fairly low number, but will be high enough that enemies will still be generated quite often. Should the chance roll pass, a new enemy will be generated and added to the game in the same way that the enemies were prewarmed before (randomly in a box as tall as the game and a bit to the right of the screen).

```
if(Math.random() < this.spawnChance) {
    var enemy = new Enemy(this.game,
                          this.game.width + 100),
                          Math.random() * this.game.
                            height,
                          this.enemyBullets
                        );
    this.enemies.add(enemy);
}
```

The last bit of the update method is to check for collisions, using the overlap method (because we don't want to transfer energy from any collisions, making it seem like the player got "knocked back" by one of the enemy's shots). There are two methods that will need to be added to make these overlaps work. One will damage the enemy hit by a player bullet and the other will damage the player for different actions.

```
this.physics.arcade.overlap (this.enemies,
  (this.bullets,
    this.damageEnemy,
    null,this);
```

```
this.physics.arcade.overlap(this.player,this.enemies,
                            this.damagePlayer,
                            null, this);

this.physics.arcade.overlap(this.player,
    this.enemyBullets,
                            this.damagePlayer,
                            null,this);
```

7.2.4.4 Increment Wave Method

The increment wave function simply increases the spawn chance by 20% every time it ticks. It is set to tick every 20 s, whenever the timer started in the create function cycles through its timer and restarts. The maximum chance that is really needed for an enemy to be spawned with 100% certainty for every frame is one (as `Math.random()` will always return a number less than one), so anything above that is just overkill. If the player manages to play that long that will be dealing with a lot of enemies on the screen, so it is not very likely that the spawn chance will need to be clamped to a maximum of one.

```
incrementWave() {
      this.spawnChance *= 1.2;
}
```

7.2.4.5 Damage Enemy Method

The next method to tackle is the damage enemy method that runs when a player's attack hits an enemy. The antagonists in this game currently aren't that robust since we didn't give them any health. One hit will off them with ease. Because it is so simple to kill these enemies, this function only needs to do three things (the "damaging" in this case being more "obliterating" than anything). First, it will reposition the particle emitter to the location of the enemy and have the emitter generate a burst of four particles that will fade away quickly. Even though the emitter may later be moved for the destruction of another enemy, these generated particles will remain at where they were generated in the world space for the duration of their lives. Next, the player's bullet and enemy are removed from the game via a `.kill()`, ready to be revived later on. Finally, the score is incremented, and the score box is fed the new score to be displayed to the player.

```
damageEnemy(enemy, bullet) {
    this.explosions.x = enemy.x;
    this.explosions.y = enemy.y;

    this.explosions.explode(2000, 4);

    enemy.kill();
    bullet.kill();

    this.score++;
    this.scoreField.setValue(this.score);
}
```

7.2.4.6 Damage Player Method

The last process is the damage player method. It actually will bring us to the end of both the game state's code and the player's gameplay, as it is the function that checks for a game over state. In this game, game over means that the player's life has hit zero, so we'll be checking the player's health to hit zero inside of this function. The player in this game can take several hits before it dies, and the player object manages the total number of hits they can take. If an overlap between a player and an enemy bullet is detected, the player's apply damage method is called, subtracting 1 from its health and bringing the player closer to death. This new state of the health is sent to the healthbar via a percentage calculation. The healthbar is programmed to reduce its size to the percentage sent in. For instance, if the player's current health is 9 and the player's max health is 10, then when the player hits something, it will take one point of damage. Its new current health property will have a value of 8, and the percentage of 0.8(8/10) will be sent to the healthbar, which will scale down to show a missing 20% gap between its rightmost side and the right of the bar container.

Next, the enemy or enemy bullet is killed, ready to be reused in the future. Finally, there is a check to see if the player is dead (if their health is less than or equal to zero). If their hp is at that low level, they have taken too much damage, and the game is over. It is time to move on to the game over state.

```
damagePlayer(playerRef, enemyRef) {
    this.player.damage(1);
    this.healthBar.setValue(
            this.player.health.current /
                this.player.health.max
    );
    enemyRef.kill();

    if(this.player.health.current <= 0) {
        this.game.state.start('gameOver');
    }

}
```

7.3 Game State Source Code

The following is the contents of the shmup game.js file in full.

```
import Player from "../prefabs/Player.js";
import Enemy from "../prefabs/Enemy.js";
import NumberBox from "../prefabs/NumberBox.js";
import HealthBar from "../prefabs/HealthBar.js";

export default class Game extends Phaser.State {

  constructor() {
    super();
  }
```

```
create() {

    this.spawnChance = .02;
    this.score = 0;

    this.game.physics.startSystem(Phaser.Physics.
      ARCADE);

    this.bg = this.add.tileSprite(0, 0, 1024,
      768, 'bg');

    this.bullets = this.add.group();
    this.enemyBullets = this.add.group();

    this.player = new Player(this.game, 0, 0,
      this.bullets);
    this.game.add.existing(this.player);

    this.enemies = this.add.group();
    for(var i = 0; i < 5; i++) {
      var enemy = new Enemy(this.game,
                            this.game.width + 100
                              + (Math.random() *
                              400),
                            Math.random() * this.
                              game.height,
                            this.enemyBullets
                            );
      this.enemies.add(enemy);
    }

    this.explosions = this.game.add.emitter
      (0,0, 200);
    this.explosions.makeParticles("hexagon");
    this.explosions.setAlpha(1, .2, 2000);
    this.setupUI();

    this.waveTimer = this.game.time.create(false);
    this.waveTimer.loop(20000, this.incrementWave,
      this);
    this.waveTimer.start();

}

setupUI() {
  this.UILayer = this.add.group();

  this.scoreField = new NumberBox(this.game,
    "circle", 0);
  this.UILayer.add(this.scoreField);

  this.healthBar = new HealthBar(this.game, 120, 40,
                                "health_bar",
                                  "health_holder"
                                );
this.UILayer.add(this.healthBar);
  }
```

```
update() {
  this.bg.tilePosition.x -= .5;

  if(Math.random() < this.spawnChance) {
    var enemy = new Enemy(this.game,
                          this.game.width + 100 +
                            (Math.random() * 400),
                          Math.random() * this.
                            game.height,
                          this.enemyBullets
                          );
    this.enemies.add(enemy);
  }

  this.physics.arcade.overlap(this.enemies, this.
    bullets,
                              this.damageEnemy,
                                null, this);
  this.physics.arcade.overlap(this.player, this.
    enemies,
                              this.damagePlayer,
                                null, this);
  this.physics.arcade.overlap(this.player, this.
    enemyBullets,
                              this.damagePlayer,
                                null, this);
}
incrementWave() {
  this.spawnChance *= 1.2;
}
damagePlayer(playerRef, enemyRef) {
    this.player.damage(1);
    this.healthBar.setValue(
        this.player.health.current / this.
          player.health.max
  );
  enemyRef.kill();

  if(this.player.health.current <= 0) {
    this.game.state.start('gameOver');
  }
}
damageEnemy(enemy, bullet) {

    this.explosions.x = enemy.x;
    this.explosions.y = enemy.y;

    this.explosions.explode(2000, 4);

    enemy.kill();
    bullet.kill();
```

```
                              this.score++;
                              this.scoreField.setValue(this.score);

                    }

                 }
```

7.3.1 Wrap Up

With the addition of the player damage code to the game state, the basic example of a shmup is completed. It is a simple introduction to the genre, but it demonstrates a lot of the essentials of game development including input, collision, and proper separation of code into state and prefabs. Make sure to master the essentials of creating UI components and extending game objects as these are techniques that will be used in every other example in this book.

The best way to learn about code (beyond simply stepping through it, like we have in this chapter) is to alter the code and see what happens when you run it again. Sometimes it breaks, which can seem frustrating, but even broken code presents you with an opportunity to really engage with the code and see why it is breaking. Never take a broken build as a failure so much as a chance to learn and ask "why?" Listed here are a few places where changing the code can produce interesting results without there being a large chance of breaking the game.

Some great places to "play with numbers" include the following:

- Change the original spawn rate of the enemies.
- Change the multiplier of the spawn rate.
- Edit the enemy movement speed.
- Edit the player movement speed or player drag.
- Change the chance that an enemy is a "shooter."
- Adjust the firing gate of the player.

While there is something to be said just for playing with the numbers for playfulness sake (sneaking in a bit of fun into the tiring process of game development), there is another reason for tinkering with numbers, especially those that control physical movement. Think back to some of the different games you have played. Did some of them feel more "right" than others? It is likely that some of them just felt better. Everything in those games moved in such a way that just moving around and existing in the game brought a lot of joy. The movement numbers here are the ones that control precisely that feel. It is quite likely that the first values one puts into player and enemy movement will be off in some way. This is where the tinkering and playtesting will have to be done to get them to be "just right." This example has included some sensible defaults for the interaction numbers, but changing them can lead to vastly different types of games. A lower drag on the player would lead to a very slidey hero, making it harder to position her right where one wanted, perhaps putting the player on edge or leading them into laughable mishaps. Higher spawn rates on the enemies would make the game very hard to dodge enemies, bringing it closer to a "bullet hell"–type experience. In short, playing with numbers will be critical to get the gameplay to act in the intended way and impart the right feeling to the player that you are trying to convey.

Of course, not all changes to code are simply numerical. While this is a working game, there remains a number of places to improve the game that could make it more fun, challenging, and interesting to a player. Adding these new features will take some addition of code and modification of the game structure itself. Here are a few ideas to get you started (some of which you probably are already thinking on):

- Add in new enemy types and path patterns.
- Add in new shot types for the player. Perhaps a double shot, large bullet, or a pass-through beam?
- Use power-ups to unlock shots or grant the player more health.
- Manage shielding for the player either via power-ups or recharging when not getting hit.
- Add in collectable currency and a store for unlocks after gameplay (advanced).

Go forth and play with the code. Break things and learn. Make something beautiful or ugly, or both. You can always come back to the original source if you need to. When you're ready to move on to the next game, a platformer, we will build upon all the base ideas from this chapter, so make sure you know them well.

When it comes to 2D games, the platformer genre rules. Nearly every major 2D game engine provides built-in support for platformers and tilemaps to give interested game developers the ability to quickly get a world set up with walls, floors, and other objects that they can jump around on. Perhaps the most notable platformer is Super Mario Brothers with its heavily tweaked movement, intelligent camera system, and memorable music. Other great and classic examples include the Sonic the Hedgehog series, Megaman (actually a combination of platformer and shooter), and Super Metroid. These games clearly stuck in the minds of future game developers, who have gone on to create new and wonderful additions to the genre including Super Meat Boy, Braid, and Thomas Was Alone (examples are shown in Figures 7.6 through 7.17).

FIG 7.6 Platformer basic gameplay.

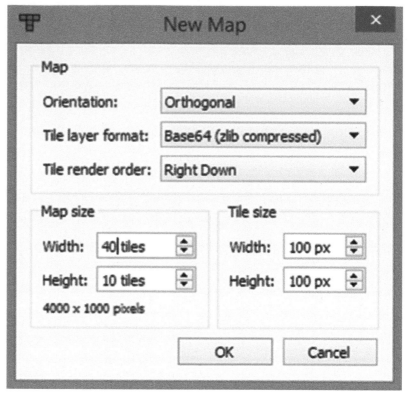

FIG 7.7 Creating a new map in Tiled.

Though the gameplay may differ slightly from game to game, there are certain elements that make a platformer what it is. In general, these elements are as follows:

- A side-on view of the character similar to a paper puppet
- A character that can move right and left, and jump
- A world for the character to navigate with solid walls and floors
- Gravity that pulls the player and game objects down
- An item or object to collect throughout the levels
- Enemies to dodge and avoid, typically with some simple AI
- Multiple stages or levels to traverse to get to the end of the game

Throughout this chapter, we will be placing all these necessities into our game, Ground Fox. To begin with, we will need to make a world that will serve as the location for the gameplay, and we will be using a new piece of software to get the job done.

7.3.2 Tiled

While it is possible to lay out whole tile-based world by editing numbers in a text file, it can be pretty hard to imagine what the final world will look

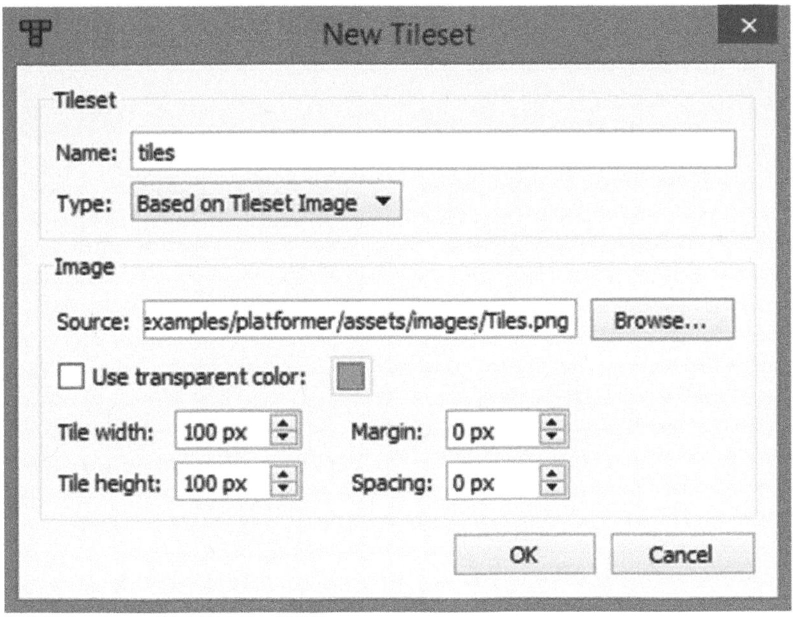

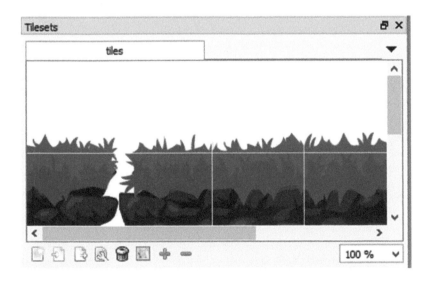

FIG 7.8 Specifying a tileset image.

FIG 7.9 Individual tiles extracted from the tileset image.

like without loading the game up and seeing how it looks with the actual tile images. Tiled is a piece of software that lets someone lay out the tiles (square bits of graphics) that make up a platformer world visually without having the reload of the game with every change. It is a popular program with a lot of great tools that make laying out a map and planning a game easier.

FIG 7.10 Example level drawn with the imported tiles.

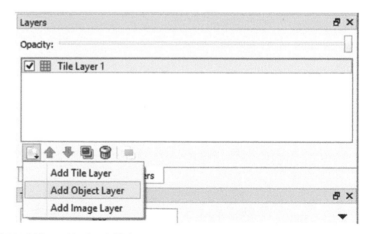

FIG 7.11 Adding an object layer in Tiled.

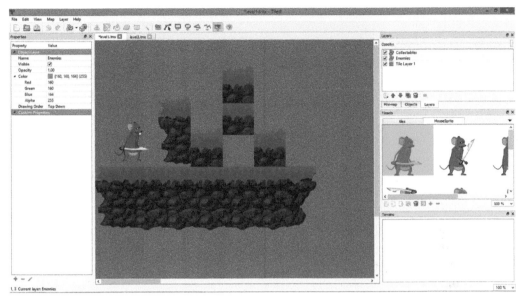

FIG 7.12 Placing objects in a layer.

FIG 7.13 Finished level layout in Tiled.

Path step, per frame

FIG 7.14 Enemy distance moved per frame with turn limits.

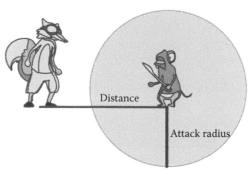

Attack radius of mouse

Distance

Attack radius

FIG 7.15 Area that an enemy will begin to attack.

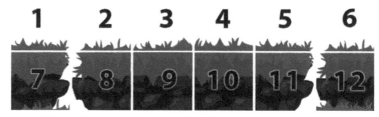

FIG 7.16 Individual tile IDs.

Viable Camera Movement Area

FIG 7.17 Camera movement bounds.

For this game, we're going to be making use of some of its nontiled, object layers in order to even lay out collectables and enemies in the game.

Before moving on, you'll need to install Tiled. You can find an installer for your operating system at http://www.mapeditor.org. This website also contains a set of documentation for the program that is worth checking out if you are interested in using the more advanced features of Tiled on this or future projects.

7.3.2.1 Laying Out a Map in Tiled

There are two steps to laying out a map in Tiled. The images for the tileset need to be imported and then those tiles can be used to stamp the images onto the map. To begin, create a new map in Tiled. Ensure that this map is orthogonal (not isometric or hexagonal) and that the tile size is 100×100. The tile sizes will vary with your games, but for the platformer in this chapter, 100×100 is the size of a single tile. Save this map as "level1" (See Figure 7.7).

7.3.2.1.1 Loading In a Tileset Image

The next step in the creation of a tilemap is to load in a tileset to the Tiled map editor. The tileset is a series of tiles laid out much like a sprite sheet, with each tile appearing to the right of the previous tile. All the tiles need to have a set width and height. The option to add a new tileset is in the file bar under map → add new tileset.

When loading in a new tileset, there are two important areas to focus on: First is the tile size, which usually is the same as the size of the tiles on the map (100×100 in this case). The second important field is the "name" field. The value you type into this field will be used later in the game scripts, so name the tiles something descriptive and memorable. For simple games that only use one tileset (like ours) "tiles" is a good standby (See Figure 7.8).

7.3.2.1.2 Drawing to the Map

Once a tileset is loaded in, they will be added to the tileset panel on the right of the program. Based on the width and height given for the tiles, the different images for the tiles will be split into individual boxes under the tileset panel (See Figure 7.9).

Clicking on any of these tiles in the tab will set it as the active tile for drawing. Once a tile is active in the tileset pane, clicking (or dragging) in the middle area of the Tiled program will draw the tiles to the game world. This is your chance to be creative, so spend some time drawing to the world (See Figure 7.10).

7.3.2.2 Adding In Metadata in Tiled

Once you finish a map, it is not much work to export it and load it into Phaser. Unfortunately, if you were to load this level into Phaser right now, it would wind up being pretty boring after the first few minutes of play. There's nothing else in the map beyond platforms and walls. Most games have objects like collectables and enemies to populate the world and make it a bit more lively.

Tiled has a second type of layer that can be used for laying out objects that are meant to fill the game world. This layer type is called an "object layer," and a new one can be added by clicking the "new layer" icon at the bottom left of the layer's pane (See Figure 7.11).

7.3.2.2.1 Placing Assets in an Object Layer

Assets that are placed in an object layer still need to be imported as tilesets into Tiled. In this example, the whole sprite sheets for the enemies will be imported in to be used for their placement in the world. Go back to map → new tileset. This time find the image for the mouse enemy and set its dimensions to 160 × 160. A new tileset will be added to the tiles panel that contains the mice.

When working with object layers, it is important to always place the same sprite on the page because that particular sprite (and only that one) will cause Phaser to place objects into the game. When placing objects like this mouse, try to rely only on the first entry in the sprite sheet.

Because object layers are not restricted to the game grid, the stamp tool that you used to lay out the world will not work. Instead you will need to place objects using the "place tile" tool. This tool can be found right above the map and looks like an image instead of a stamp or shapes (see top of Figure 7.12). To put some enemies on the screen, select the enemy layer in the layers panel, select the first enemy of the enemy sprites in the tiles panel, and make sure the "place tile" tool is the currently active tool. Once these three conditions are met, clicking anywhere in the map view will place a new enemy. Try to place them above the ground, with a little bit of walking room because we'll be writing some code in a bit to make them patrol back and forth.

Any object can be laid out in this manner in the map, and the different layers can have many different objects in their layers. Later on if development of this game were to continue, the enemy layer might also contain hedgehogs or bees in addition to the mice. For this chapter, other layers will also be set up to hold coins for the character to collect and doors to progress the player through the game. The process of making more layers is the same as for the enemies. Start with a new layer, import an image as a tile sheet, and lay the objects out on that layer with the place tile tool. See Figure 7.13 for an example of a finished map.

7.3.2.3 Exporting a Tiled Map for Phaser

Once the map is completely laid out (or far enough along that is worthwhile testing), the next step is to get the map into a format that Phaser can understand and render. Phaser imports and reads the JSON export format from Tiled (called tiledJSON inside of the Phaser engine). Maps can be exported by going to file → export and selecting the JSON format from the list of options. When saving the file, make sure the file gets saved into the assets folder.

Before moving on, take a moment to open up the exported JSON file and look through it. When creating the enemies and collectables, the GIDs of the objects in this file will need to be passed to Phaser. These GIDs can be found in the JSON in the objects layer data. Here is a snippet of the JSON for the enemy layer. If you are working on your own map, take note of your object GIDs because it will likely differ from this map's data.

```
{
    "draworder":"topdown",
    "height":15,
    "name":"Enemies",
    "objects":[
        {
            "gid":225,
            "height":160,
            "id":5,
            "name":"",
            "properties":
                {
                },
            "rotation":0,
            "type":"",
            "visible":true,
            "width":160,
            "x":436,
            "y":1388
        }
    ]
}
```

7.4 Making the Ground Fox Platformer

The example in this chapter is used to demonstrate the 2D platformer genre is a simple fox platformer game. It is going to have two levels for player to navigate that will be filled with collectables and terrifying mice with swords. The player's goal is to finish the game with as many coins as possible, but they will need to avoid the mice who will take a coin from them with every collision. Everything in the level, including the enemy placements, player start positions, and collectable locations, will be laid out in Tiled first and then pulled into Phaser.

To begin with, create the basic project structure described in chapter five. We will be adding to that base throughout this exercise. Should you need to see the finished code or to get the assets for the game, you can find the full source at https://github.com/meanderingleaf/PhaserBookExamples/tree/master/platformer.

7.4.1 Level Layout

Take a moment to look through the levels in Tiled (you can find the maps in the project's assets folder). The map files for this game have two tile layers and four object layers. There is one tile layer that is just the background and is made of up a number of tiles that make up a full image. It is separate from the foreground ("tiles") layer because it will be scrolled slower to give the game the appearance of parallax. The object layers are player, doors, enemies, and collectables. Each of the object layers is used to specify where an object should appear when the level associated with this map is loaded.

7.4.2 App.js

The app will need to load in a few extra states and add them to the state list. Also, the size of the game is changed from its defaults to 1024 × 768 to give us a bigger view into the world.

```js
var game;

import Boot from "./states/Boot.js";
import Preload from "./states/Preload.js";
import Game from "./states/Game.js";
import Level1 from "./states/Level1.js";
import Level2 from "./states/Level2.js";
import GameOver from "./states/GameOver.js";

window.onload = function () {
  game = new Phaser.Game(1024, 768, Phaser.AUTO,
    'game');
  game.state.add('boot', Boot);
  game.state.add('preload', Preload);
  game.state.add('game', Game);
  game.state.add('Level1', Level1);
  game.state.add('Level2', Level2);
  game.state.add("GameOver", GameOver);
  game.state.start('boot');
};
```

7.4.3 Preloading

This game will load in a lot of image and sound files. It needs sprite sheets for the animated player and mouse, which have some beautiful animations and images that will be used for the world foreground and background. The map data for the two levels is loaded in, using the tiled_json format, so we can access the extra data that Tiled exports with its specific maps. Some images are loaded in for other game objects, like the signs, collectables, and UI elements. Finally, an audiosprite (with multiple sounds inside of it) is loaded. Multiple audio formats are passed to the sprite, so the browser can select which format it can actually play.

```js
this.load.spritesheet(
  'player', 'assets/images/sprites/FoxSprite.png',
    210, 210
  );
this.load.spritesheet(
  'mouse', 'assets/images/sprites/MouseSprite.png',
    165, 160
  );
```

```
this.load.image('gamebg', 'assets/images/Background.
  png');
this.load.tilemap(
      'level1', 'assets/levels/level1.json',
      null, Phaser.Tilemap.TILED_JSON
  );
this.load.tilemap(
      'level2', 'assets/levels/level2.json',
      null, Phaser.Tilemap.TILED_JSON
  );
this.load.image('Tiles', 'assets/images/Tiles.png');
this.load.image('coin', 'assets/images/coin.png');
this.load.image('scoreholder', 'assets/images/
  scoreholder.png');
this.load.image('sign', 'assets/images/sign.png');
this.load.image('gameover_bg', 'assets/images/
  gameover_bg.png');
this.load.audiosprite(
      'sfx',
      [ 'assets/sounds/sfx.mp3', 'assets/sounds/
        sfx.ogg' ], "assets/sounds/sfx.json"
  );
```

7.4.4 Player Character Prefab

The player character in this game is a rather fast-looking fox. This game is built to run on the keyboard, so the fox is going to need to respond to the standard cursor keys for left and right movements and the spacebar will cause him to jump.

```
export default class Player extends Phaser.Sprite {

    constructor(game, x, y) {
        super(game, x, y, 'player', 0);

        //game object level variables
        this.speed = 400;
        this.airSpeed = 300;
        this.jumpPower = 600;
        this.inAir = true;
        this.hitGround = false;

        //animations
        this.animations.add("idle",
          [0,1,2,3,4,3,2,1]);
        this.animations.add("jump",
          [0,5,6,7,8,9]);
        this.landAnimation = this.animations.
          add("land", [7,6,5]);
        this.animations.add("run",
          [11,12,13,14,15,16,17]);

        this.game.physics.enable(this, Phaser.
          Physics.ARCADE);
```

```
        this.body.collideWorldBounds = true;
        this.body.drag = { x: 600, y: 0 };
        this.body.setSize(60, 100);
        this.anchor.setTo(.5, 1);
        this.cursors = this.game.input.keyboard.
          createCursorKeys();
        this.jumpButton = this.game.input.keyboard.
          addKey(Phaser.Keyboard.SPACEBAR);
        this.jumpButton.onDown.add(this.jump, this);

        this.animations.play("idle", 9, true);

        this.flashEffect = this.game.add.
          tween(this)
            .to( { alpha: 0 }, 50, Phaser.
              Easing.Bounce.Out)
            .to( { alpha: .8 }, 50, Phaser.
              Easing.Bounce.Out)
            .to( { alpha: 1 }, 150, Phaser.
              Easing.Circular.Out);
    }

    animationState() {
        if(this.hitGround) {
            this.animations.play("land", 15);
        } else if(!this.inAir && !this.
          landAnimation.isPlaying) {
            if(Math.abs(this.body.velocity.x)
              > 4) {
                this.animations.play("run", 9,
                  true);
            } else if( this.body.onFloor() ) {
                this.animations.play("idle",
                  9, true);
            }
        }
    }

    update() {

        this.hitGround = false;
        var wasAir = this.inAir;
        this.inAir = !this.body.onFloor();

        if(this.inAir != wasAir && this.body.
          velocity > 0) {
            this.hitGround = true;
        }

        this.animationState();

        this.speedToUse = this.inAir ? this.
          airSpeed : this.speed;

        if(this.cursors.left.isDown) {
            this.scale.x = -1;
```

```
            this.body.velocity.x = -this.
               speedToUse;
        }

        if(this.cursors.right.isDown) {
            this.scale.x = 1;
            this.body.velocity.x = this.
               speedToUse;
        }
    }

    jump() {

        if(this.body.onFloor() == true) {
            this.body.velocity.y = -this.
               jumpPower;
            this.animations.play("jump", 30);
            this.doubleJump = true;

        } else if(this.doubleJump == true) {
            console.log(this.doubleJump);
            this.doubleJump = false;
            this.body.velocity.y = -this.
               jumpPower;
            this.animations.play("jump", 30);
        }
    }

    flash() {

        if(!this.flashEffect.isRunning) {
            this.flashEffect.start();

        }
    }
}
```

7.4.4.1 Player Prefab Constructor

The fox constructor starts the process of getting the fox read to move and animate fluidly. To get things started, there are a series of object-level variables that will be used throughout the lifespan of this fox. The first three variables are used to control the speed that the character moves. For this game, to give the fox a bit more responsive feel, he will have a different speed when in the air. The first condition requires that the fox was in the air last frame and has hit the ground on the current update frame.

```
this.speed = 400;
this.airSpeed = 300;
this.jumpPower = 600;
this.inAir = true;
this.hitGround = false;
```

The next sections of constructor code set up the player physics and animations. Much of it is basic animation setup, but there are a few important parts of the setup that either are tweakable or will come up later in the player object. The first line of code of interest is the landing animation that will need to be referenced later on, so it is stored in an object-level variable.

```
this.landAnimation = this.animations.add("land",
    [7,6,5]);
```

Drag is an important property to tweak to get a character's motion feeling correct. In this case, we want him to have a snappy start and stop feeling when moving horizontally. A large drag in the x direction will pull him to a stop quickly. The drag is set to zero for the y-axis because the fox doesn't need any effects of air resistance in this game. The hitbox for this character starts out quite large, especially because it is sized to encompass his long tail. The hitbox is reduced to a size that won't aggravate the player via the setSize method of the physics body. The new collision box is located in the middle of the character. Finally, the anchor point (from which he will rotate and scale around) is set to the center bottom point of the sprite. Later on, we will be "flipping" this character to face right and left by changing his scale, and this prevents him from flipping around on the back of his tail.

```
this.body.drag = { x: 600, y: 0 };
this.body.setSize(60, 100);
this.anchor.setTo(.5, 1);
```

The last interesting part of the setup function is the addition of a chained tween to the sprite. This animation tweens to zero visibility and back to full visibility creating an extra flash in between from the bounce easing (which will cause it to flicker as it "bounces" the alpha back before settling). This animation is stored in an object-level variable, so it can be stopped and reused without having to create a new animation every time a flash is needed.

```
this.flashEffect = this.game.add.tween(this)
        .to( { alpha: 0 }, 50, Phaser.Easing.
            Bounce.Out)
        .to( { alpha: .8 }, 50, Phaser.Easing.
            Bounce.Out)
        .to( { alpha: 1 }, 150, Phaser.Easing.
            Circular.Out);
```

7.4.4.2 Player Prefab Update

Now that the player is set up, the next step is to implement the player's custom update method. The first step of this process is to place the object into the right animation state. This game object has animations for running, standing, jumping, falling, and hitting the ground. For the animations to work properly, the prefab needs to track the properties that relate to those animations and trigger a change when something significant happens. The factors that affect the player's are if it is currently airborne of it hit just hit the ground and should trigger the hit ground animation.

The start of the update method tracks these states. First, the inAir state of the object is stored from the last frame, which will be contrasted later on with the current in air state to determine if the player just hit the ground. Next, using `this.body.onGround`, the player updates its inAir state. Finally, the hitGround property is set to false to ensure the value will only be "true" frame when it hits the ground. There are two conditions that need to be met for the hitGround property to be true. First, the fox needs to be in the air last update, and on the ground this update. Also the player needs to be falling downward (meaning they need a downward velocity greater than zero).

Once the general state of the player has been properly set, a method is called to actually figure out which animation should be currently playing.

```
this.hitGround = false;
var wasAir = this.inAir;
this.inAir = !this.body.onFloor();

if(this.inAir != wasAir && this.body.velocity > 0) {
    this.hitGround = true;
}

this.animationState();
```

The next step in the update is to move the player. The actual movement code is a simple test to see if the left or right arrows are depressed and to add velocity to the object if they are. Because the player has a varied speed based on his grounded state, the speed to use as his velocity is stored in a variable beforehand. If the player is in the sky, then speedToUse will default to the left side of the colon in the first line (`this.airSpeed`). If the player is grounded, the right side of the colon (`this.speed`) will be the speed that will be used for the player motion. Based on the direction the player is inputting to the keyboard, the player sprite will be flipped right or left by changing its scale.x to be positive (facing right) or negative (facing left).

```
this.speedToUse = this.inAir ? this.airSpeed :
  this.speed;

if(this.cursors.left.isDown) {
    this.scale.x = -1;
    this.body.velocity.x = -this.speedToUse;
}

if(this.cursors.right.isDown) {
    this.scale.x = 1;
    this.body.velocity.x = this.speedToUse;
}
```

7.4.4.3 Player Prefab Animation Controller
In the update method, the process of animating was handed on to the animation controller method. This has been placed into a separate method so as much of the animation can be done in one place and not get lost throughout all the other portions of the player's update and state code.

First, if the player has just hit the ground, then the landing animation is triggered. While it is only a few frames, the bit of down and compression on the character when he lands imparts a good and solid "landing feeling."

If the player is not in the process of landing and they are on the ground, the game then checks the player's speed. If they're moving fast enough on the x-axis (the `Math.abs` removing the need to deal with negative speed), then the run animation is activated for this sprite. If the player isn't moving fast enough to warrant a run animation, the idle is played instead. Because the check for the switch to idle transition still contains some movement for the character, fox will slide slightly to a complete stop.

```
animationState() {
    if(this.hitGround) {
        this.animations.play("land", 15);
    } else if(!this.inAir && !this.landAnimation.
      isPlaying) {
        if(Math.abs(this.body.velocity.x) > 4) {
            this.animations.play("run", 9,
                true);
        } else if( this.body.onFloor() ) {
            this.animations.play("idle", 9,
                true);
        }
    }
}
```

7.4.4.4 Player Jump Method

So far, we've gotten the player to run to the right and the left, but the player still is lacking the critical jump capability that makes a platformer enjoyable. The jump is handled by a key down handler that is set up in the player's constructor.

```
this.jumpButton = this.game.input.keyboard.
  addKey(Phaser.Keyboard.SPACEBAR);
this.jumpButton.onDown.add(this.jump, this);
```

The handler will implement a double jump, so there are two sets of jump conditions to be validated. For the first jump, it is only necessary to check to see if the player is on the ground. If they are, they are given an upward velocity equal to the jump power configured in the constructor. The jump animation is triggered and the doubleJump flag is set to true.

If the jump button is pressed and the player is not on the ground, the double jump flag is checked. If it is "true," then the player can jump again. The same impulse and animation are applied, and the double jump flag is deactivated. The player will not be able to use another jump in the sky until they jump from the ground again and reset the doubleJump variable.

```
jump() {
        if(this.body.onFloor() == true) {
                this.body.velocity.y = -this.
                    jumpPower;
                this.animations.play("jump", 30);
                this.doubleJump = true;
        } else if(this.doubleJump == true) {
                console.log(this.doubleJump);
                this.doubleJump = false;
                this.body.velocity.y = -this.
                    jumpPower;
                this.animations.play("jump", 30);
        }
}
```

7.4.4.5 Player Flash Method

The final method in the player prefab is the flash method. It is a simple
method that will play the flash animation that was configured in the
constructor. The only other special consideration in this method is to ensure
that it will not restart the animation every time the flash method is called.
This will give the animation the time it needs to actually play through its
whole duration, so the player will actually flash and not just fade.

```
flash() {
        if(!this.flashEffect.isRunning) {
                this.flashEffect.start();
        }
}
```

7.4.5 Mouse Prefab

The next unique prefab in this game is the mouse prefab that will act as the
enemy and obstacle in the game. They're not going to be the smartest of
mice and will simply patrol back and forth. Should the fox get near enough to
them to bother them, they will stop and slash at the player, but the moment
the fox gets out of their "anger range," they will resume their patrol. The
following is the entirety of the code for the mouse prefab.

```
export default class Mouse extends Phaser.Sprite {
        constructor(game, x, y) {
        super(game, x, y, 'mouse', 0);

        //game object level variables
        this.speed = 200;
        this.stepLimit = 90;
        this.currentStep = Math.floor(Math.
          random() * this.stepLimit);

        //animations
        this.animations.add("stand", [0]);
```

```
        this.swingAnimation = this.animations.
          add("swing", [0,1,2,3,4,5,6,7]);
        this.animations.add("run",
          [8,9,10,11,12,13,14]);

        this.game.physics.enable(this, Phaser.
          Physics.ARCADE);
        this.body.collideWorldBounds = true;
        this.body.drag = { x: 600, y: 0 };
        this.body.setSize(60, 80);
        this.anchor.setTo(.5, 1);

        this.animations.play("run", 9, true);
    }

  update() {

        var dist = Phaser.Math.distance(this.x,
          this.y, this.player.x, this.player.y);

        if( Math.round(dist) < 210 ) {
            this.animations.play("swing", 9);

            if(this.x < this.player.x) {
                this.scale.x = 1;
            } else {
                this.scale.x = -1;
            }

        }

        if(!this.swingAnimation.isPlaying) {

            this.currentStep++;
            this.body.velocity.x = this.speed;

            this.animations.play("run", 9,
              true);

            this.scale.x = (this.speed > 0) ?
              1 : -1;

            if(this.currentStep >= this.
              stepLimit) {
                this.speed *= -1;
                this.currentStep = 0;
            }

        }

    }

}
```

7.4.5.1 Mouse Constructor
The constructor for the mouse does many of the basic setup functions to get a sprite into a 2D world including setting up its drag, adding animations, and placing the anchor at the center of the sprite so it can be flipped widthwise.

The important new additions to this sprite are a set of variables that will control its patrol area and where it starts on its patrol.

```
this.stepLimit = 90;
this.currentStep = Math.floor(Math.random() * this.
    stepLimit);
```

The first variable, stepLimit, is the number of steps that the mouse can take in any direction before it will turn around and start walking in the other direction. The currentStep is where the mouse is on its step limit and is initialized as a random number within the step limit. Setting each mouse to a random starting point in its patrol helps to randomize the directions the mice in the game are facing. With the random starting points, the mice will change directions at different times in the game instead of all of them doing an about-face at exactly the same time (which has the potential to just look a bit jarring to the player). (See Figure 7.14).

7.4.5.2 Mouse Update

Like most prefabs, the meat of the code for the mouse is going to come in the update method. The update method handles moving the mouse forward, flipping it around when it has reached the limits of its patrol, and attacking the player when it gets too near.

The first consideration is checking to see if the player is near enough for an attack to make sense and stopping to play the attack animation if that is the case. To begin with, the distance between the mouse and the player is calculated using Phaser's built-in distance method. Distance in this case is the length of the line from the player's anchor point to the mouse's anchor point (i.e., from the bottom center of the player to the bottom center of the mouse). (See Figure 7.15).

```
var dist = Phaser.Math.distance(this.x, this.y,
    this.player.x, this.player.y);
```

The next portion checks to see if the player qualifies as "close enough" based on the distance between the mouse and player. The "magic number" of 210 has been provided in here because it gives a very good feel to the reaction time of the mouse, but you are free to play with this number to get values for a very lazy mouse or one that really just wants to swing its sword a lot. If the player is close enough, the swing animation is triggered, and the mouse is flipped to face the player. The flip (scaling left or right) is based on the location of the mouse relative to the player. If the player's x location is less than the mouse's x position, then the mouse needs to face left to swing, or vice versa, for right.

```
if( Math.round(dist) < 210 ) {
    this.animations.play("swing", 9);

    if(this.x < this.player.x) {
        this.scale.x = 1;
    } else {
        this.scale.x = -1;
    }
}
```

183

> **Where Does the Player Object Come From?**
>
> Nowhere in the mouse's code is the player explicitly set. The player reference will be provided in the game state code right after the mouse is created. Look for the line `this.enemies.setAll("player," this.player)` to see how the reference is provided.

The patrol code finishes off the sprite's update method. In order to ensure that the mouse only patrols when it is not attacking, the patrol code is wrapped in a condition that will run only when the attack animation is not playing.

During each update call when on patrol, the current step is incremented by one, bringing it closer to the maximum number of steps it can take in one direction. The velocity is set back to full to override any effects of friction, and the running animation is played so it can continue to animate its steps. Because the sprite might flip around to attack the player, the scale is set to face the direction the mouse is moving. A negative velocity will force its scale to be negative one, while a positive velocity will result in a positive scale to make it face right.

The final bit of code checks to see if the step limit has been reached. If that is so, the walking speed of the mouse is reversed, which will cause it to move in the opposite direction starting with the next frame, and its step limit is reset. It will need to walk in this new direction for as many frames as it takes to get to the step limit again before it will turn around once more (See Figure 7.15).

```
if(!this.swingAnimation.isPlaying) {
        this.currentStep++;
        this.body.velocity.x = this.speed;

        this.animations.play("run", 9,
          true);

        this.scale.x = (this.speed > 0) ?
          1 : -1;

        if(this.currentStep >= this.
          stepLimit) {
            this.speed *= -1;
            this.currentStep = 0;
        }
}
```

7.4.6 UI Components

There is exactly one UI component that will be used in this game, and thankfully it is a reused component from the last game example. The number box from the shoot 'em up will be brought into this game to give the user feedback about how many coins they have collected during gameplay.

7.4.6.1 Fixed to Camera

Unfortunately, when the number box is added to the game, it is added into the game world space. This works fine for a game where the camera never moves, but it won't look quite so good the moment the game camera begins to budge. As the camera moves away from its starting position, the number box will move with the rest of the objects, as if it were an object in the fox's world. The fix to this problem is to affix your UI components to the camera so that when the camera moves, so does the UI element. This is done by setting UI element's "fixedToCamera" property to "true." In the game state's constructor, you will see this is done on the number box right after it is created and added to the world.

7.4.7 Game State

This game has multiple levels, which means that it has more than one state that implements the gameplay. For this project, the game state is going to start the score for the gameplay and then bounce the player to the first level of our game. This score object is added to the game itself, so it can exist throughout the life of all the states. It will move from level one to level two unaffected because it is not in the level's scope. Watch for it to be used in three separate states and keep its value each time the state changes.

```
create() {
    this.game.score = 0;
    this.game.state.start("Level1");
}
```

7.4.8 Level State

A level state in this game takes all of the prefabs and adds the final logic of the game. It handles the creation of the game world, changing levels, collisions between player and game objects, and player feedback. For each level in your game, you will need to create a separate level object that will help with writing special code that is associated with the level. In this game, there are two different levels. When the player reaches the end of the first level, they are taken to the second level. Completing level two will bring the player to the game over screen. The following is the template for a level state that will undergo some small modifications for the level two state.

```
//require other components
import Player from "../prefabs/Player.js";
import Mouse from "../prefabs/Mouse.js";
import NumberBox from "../prefabs/NumberBox.js";

export default class Level1 extends Phaser.State {

  constructor() {
    //object level properties
```

```
        super();
    }

    create() {

        //physics
        this.physics.startSystem(Phaser.Physics.
          ARCADE);
        this.physics.arcade.gravity.y = 800;

      //map start
      this.map = this.add.tilemap("level1");

      //parallax background
      this.map.addTilesetImage('gamebg');
      this.bg = this.map.createLayer('bg');
      this.bg.scrollFactorX = .6;
      this.bg.scrollFactorY = .6;

      //walkable tiles
      this.map.addTilesetImage('Tiles');
      this.layer = this.map.createLayer('Level');

      //collision
      this.layer.resizeWorld();
      this.map.setCollisionBetween(6,25,true,this.
        layer);

      //coin layer
      this.coins = this.add.group();
      this.coins.physicsBodyType = Phaser.Physics.
        ARCADE;
      this.coins.enableBody = true;
      this.map.createFromObjects("Collectables", 41,
        'coin', null, true, false, this.coins);
      this.coins.setAll("body.gravity", 0);

      //place doors
      this.doors = this.add.group();
      this.doors.physicsBodyType = Phaser.Physics.
        ARCADE;
      this.doors.enableBody = true;
      this.map.createFromObjects("Doors", 242, 'sign',
        null, true, false, this.doors);
      this.doors.setAll("body.gravity", 0);

      //player
      this.map.createFromObjects("Player", 243, null,
        null, true, false, this.world, Player);
      this.player = this.world.getTop();

      //place enemies
      this.enemies = this.add.group();
      this.map.createFromObjects("Enemies", 25, null,
        null, true, false, this.enemies, Mouse);
      this.enemies.setAll("player", this.player);
```

```
        //UI
        this.UIGroup = this.add.group();
        this.scoreField = new NumberBox(this.game,
          "scoreholder", this.game.score, this.UIGroup);
        this.scoreField.fixedToCamera = true;

        //sound
        this.sfx = this.add.audioSprite('sfx');

          this.camera.follow(this.player);
    }
    update() {
        this.physics.arcade.collide(this.player, this.
          layer);
        this.physics.arcade.collide(this.enemies, this.
          layer);
        this.physics.arcade.overlap(this.player, this.
          coins, this.collectCoin, null, this);
        this.physics.arcade.overlap(this.player, this.
          doors, this.hitDoor, null, this);
        this.physics.arcade.collide(this.player, this.
          enemies, this.hitEnemy, null, this);
    }
    collectCoin(playerRef, coinRef) {
        coinRef.kill();
        this.game.score ++;
        this.scoreField.setValue(this.game.score);
        this.sfx.play("coin");
    }
    hitDoor(playerRef, doorRef) {
        this.game.state.clearCurrentState();
        this.game.state.start("Level2");
    }
    hitEnemy(playerRef, enemyRef) {
        if(!playerRef.flashEffect.isRunning) {
            playerRef.flash();
        this.sfx.play("hit");
            if(this.game.score > 0) {
                this.game.score - -;
                this.scoreField.setValue(this.game.
                  score);
            }
        }
    }
  }
}
```

7.4.8.1 Game State Constructor
The constructor is responsible for setting up the world, loading in the tilemap, placing the player into the world, creating all the collectables, and instantiating all the enemies. All of that work is accomplished based on the

data that have been set up and exported from the Tiled map editor. Among the miscellaneous items the constructor accomplishes are getting the sounds ready to play and placing the UI elements on to the stage.

To start everything, a new tilemap is added to the world. This is the map that will display all the "world tiles" in the game and the background. The world tiles will specify where a player can and cannot walk, so there will be some setup required to tell Phaser which tiles are solid.

```
this.map = this.add.tilemap(levelName);
```

Once the map is added, the next step is to add the first layer to the map that shows the background of the game. This background is actually a collection of background tiles that will be rendered behind the foreground elements and cannot collide with anything. To load in a tile layer, first you specify the tileset image to use and then create a tilemap. Make sure when creating these layers that the ID for the layer is the same as the ID of the layer in the map's JSON file. In this case, in the JSON file, there is a layer named "bg" that has the data for the background tiles, so the create layer method must reference the "bg" layer when it is called. (See figure 7.2k.)

The last part of the setup of the background reduces its scroll factor. The scroll factor is how fast the tile layer moves relative to a camera movement. A value of one means it will move equally as much as the camera, so if the camera moves 20 pixels to the right, the background will show 20 more of its pixels to the right. Lesser scroll factors make the background move less quickly than the camera. In the following example, the background will move about 60% as fast as the foreground. When the camera moves 20 pixels to the right, the background will only move 12 now.

```
//parallax background
this.map.addTilesetImage('gamebg');
 this.bg = this.map.createLayer('bg');
 this.bg.scrollFactorX = .6;
 this.bg.scrollFactorY = .6;
```

Parallax

The scroll factors establish the effect of parallax for the game world. Parallax is the tendency for faraway objects to appear to be moving less quickly than ones nearby. It is actually a depth cue that helps one determine the relative distances of objects. By adding parallax to a game, you add an extra bit of depth to something that would otherwise look flat. The overall effect is a nice bit of polish that makes the game read and feel very solid.

After the background comes the foreground tiles. First, the tileset for the foreground is added and then the tiles are drawn to the foreground via this. map.createLayer. These two calls will create the actual platforms and ground for the player to stand on, but they don't make them solid objects in the physics system.

The first step in making the visible tiles of the foreground solid is making the world big enough to hold them all. Currently, the world space is as big as the screen. Anything beyond the bounds of the screen doesn't exist physically. Map layers have a method (resizeWorld) that will increase the bounds of the world space to contain all the tiles in the layer. Now that all of the tiles in the layer can potentially be collided with, the next step is to tell the game which of the tiles should be "solid" tiles in the world. The method setCollision between will set all of the tiles with IDs between the first two arguments as being solid. These tiles then will work as platforms and walls for the game.

```
//walkable tiles
this.map.addTilesetImage('Tiles');
this.layer = this.map.createLayer('Level');

//collision
this.layer.resizeWorld();
this.map.setCollisionBetween(6,25,true,this.layer);
```

Where to Find Tile IDs

If you are looking for the ID of the tiles, the best place to find them is in the tilemap JSON file. Open up the JSON and look at the IDs of the tiles that appear in the layer's data property and in the tileset property. For this game, the tiles being used as the foreground start at ID 1. You can then count forward from the starting ID to figure out which tiles count as "collidable" on the tilesheet. The tile on the far left will start at the first GID and move upward from there.

```
"tilesets":[
        {
        "firstgid":1,
        "image":"..\/images\/Tiles.png",
        "imageheight":400,
        "imagewidth":600,
        "margin":0,
        "name":"Tiles",
        "properties":
            {
            },
        "spacing":0,
        "tileheight":100,
        "tilewidth":100
        },
```

After the world space has been set up and properly configured, the next step is to get the game objects into the world. There are four different object layers in the game map files. These objects are the enemies, the coins to collect, the player, and the sign that leads to the next room. Each of these objects will be added to the game using a method of Phaser's map system that can create objects at the same location they were placed in the map editor. The different objects will all need a bit of custom configuration, so we will discuss each in turn, starting with the coins.

The coins have been placed onto the "collectable" layer in the map. In order to create sprites at the same location as the coins in the layer, the createFromObjects method is invoked. The arguments to this method tell it to search through the "Collectables" layer in the map file for any object with a GID of 41. If it finds that object, it will create a "coin" at the same location in the game. The next few arguments (null, true, and false) are simply needed to get to the final input, this.coins. This will place all the created coin sprites into the newly created coins group.

The coins have a problem though. They need to collide with the player, but we want them to also float in midair. We've already set their physics bodies up with the physicsBodyType and enabled their bodies, but gravity will still tug them to the ground the first moment it gets a chance. To stop gravity's pull on the coins the gravity for each individual coin's body is set to zero using a call to this.coins.setAll (a method of Phaser's group object), telling it to give each coin no gravitational pull.

```
//coin layer
this.coins = this.add.group();
this.coins.physicsBodyType = Phaser.Physics.ARCADE;
this.coins.enableBody = true;
this.map.createFromObjects("Collectables", 41,
  'coin', null, true, false, this.coins);
this.coins.setAll("body.gravity", 0);
```

The signs are actually set up the same way as the coins. The only change is that a signs group is created, and the doors layer is referenced when creating the signs using the createFromObjects method.

```
//place doors
this.doors = this.add.group();
this.doors.physicsBodyType = Phaser.Physics.ARCADE;
this.doors.enableBody = true;
this.map.createFromObjects("Doors", 242, 'sign',
  null, true, false, this.doors);
this.doors.setAll("body.gravity", 0);
```

Next on the list of layers to import from the Tiled map is the player. Unlike the coins and the doors, we want to add a custom object at the player location. To create a custom object, "null" is passed in as the name for the sprite and the last argument is the class that should be used to create the new object on the stage.

The player itself is easy to create and position, but the game also needs to know what object the player is so it can have the mice give chase and collide the player against different objects in the game. The createFromObjects method does not return a reference to the object created, but it is possible to find the last object added to a group using the getTop method. Since the player is added into the root "world" group, we'll store a reference to the player via `this.world.getTop()`, which will return the last objects added to the world (our player, in this case).

```
//player
  this.map.createFromObjects("Player", 243, null,
    null, true, false, this.world, Player);
this.player = this.world.getTop();
```

The mice are the final bit of object instantiation done in the constructor. They are on the enemy layer in the Tiled map and are created as custom objects in the enemy group in the game. For their simple AI to work properly, each enemy needs to know what object the player is. The reference to the player is set the same way the gravity was turned off on the coins, via a set all that tells each enemy where the player object is.

```
//place enemies
this.enemies = this.add.group();
this.map.createFromObjects("Enemies", 25, null,
  null, true, false, this.enemies, Mouse);
this.enemies.setAll("player", this.player);
```

For the UI, we will be reusing the `NumberBox` from the last game. Without fixing it to the camera, it would fly off the screen, so after creating this score box and adding it to the stage, its fixedToCamera property is set to true to keep it always visible in the upper left-hand corner of the game.

```
//UI
this.UIGroup = this.add.group();
this.scoreField = new NumberBox(
            this.game, "scoreholder", this.game.
              score, this.UIGroup
            );
this.scoreField.fixedToCamera = true;
```

The final two lines in the setup function create a sound to play when collisions happen between objects. This is an audio sprite that has two sounds. One sound is for coins and the other sound is for each instance the player collides with an enemy.

Finally, the camera is told to follow the player. If this line was not here, the camera would never budge from its original position. Once the player spawned and walked too far to the right (or jumped too far up), they would wind up off screen and unable to play the game. The camera follow method will follow whatever object it is told to follow, which is the player character in this case. The camera will not move further if the world bounds have been reached, instead it will move to be fully flush with the edge of the world and stay still until the player moves in a direction that does have space and new objects to render (See Figure 7.17).

```
this.sfx = this.add.audioSprite('sfx');
this.camera.follow(this.player);
```

7.4.8.2 Update Method

Because the majority of the update code for this game has already been written in the individual sprite update methods, the game state's update code is just a series of physics calls. The first two collide the player and mice against the tilemap layer, which will keep them on the ground and unable them to walk through walls. The others check for collisions between player and objects in the game (collecting coins, hitting enemies, or reaching a door). Each of these final collide calls has collision response handlers, which will be discussed next.

```
update() {
    this.physics.arcade.collide(this.player, this.
        layer);
    this.physics.arcade.collide(this.enemies, this.
        layer);
    this.physics.arcade.overlap(this.player, this.
        coins, this.collectCoin, null, this);
    this.physics.arcade.overlap(this.player, this.
        doors, this.hitDoor, null, this);
    this.physics.arcade.collide(this.player, this.
        enemies, this.hitEnemy, null, this);
}
```

7.4.8.3 Hit Enemy Handler

When the player hits the enemy, this game is going to have the fox flash to give the player some feedback that they messed up. Additionally the mouse, apparently trickier than the fox, will steal one coin from the fox (so long as the player has any coins to be stolen). All of this code is only executed if the fox is not currently in a flash animation, so all the coins don't get zapped away for every frame the fox touches the mouse. As a reminder, the flash effect is not built into Phaser sprites, but it is a method added to the player that runs an animation that animates the transparency of the sprite to give it a flashing effect.

```
hitEnemy(playerRef, enemyRef) {
    if(!playerRef.flashEffect.isRunning) {
        playerRef.flash();
        if(this.score > 0) {
            this.score - -;
            this.scoreField.setValue(this.score);
        }
    }
}
```

7.4.8.4 Hit Door Handler

The hit door handler will be run whenever the player collides with the "forward" sign that has been placed at the end of each level. The response that is caused by hitting the sign differs based on which level the player is currently engaged in.

For the first level, the hit door handler will transition the game to level two. Because many of the properties and objects are the same between level one and level two, the current state needs to be explicitly cleaned up so objects can be reconstructed in the new state without having any leftover properties from their old level.

```
hitDoor(playerRef, doorRef) {
    this.game.state.clearCurrentState();
    this.game.state.start("Level2");
}
```

The hit door handler for level two loads in the game over scene. Because this scene does not share objects like player, map, or mice, it only needs the state start call.

```
hitDoor(playerRef, doorRef) {
    this.game.state.start("GameOver");
}
```

7.4.8.5 Hit Coin Handler
When the player hits a coin, it is removed from the game, the score is incremented, and the UI is updated to show the new number of coins the player has collected.

```
collectCoin(playerRef, coinRef) {
    coinRef.kill();
    this.score ++;
    this.scoreField.setValue(this.score);
}
```

7.4.9 Game Over State

The game over state adds an image to the back of the display list to act as grounding to the text. It also shows the final score of the player, using the "this.game.score" variable that has now been used between the game and the level one and level two states. If the player presses down on the screen, the score will be reset and they will be able to play through the two levels again.

```
export default class GameOver extends Phaser.State {
  create() {
      this.add.sprite( 0,0,'gameover_bg');

      var style = { font: "30px Arial", align:
        "center", fill: "#fff" };
      this.txtValue = this.add.text(
            512, 534, this.game.score.toString() +
              " points", style
      );
```

```
        this.txtValue.anchor.setTo(.5, .5);
        this.game.input.onDown.addOnce(this.
          switchState, this);
    }

    switchState() {
        this.game.score = 0;
        this.state.start("Level1");
      }
    }
```

7.4.10 Conclusion

The process that goes into making maps, placing items, tweaking values, creating animations, and transitioning between levels is engaging and intricate work. We have breezed through a number of concepts in this chapter, and you might feel a need to take further study of the underlying concepts. There are a number of great examples on the web that can be found with a web search that can give you another angle on what is going on behind the scenes to make all of this work. Look for "Tiled map tutorials" and "tile engine creation" examples in specific to get a good start.

This game gives you the basics of a platformer and really actually pushes Phaser and HTML5 games to a high degree with its large render area, lots of moving parts, and big graphics to animate. As always, I encourage you to have fun with it and make it your own. Swap out graphics, make new animations, and break things so you can fix them. Here are a few places where you can play with numbers or ideas that can add to advancement of the game:

- Change gravity and friction on the characters.
- Adjust speed and jump power.
- Play around with collider sizes on the characters.
- Change the collideable tiles in the world (dangerous but fun).
- Adjust the mouse AI chase range.

Also, here are some things that will prove more advanced techniques:

- Add more levels.
- Add extra doors that go to different levels, or back to old ones.
- Add new enemies or collectables.

The next examples in this book are going to take a step back and focus on less complex world interactions and mobile input, so continue reading from here if "simpler" mobile games are of interest to you.

7.5 Tower Defense

Tower defense games are a great combination of several different major areas of game development. They bring together map making, real-time AI, and even pathfinding. When a tower defense game is made in a 2D engine, there is also an additional challenge of how to show depth (or 3D space) in a system that was not originally built for the task. All of these tasks can be quite complex to tackle, so we'll be using the work of others in order to get our game done faster, pausing only to look at the concepts behind the code libraries that will be used without actually implementing the algorithms completely.

7.6 Spatial Cues

Our brains use a number of different cues to discern how far away objects are. These cues are separated into monocular and binocular cues. Binocular cues require both eyes to be open and each eye to see a different, slightly offset view of the world. This is a task that VR viewers like the Oculus Rift can tackle, but it is pretty much impossible for phone and computer screens to accomplish. Thankfully, monocular cues work just as well with only one image (or an eye closed). We use monocular cues all the time to interpret space on screens and on paper, even though the image itself is only in two dimensions. They are important enough that artists will study these cues and practice their implementation so they can accurately show them in their work.

Why Study Depth Cues

It may seem odd to be reading about depth cues in a technical manual, but as mentioned earlier, they are part of the trade of an artist. Unfortunately, while an artist can make some beautiful assets for a game, it is up to the developer to finish the job and assemble them into a fully functioning world. The developer will need to figure out how and when to work these depth cues into the game. The proper setup and implementation of a depth cue can really make a game world feel alive and vivid, making them important considerations of any game developer.

See Figures 7.18 through 7.26.

Some of the more commonly used monocular depth cues include perspective, shading, relative heights, atmospheric effects, and occlusion. Lines that converge until they hit a point on the horizon are the hallmarks of perspective and they give the viewer a very strong sense of depth. Shading indicates where light is and how an object is illuminated. A well-shaded scene and object can show what parts of an object is where based on how bright portions of the object are relative to the light source. Relative heights describe how our brains interpret distance based on sizes. The closer something comes to us, the bigger it gets. This works really well with objects we know their general heights (like people, books, or cars). When we see a human figure, but it is tiny and takes up a small amount of space in our field of view, we can assume that the human and other objects near it are far away (See Figure 7.18).

Pespective   Shading

Relative heights   Overlapping objects

FIG 7.18 Some of the major depth cues.

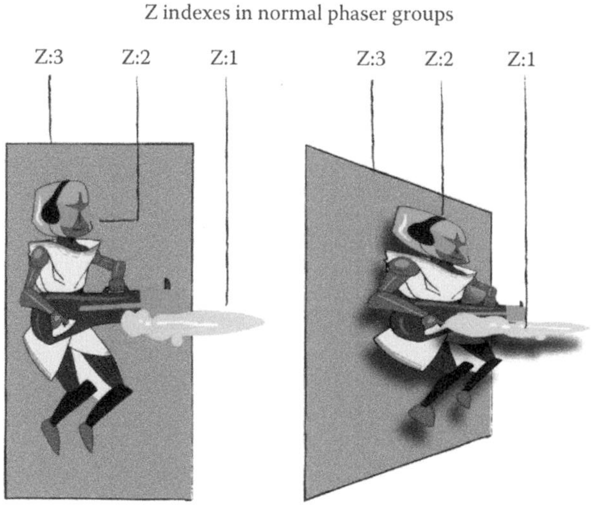

Z indexes in normal phaser groups

Z:3   Z:2   Z:1   Z:3   Z:2   Z:1

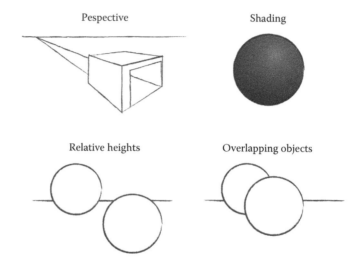

FIG 7.19 Z indexes and corresponding layering.

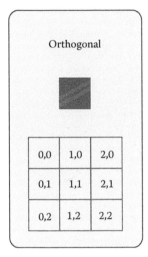 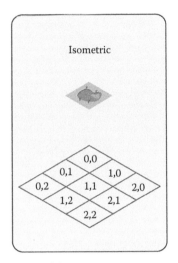

FIG 7.20 Appearance differences between isometric and orthogonal tiles.

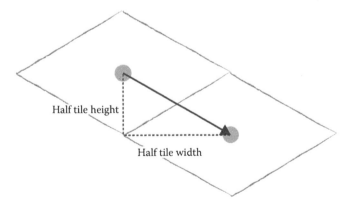

FIG 7.21 Determining layout position in isometric space.

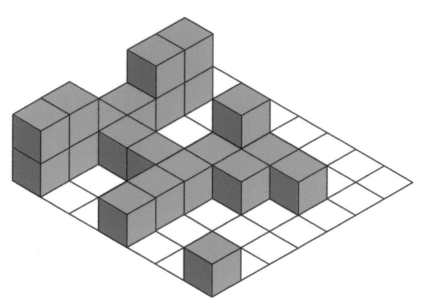

FIG 7.22 Sample isometric grid with cube placements.

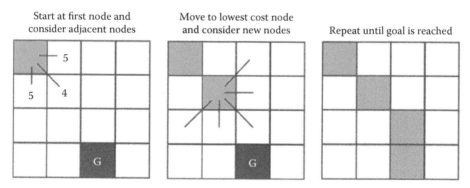

FIG 7.23 Visualization of a simple pathfinding approach.

Out of all of the cues, occlusion is the most important and perhaps easiest to implement. If something is overlapping something else, we assume it is closer. Cars closer on the highway obscure cars further away, and a fence between you and someone else obscures some of their form behind the fence (See Figure 7.18).

The actual calculations to create a fully 3D space are quite intense. When 2D games emulate 3D space, they typically strip out as much of the calculations as possible and cheat the other cues into the rendering process. Some cheats include background images that are drawn in perspective, sprites with shading added before being added to the game, and drawing more distant objects in a much hazier style. All of this work offloads the task of figuring

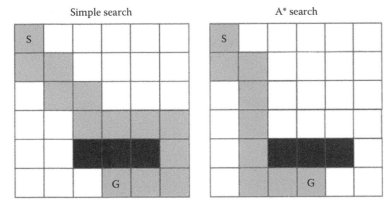

FIG 7.24 Difference in a path found between a simple pathfinder and an A* search.

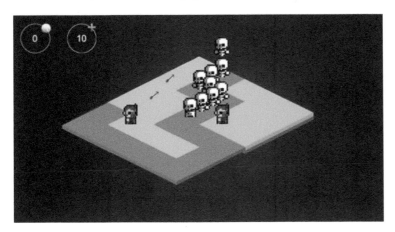

FIG 7.25 Screenshot of the finished defense game.

Tile drawing process

(1) Place first tile   (2) Build first x-axis row   (3) Continue for each y-axis row

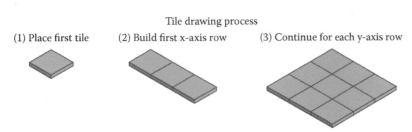

FIG 7.26 Visualization of an isometric tile layout order.

out spatial cues to the artists and leaves the developer with less they need to implement. Often when working on a "faked" 3D world, the developer will only have to figure out what size an object should be based on its depth and manage the proper overlapping of the game objects.

Most games will bypass the need to scale sprites by keeping the relative difference in distance from camera low enough that the minute reduction in scale would not be noticeable. Brawler games are a common example of this approach. In these games, the characters on the screen are able to move away from the viewer but never very far and keep their size the same the whole time. This winds up giving a game a 2.5D feeling, where there is some very limited depth to the game world.

Removing scaling from the spatial depiction of objects can cause some issues for viewers of the world. Things that are far away will never look quite right in a game with even faked perspective. They would appear to grow larger the further away they moved from the camera. If a game's goal is to present a world that has some significant depth to it, but still doesn't need to figure out the correct scale and position for a sprite in the world, the best goal would be to remove perspective from the world altogether. Isometric worlds discard the calculations of perspective and shrinking objects as they move into the background. In an isometric world, all distances (left, right, and back) have a set measurement, and objects are laid out in a grid based on these measurements. This makes it easy to lay out a whole world with objects that always remain visible, but it becomes difficult to tell the distance between objects because the only depth cue left to rely upon is overlapping objects.

7.6.1 Overlapping Objects

The display list is how Phaser and other games can create the depth cue of overlapping objects (see Figure 7.19). As objects move around in the world space, the display list will need to be resorted to make sure that any objects that have moved behind others actually appear behind the other objects in the game. Phaser's group object has a built-in sort method that can be used to achieve this effect by reordering the items in the array based on a metric given to the sorting function. Typically this metric is a position in space. In most programming environments, the depth (how far away the object is) of an object is stored in the "z" property.

Before delving into simulating space with a z property and the calculations that go into isometric games, it might be helpful to explore the easiest way to simulate depth in a game: y-sorting. This form of depth sorting is the kind that gives a sort of 2.5D look to a game. It is commonly used in the brawler and 2D adventure game genres because it is fairly quick and simple to implement. When y-sorting, objects that are lower on the screen are sorted to the top of the display list, making them render first. The closer the object gets to the bottom of the screen, the closer the object will appear to the player.

```
function create() {
    game.physics.startSystem(Phaser.Physics.
      ARCADE);

    sortGroup = game.add.group();
    sortGroup.enableBody = true;

    for(var i = 0; i < 200; i++) {
        var sprite = sortGroup.create(Math.
          random() * game.width, Math.random() *
          game.height, "particle");
```

```
                sprite.body.velocity.x = Phaser.Utils.
                    randomChoice(-20, 20);
                sprite.body.velocity.y = Phaser.Utils.
                    randomChoice(-20, 20);
            }
        }

    function update() {
            sortGroup.sort('y', Phaser.Group.
                SORT_ASCENDING);
        }
```

This code snippet shows an example of sorting a layer based on its y position. Objects higher in the frame will be sorted such that they will appear behind objects that are lower in the frame. Because objects are moving around in the scene, the sort needs to be done once per frame to ensure that changed depths are shown with the update.

Solid Depth Objects

If you implement this code and watch the objects moving around in the sample scene, you'll notice that the objects will just "snap" through other objects, warping through each other as if they were never really there. A good solution for this distracting effect is to add a reduced collision box to these objects that is about one-third of the sprite's original height.

7.7 Rendering an Isometric Grid

Isometric games implement their world with a 2D array of data, much like a tile system does. These two different grids are shown in Figure 7.20. The original on the left is a standard tile system, with the tiles laid out in an axis-aligned way. The second is an isometric view, with the "camera" or view rotated 45° to the right and 30° down. Above each grid is an example of a single tile asset that might be used in the respective engine.

Because the boxes are no longer laid out on an axis-aligned grid, a new algorithm will be needed to place these tiles. The process for placing an isometric tile starts with getting a point in 3D space (x-, y-, and z-coordinates) and then translating that point into a 2D point. The two most important factors of this translation is that a move in any direction on an isometric grid will affect both the x and y positions and that the distance moved in both directions is half of the original width and height of the tile (See Figure 7.21).

Here is the method to turn an isometric point into a screen position. The equation needs to know the half width and half height of the isometric tiles.

```
function isoToCartesian( isoCoords ) {
    var cartesianCoords = {}
    cartesianCoords.x = (isoCoords.x -
        isoCoords.y) * tileHalfWidth;
    cartesianCoords.y = (isoCoords.x +
        isoCoords.y) * tileHalfHeight;
    return cartesianCoords;
}
```

Isometric Tile Sizes

Because the calculations to convert to and from isometric coordinates require dividing the height and width of the tile by two, it is important to keep the tiles sized to something that comes out to a whole number when halved. If they are set to an odd number, such as 74 × 37, the final positioning will continue to be off by half-pixels height-wise (as 37/2 is 18.5), eventually ruining the grid.

Common sizes for isometric tiles include 32 × 16 and 64 × 32. All of these are sizes that are common for other artists working with tiles and typically can be rendered faster by graphics engines optimized for power-of-two graphics. They aren't steadfast sizes though. If you feel your game looks simply amazing at 72 × 36, then it is fine to create tiles at that size as well.

7.7.1 Isometric Depth Sorting

Sorting based on y position is a cheat that only works for one fixed camera angle. The sense of depth to objects is quite limited in this view because all the objects must face the camera head on. You really only see an object's front, with no depth. A box in the view that a y-sorted game grants would only look like a square sitting on the screen. Shifting the camera so that objects could be viewed on an angle will let the game display the side of the box as well, granting more depth to the game. An isometric projection will turn the camera so its look at the game objects at a 90° angle and keep all the x, y, and z measurements the same. This will create fixed foreshortening where nothing ever converges into the distance and objects never shrink as they move further back. Note in Figure 7.22 how there is now depth to the grid in two different directions (slanted in both directions), and it becomes somewhat easier to interpret the space something takes up.

7.7.2 Picking Grid Locations via Screen Position

The player of this game is going to need to be able to interact with the game world somehow, and the most intuitive (especially for mobile deployment) is via targeting using the pointer. The process for getting a tile that is under a click requires getting the x and y positions of the click and putting it through the opposite of the layout positioning equation. This will return a grid position of the tile in the isometric world. If the user were to click in the middle tile of an isometric world of size 10 × 10, this function would return a point with values {x: 5, y:5}.

```
function catesianToIso(cartesianCoords) {
    var isoCoords = {};
    isoCoords.x = (cartesianCoords.x /
        tileHalfWidth + cartesianCoords.y /
        tileHalfHeight) /2;
    isoCoords.y = (cartesianCoords.y /
        tileHalfHeight - (cartesianCoords.x /
        tileHalfWidth)) /2;
    return isoCoords;
}
```

7.8 Phaser Isometric Plugin

Given the math discussed earlier, it wouldn't be too much work to implement a working isometric system for a Phaser game. The major problem is that the time to make the isometric engine would be time not spent actually making a game. Thankfully, there already exists a plugin for Phaser that has all the tools a developer needs for an isometric game without having to go through the process of making the engine, testing it, and squashing all the little bugs that are inevitable with software development.

The Phaser Isometric Plugin is a plugin developed by Lewis Lane that provides isometric layout, depth sorting, and a number of other isometric features for Phaser. It does this with an API that won't look out of place next to the other Phaser code in a game. Its homepage (http://rotates.org/phaser/iso/) contains a number of code samples that can help one get started with the plugin, and the Github repository (https://github.com/lewster32/phaser-plugin-isometric/) contains the plugin itself that can be integrated into Phaser.

For this library and the pathfinding library that will be used later on in this chapter, we'll use Bower to install and manage the dependency. To install the isometric plugin, open your console at the project root and type in this command. This will download and install the isometric plugin to your bower components. Make sure to exit and rerun grunt after running the script, so the bower-main-files task can move the plugin to your scripts folder.

```
bower install phaser-plugin-isometric --save
```

In order to use this script with Phaser, it will have to be included in the html page, after Phaser but before the game's script.

```
<script src="bower_components/phaser/build/phaser.
    min.js"></script>
<script src="scripts/phaser-plugin-isometric.min.
    js"></script>
<script src="scripts/app.js"></script>
```

Once the plugin is included, before using any of the plugin's capabilities, activate it with the Phaser core. This line of code is added in the game state's creation function.

```
this.game.plugins.add(new Phaser.Plugin.
    Isometric(this.game));
```

Once activated, it will be possible to use all the isometric code provided by the plugin throughout the rest of the game.

7.8.1 Pathfinding

A major feature of any tower defense game is the path or walkable areas that the enemy units can advance upon. Many tower defense games will have set paths that enemies use, though some variations of the game genre give the enemies larger walkable areas and let the opposing units find the ideal path to their goal. In either case, there has to be a pathfinding step during development or during gameplay to find a path from where the attacking units can walk across to their end goal.

7.8.1.1 Hardcoded Paths

Before delving into the implementation of a pathfinding algorithm, it will help to think through the process of doing it manually. This will help when reading about the actual pathfinder because it will be easier to visualize what the pathfinding algorithm is doing and the final encoding of the path.

First, we will need a world to find a path in. Here is a simple 2D grid, where "1" will count as a walkable space and "0" as a nonwalkable space.

```
[
    [ 1,1,1,1,0,0,0 ],
    [ 0,0,0,1,0,0,0 ],
    [ 0,1,1,1,0,0,0 ],
    [ 0,1,0,0,0,0,0 ],
    [ 0,1,1,1,1,1,1 ]
]
```

One way to encode the path for the enemies to take is to create a series of locations that they should visit on the map in order. Taking a look at the grid, we can easily trace the path that needs to be followed. It starts at the top left at position (0, 0) and progresses to the right, eventually hitting (3, 0). It moves down to (3, 2) and continues on its way to the left, around, and down. Now all that needs to be done is to manually enter each of these values into an array for the unit to follow. Here is that final path array.

```
[
  [0,0], [1,0], [2,0], [3,0], [3,1], [3,2], [2,2],
    [1,2], [1,3], [1,4], [2,4], [3,4], [4,4], [5,4],
    [6,4]
]
```

In order to have a unit walk this path, they should be told: "Move to the first point in this array." Once they get to the first point in the array, the program should find the next point, and have the enemy move to the next point. In this example, they would move from [0, 0] to [1, 0] onward, until they hit their destination of [6, 4].

7.8.1.2 Pathfinding Algorithms

The work of figuring out a path for the units to follow and then encoding that into an array literally can be quite an amount of effort. If the game developer wants the unit to be able to choose new paths at runtime as circumstances change in the world, it would be impossible with only predefined paths. It would be much better if the computer could figure this path out at runtime instead. The process of finding a route from a start and end points on a grid is called pathfinding, and there are a number of algorithms that tackle the problem of finding the most efficient route on a grid. The most common pathfinding algorithm used in game development is named A* (pronounced A Star).

7.8.1.2.1 Basic Pathfinder

Running an A* search will return a path of nodes just like the node list we precomputed. While it is possible to find an implementation of A* in just about every programming language out there (and we will be using one for this game), understanding the basics of the implementation will help you when it comes to setting up game maps or when choosing which implementation of A* you want to use with your game.

Here are the steps to write a simple pathfinder. This will be lacking some critical components of the A* algorithm that make it such a strong approach, but it will give you the fundamentals to understand how it approaches the problem:

1. Look at open spaces around the current location.
2. For each open space, figure out how much closer the open space is to the goal.
3. Calculate the cost associated with the move.
4. Figure out which of the considered spaces get closest to the goal with the least cost.
5. Move to that space and add it to the node list.
6. Return to step one if not at the goal yet.

Figure 7.23 shows how the process works in general. When considering the next grid positions to take on the path, potential moves might be either the four compass directions (up, down, left, or right) or the diagonals. Each of these spaces needs to be considered in turn as the algorithm decides how desirable it is to move to the different locations via something called a heuristic. When considering each space, the heuristic (a function) guesses at how much closer the cell is to the destination. There are different ways to make the guess, but the simplest is just the distance between the location being considered and the goal. The application of the distance heuristic means that for each space considered the program would figure out the distance from that cell to the goal, and the cell that has the lowest distance to the goal would be the next step on the path.

Here is the general idea of an implementation of the pathfinder discussed earlier, a type often called a "greedy best first" search. It is not a fully working Javascript, but it should give you an idea of the approach.

```
path = []
current_node = start_node

while (current_node != end_node) {
        considered_nodes = []

        neighbors = current_node.getNeighbors()
        neighbors.each(neighbor) {
                if(neighbor.walkable) {
                        neighbor.pathValue =
                           heuristic(neighbor, end_node)
                        considered_nodes.push(neighbor)
                }
        }

        considered_nodes.sort("pathValue")
        current_node = considered_nodes[0]
        path.push(current_node)
}
```

This assumes there is a method named heuristic that will return how far something is from its goal. The simplest implementation is distance. Many A* searches use a variation of the distance calculation called Manhattan distance that calculates how far something is when only vertical and horizontal movements are allowed (like driving through a city). Both versions are shown in the following, though you'll note that Manhattan distance is easier to calculate (though it will return a higher number than the normal calculation because it is not calculating "as the bird flies" but rather "as the cab drives").

Euclidean Distance

```
function heuristic(current, goal) {
        var difference_x = goal.x – current.x;
        var difference_y = goal.y – current.y;
        return Math.sqrt( differenceX*differenceX +
          differenceY*differenceY );
}
```

Manhattan Distance

```
function heuristic(current, goal) {
        return abs(goal.x – current.x) +
          abs(goal.y – current.y)
}
```

> ### What Differentiates A*
>
> The problem with a greedy search is that it doesn't really think ahead and will always move toward the goal, even if there is a wall in the way and it would have been much easier to go around the wall first. A* has an additional step to its calculations that safeguards against creating a path that walks into a room with only one door, get to a walls, and turns around (or worse, it stops entirely). The safeguard is that it favors paths that are closer to where it has already been, so it won't go wandering too far as it selects its best route (See Figure 7.24).

7.8.1.2.2 Easy Star

Knowing the basics of a pathfinding algorithm, we could go on to implement a variation for this game that would find a path for our enemies to traverse at runtime. This is an enjoyable challenge to tackle and very rewarding when successfully implemented. In the interest of both time and learning how to make use of external code libraries, we're going to find a package that can do the searching for us. There are a number of great implementations of A* that can be used in a Javascript project (Phaser now has one built in for its tilemaps).

The pathfinding package we'll be using for this game is named "easystar.js," and information about it can be found at http://www.easystarjs.com/. Some of the key features of this package include its small size, asynchronous solutions (so the game can continue to run until a path is found), and its ability to be installed via Bower. The first step in using easystar is to install it.

```
bower install easystarjs -save
```

7.8.1.2.3 Working with Easystar

Easystar works on a grid of nodes that can either be walkable or not walkable, just as in our manual pathfinding process. Here is a grid that can work for the pathfinding algorithm.

```
var map = [
    [ 1,1,1,3,1,1,0 ],
    [ 0,0,0,3,0,0,0 ],
    [ 0,2,2,2,3,3,0 ],
    [ 0,0,0,0,0,0,0 ],
    [ 0,1,1,1,1,1,1 ]
]
```

Easystar can find paths on this world but it needs to know what the world looks like and what it can walk on. These next three lines of code start up easystar and get it ready to search.

```
var easystar = new EasyStar.js();
this.easystar.setGrid(map);
this.easystar.setAcceptableTiles([0]);
```

Finally, easystar needs to know its starting and stopping points, and then it can find a path. This is done via the findPath method. The first two arguments of the method are the starting point, while the second two are the final goal. This is an asynchronous function, so the final argument is a callback that will be called when the path is found. Once a path is found, it calls the callback function and passes in that path that is an array of points like we had calculated before.

```
this.easystar.findPath(1, 0, 0, 4, function(path) {
    //start walking the path
});
```

7.8.1.2.4 Walking through a Path

Once we have a path from either hardcoding it or by using a search algorithm, the next step is to have an object actually walk through the whole path. While it is fairly simple to have a loop iterate over all the entries in the node list and put the object at the locations specified in the list, the loop will run so quickly that there will be no delay between each move. In the end, it won't look like the object has walked the path, but just warped from the starting point to the end point.

To make it look like the game object is actually walking the path, there needs to be a delay in between each step the object takes. The time in between those grid moves would ideally be filled with an animation to make it look like the unit is actually moving from grid space to grid space. One solution to this is to let the unit remember the path it is meant to take and then animate the transitions from point to point along the path using Phaser's tween engine. The unit will need to store its current index on the path so that when the animation ends it can look up the next point it needs to move to on the path. Then, when a tween's onComplete signal fires, it can check for the next point and start a new tween. Over time the unit will tween itself from position to position appearing as if it is smoothly walking a path. The following is a simple implementation of a path walker.

```
export default class PathWalker extends Phaser.
  Sprite {

    constructor(game, x, y, frame) {
        super(game, x, y, 'spriteKey', frame);
    }
    setPath(path) {
        this.path = path;
        this.pathPosition = -1;
        this.advanceTile();
    }

  advanceTile() {
        this.pathPosition ++;

        if(this.pathPosition < this.path.length) {
            //tween
```

```
        this.walkMotion = this.game.add.
          tween(this).to(
              { isoX: this.path[this.
                pathPosition].x,
                isoY: this.path[this.
                  pathPosition].y
              },
              2000, Phaser.Easing.Linear.
                None, true);
        this.walkMotion.onComplete.add(this.
          advanceTile, this);

      }
    }
  }
```

7.9 Skeleton Shootout Project Design

The gameplay for this tower defense game draws from a number of common features in the genre. The core features of this game are as follows:

1. A set path or walkable area for opposing units to traverse.
2. A goal the opposing units are walking toward.
3. Enemies damage the player "health" once they reach their goal: this is a one-time effect, with the enemy unity being destroyed after their attack.
4. Enemies are spawned in set waves or patterns as needed, getting more difficult as the game progresses.
5. The player places units throughout the level that automatically attack the enemy units: These units must be purchased at a cost.
6. Game money is typically earned via the defeat of enemies.
7. The map for this world will be custom coded and stored in a JSON file.

To begin with, create the basic project structure described in chapter five. We will be adding to that base throughout this exercise. Should you need to see the finished code or to get the assets for the game, you can find the full source at https://github.com/meanderingleaf/PhaserBookExamples/tree/master/slice.

7.9.1 Asset Pack

In the previous games, the loading was all done inside of a state built to do the loading. There was line after line of code to load in images, sprites, sounds, and map files. While this approach is not terrible, it does lend the project to be strongly linked to the assets in the game code itself. A better approach would be to specify assets to be loaded outside of the code to keep the data and the application separate, much like how map files are encoded in external data files. This gives other programs the capability to generate the listing of assets to be loaded into the game and lets the developer keep management of assets and game logic separate.

Phaser supports this sort of separation of code and assets through a feature called an asset pack. Asset packs are JSON files that specify assets for a Phaser game project, the keys they will be stored under in the cache, and the URL where the asset can be loaded from. Later, when loading in assets for the game, a single line of code is needed to load in all the files specified in the asset pack. When using asset packs, your loading state will look much simpler than before and will be more easily portable from project to project.

Here is a sample asset pack:

```
{
    "level1": [
        {
            "type": "image",
            "key": "gameoverText",
            "url": "assets/images/gameoverText.png",
            "overwrite": false
        },
        {
            "type": "spritesheet",
            "key": "skeleton",
            "url": "assets/images/sprites/Skeleton/
                skeleton.png",
            "frameWidth": 60,
            "frameHeight": 60
        }
    ],
    "meta": {
        "version": "1.0"
    }
}
```

When it is time to load in the assets instead of all the different calls to the load object, you will just need to use a single call to the load object's pack method. In order to load in a pack, you need to still create a key for the pack to be stored at in the cache, in addition to the URL for the pack.

```
this.load.pack('level1', 'assets/assetPack.json',
    null, this);
```

Why Level Packs

It might be a bit confusing that there can be different levels or subsets of items to load in an asset pack, but there is a good reason for it. It takes time to load in assets and the longer a user has to wait, the more likely they are to leave a game instead of playing it. This feature of an asset pack makes it easy to break the assets up into the different chunks that can be loaded in between gameplay, loading them only when required. This spreads the loading out over the course of a game with shorter bursts of loading that hopefully will keep the player around for the whole game.

7.9.1.1 Tilemap

Take a moment to look through the assets in the asset pack for this project. At the bottom of the asset list is a JSON asset that we haven't encountered yet. This will load and parse JSON data, adding the parsed object to the asset cache. If you take a look at the JSON file, you'll see that it is a tilemap and also the name of a few tiles. We'll be using these data in the game state to manually construct the world for the game.

7.9.2 Prefabs

There will be three prefabs in this game that can later be used as bases to build out the multitude of different opposing forces that would typically be in a tower defense–type game. Our UI will be handled by NumberBoxes, which we have seen before in the shmup and platformer games. The prefabs in the game will be a human to defend the towers and skeletons who are trying to get to the treasure at the end of the path.

7.9.2.1 NumberBox

This game is going to use a number box, which is a text field that is grounded by a graphic asset behind it. There is no change in how this number box is coded from the one created for the shmup, so refer the code in chapter 7.1 and place the resulting NumberBox.js into the prefabs folder (or, if you have it already, simply copy the file over to your new project).

7.9.2.2 Human

These humans are not terribly smart ones, but they get the job done. Their tasks in this game are to wait until they see skeletons, face the closest one they can find, and fire as many arrows at that skeleton as they possibly can.

The human starts off by adding an idle animation to give him a bit of a living feeling (else he would be more like a turret than a living being). The anchor for this human (and every other asset that will be placed into this world) is set to the middle of the sprite, because our positioning code that will be used later on will return a point in the middle of the iso tile.

This class needs to know about the enemies and the arrows group. The arrows group will be used to generate the player's attacks and the enemy group will help this human look through all the skeletons and decide which one to shoot at.

Finally, a shot interval is set up that works much like the fire gate in the shoot 'em up example. The game chooses a time in the future for when it will be okay to fire a shot again. The update method will check every frame to see if the future time has been reached. If it is time to fire another arrow, the prefab asks the enemy layer to find the nearest enemy to it. Find nearest is not a built-in Phaser function. If you want to know how this function is implemented, look at the game state's construction for an explanation.

If there is something to shoot at, an arrow is created or recycled and placed at the location of the player firing it. This is the 2D screenspace position of the human because this arrow is a bit of a cheat. It is only a simple Phaser sprite and not an isometric object. These arrows will never be sorted behind any other element, but its lifespan of 4 s and the fact that it disappears the moment it hits an enemy means it can exist believably outside of the isometric world space. Finally, taking advantage of the fact that this is just a 2D sprite, the arrow is rotated toward the skeleton and sent flying with the Phaser's arcade physics moveToObject method.

How Does the `moveToObject` **Method Work?**

The moveToObject method will rotate the sprite toward the target and move it toward that object at a set velocity. The task of finding the rotation angle is a matter of trigonometry applied to the distance between the arrow and the enemy separated into its x and y directions. This x and y distances act as the two sides of a triangle that can be used to get the angle. The inverse trigonometric function arctan gets an angle from these two lengths (`Math.atan(distanceY/distance` in Javascript).

In order to move the object toward its target, a single speed is split between the object's x and y velocities. Sines and cosines can be used to get the amount of speed that should be applied to each velocity by breaking up the velocities into relative speeds based on the relative distance between the two points. These method calls will return a number between zero and one and will return smaller numbers for the side that is the lower of the two distances. These numbers can then be used as scalers on the intended speed of the object. The final lines of code would be `Math.cos(facingAngle)*` desiredVelocity for the x speed and `Math.sin(facingAngle)*` desiredVelocity for the y speed.

```
export default class Human extends Phaser.Plugin.
Isometric.IsoSprite {

    constructor(game, x, y, enemies, arrows) {
        super(game, x, y, 0, 'human', 0);

        // initialize your prefab here
        this.animations.add('idle', [10,11]);
        this.animations.play('idle', 2, true);

        this.anchor.setTo(.5, .5);
        this.enemies = enemies;
        this.arrows = arrows;

        this.shotInterval = 400;
        this.shotTime = this.game.time.now+this.
          shotInterval;
    }

    update() {

        if(this.game.time.now > this.shotTime) {
```

```
                        this.target = this.enemies.
                          findNearest(this.x, this.y);

                    if(this.target) {
                            var arrow = this.arrows.
                              getFirstDead();
                            if(!arrow) arrow = this.
                              arrows.create(0, 0,
                              "arrow");

                            arrow.revive();
                            arrow.x = this.x;
                            arrow.y = this.y;
                            arrow.lifespan = 4000;

                            arrow.rotation = this.game.
                              physics.arcade.
                              moveToObject(arrow, this.
                              target, 120)

                            this.shotTime = this.game.
                              time.now+this.shotInterval;

                    }
                }
            }
        }
```

7.9.2.3 Skeleton

This walking skeleton person is going to serve as your antagonist for the game. The primary concerns of the skeleton are following the path to the treasure, attacking and damaging the treasure chest, and managing its own health to let it take a few hits before it is destroyed.

There's not much to note in the constructor that is new, beyond the fact that it is inheriting from the IsoSprite giving it a z position and the ability to exist in isometric space. All of our IsoSprite are going to start at z position of zero, which is the third argument to the constructor. Next, a signal is created that will be fired when the skeleton reaches its goal and the other tasks are animation and physics setup.

The majority of this class is a variation on the path walker that was described earlier in this chapter. The two major additions include some scaling code that will flip the sprite left or right based on the next tween's direction. Here is the check to see what direction the skeleton should flip in. It tests if the next point on the path is to the left or right and if it swaps scale accordingly.

```
if( this.path[this.pathPosition].x > this.isoX ) {
        this.scale.x = 1;
} else {
        this.scale.x = -1;
}
```

The walker also has a conditional that runs when the skeleton has reached its target. Once at the target, the skeleton will play its attack animation to give the player some feedback (and one last moment to kill the skeleton). When the animation completes, the attackOver signal is fired. The game state has a listener to the event that will respond to by decreasing player's life and killing the skeleton.

```
export default class Skeleton extends Phaser.Plugin.
  Isometric.IsoSprite {

    constructor(game, x, y, frame) {
        super(game, x, y, 0, 'skeleton', frame);

            // initialize your prefab here
            this.walkAnim = this.animations.
              add('walk', [10,11]);
            this.animations.add('hurt', [12]);
            this.animations.add('attack',
              [13,14,13,14,14,13,14]);

            this.animations.play('walk', 2, true);

            this.anchor.setTo(.5, .5);

            this.game.physics.enable(this, Phaser.
              Physics.ARCADE);

            this.path, this.pathPosition;

            this.health = 5;
            this.worth = 20;

            this.pathFinished = new Phaser.Signal();
    }

    setPath(path) {
            this.path = path;
            this.pathPosition = -1;
    }

    advanceTile() {

            this.pathPosition ++;

            if(this.pathPosition < this.path.length) {
                //tween
                if( this.path[this.pathPosition].
                  x > this.isoX ) {
                      this.scale.x = 1;
                } else {
                      this.scale.x = -1;
                }

                this.walkMotion = this.game.add.
                  tween(this).to(
```

```
                         {
                            isoX: this.path[this.
                               pathPosition].x,
                            isoY: this.path[this.
                               pathPosition].y
                         },
                         2000, Phaser.Easing.Linear.
                            None, true);
                      this.walkMotion.onComplete.
                         add(this.advanceTile, this);

                } else {
                      this.animations.play("attack", 2);
                   this.animations.currentAnim.onComplete.
                      addOnce(this.attackOver, this);
                }
         }

      attackOver() {
            this.pathFinished.dispatch(this);
      }
   }
}
```

7.9.3 Game State

The game state will snap these prefabs all together into a working game system. This state handles the creation of the map, user input, player and enemy interactions, and scoring.

7.9.3.1 Imports

To start, this state will be working with our prefabs, so they will need to be imported at the top of the file to make them available throughout the state.

```
import Human from "../prefabs/Human.js";
import Skeleton from "../prefabs/Skeleton.js";
import NumberBox from "../prefabs/NumberBox.js";
```

7.9.3.2 Create

The create method will draw the map, add the layers for the enemies and UI, and start the wave timer. There's a lot that goes into this game, so the setup method is going to be particularly long.

7.9.3.2.1 State Properties

There are a few state-level properties that need to be set up for the game to run properly. This includes how many hits the player can take before the game is over, the amount of money the player has to spend, and the time that should elapse in between spawning enemies.

```
this.playerLife = 10;
this.money = 100;
this.spawnTime = 1000;
```

7.9.3.2.2 Miscellaneous Setup

Before getting the rest of the game configured, a background is added to the game to give the tiles a bit of grounding, and the physics system is initialized.

```
this.game.physics.startSystem(Phaser.Physics.ARCADE);
this.game.time.advancedTiming = true;
this.game.add.sprite(0,0, "gamebg");
```

7.9.3.2.3 Setting Up the Isometric World

In order to set up the isometric world, groups will need to be created for the objects, the isometric engine needs to be started, and the data for the map will need to be loaded and used to draw the tiles to the screen.

```
this.game.plugins.add(new Phaser.Plugin.
    Isometric(this.game));
this.game.iso.anchor.setTo(0.5, 0.2);
this.isoGroup = this.game.add.group();
this.isoChars = this.game.add.group();
this.mapData =  this.game.cache.getJSON('mapdata');
this.spawnTiles();
```

Before the isometric plugin can be used, it needs to be plugged into the Phaser game engine. When the isometric engine starts, the center of its world space is the upper left corner of the screen, which isn't really where we want our tiles positioned around. To get the iso world further into the game view, its center point is repositioned closer to the middle of the screen. Then two groups are added for different levels of the game. The first group (isoGroup) will hold the game world tiles and the second (isoChars) will contain the skeletons and humans in our game.

Finally, the map data is loaded and used to spawn the tiles. The isoengine does not have a built-in tile layout method like we used in the platformer example. Instead we will have to write our own. For reference, here is a map data that is a JSON file that contains an array of tile numbers and the images that should be used to draw those tiles.

```
{
    "tileNames": [ "beach", "dirt" ],
    "tileMap": [
            [ 0,1,0,0,0 ],
            [ 0,1,1,0,0 ],
            [ 0,0,1,0,0 ],
            [ 0,0,1,1,1 ],
            [ 1,0,0,0,1 ],
            [ 1,1,1,1,1 ]
    ]
}
```

This data are then passed into the spawn tiles method as "this. mapData." Before the tiles can be laid out, we need to know the width and height of the map so that we can set up a loop to iterate through all the tiles in the map.

Two loops are required to iterate through 2D map in Javascript. The first, exterior, loop will iterate down the x direction and create arrays for the x direction of the grid. The second, interior, loop will step through the x positions on the stage in a similar manner to the y loop (See Figure 7.26).

Inside of those nested loops, the tile is actually created and placed onto the stage. The first step of creating the tile is to figure out what number is at the current index in the map data. The line `this.mapData.tileMap[y][x]` will return the tile index from the map at that x and y positions. For instance, for the position (3,2), the number returned would be zero. Because this game is using individual assets for the tiles instead of a tile sheet, the numbers need to be mapped to the images individually. That is done with the next line that uses the mapping in the tile names array from the map json file. Zeroes will return a "beach" tile, while ones will return a "dirt" tile. These names need to link to the asset keys in the Phaser cache.

Next, a tile is added to the stage that makes use of the position and tile name. By stepping forward 55 pixels for each iteration, the tiles will be laid out in a grid (going through 55 pixel jumps in the width of the game and then jumping 55 pixels down to lay out another row when the "y" variable increases). The image created is the one that is found from the mapping of tile number to asset name (either ground or dirt). Finally, these tiles are added to the isoGroup. After running through both loops, the ground of the game will have been built and added to the stage.

We don't want the player to be able to add their player units to the path that the enemies are walking on. In order to restrict the open tiles, a buyable property is added to the tile objects. If the tile is a zero, it will not be part of the path and it will be set to buyable. Finally, this tile is added to an internal listing of tiles that will be used later on for selecting, buying, and placing characters.

```
spawnTiles() {
    var size = 55;
    var map_width = this.mapData.tileMap[0].
      length - 1;
    var map_height = this.mapData.tileMap.
      length - 1;

    this.gameTiles = [];

    var i = 0, tile;
    for (var y = 0; y <= map_height; y ++) {

        this.gameTiles[ y ] = [];

        for (var x = 0; x <= map_width; x ++) {
            var tileNumber =  this.mapData.
              tileMap[y][x];
            var tileName = this.mapData.
              tileNames[tileNumber];
```

```
                              tile = this.game.add.isoSprite(
                                          x*size, y*size, 0,
                                              tileName, 0, this.
                                              isoGroup
                                   );
                              tile.anchor.set(0.5, 0);
                              tile.buyable = (tileNumber == 0) ?
                                true : false;

                              this.gameTiles[y][x] = tile;
                         }
                    }
               }
```

7.9.3.2.4 Further Setup of the Groups

The next step is to add the groups that will hold the game objects. The groups for the characters and enemies will be added to the isoChars group to keep them in isometric space. The arrows group will also be added to the world and added to the physics system so that we can check collisions between the arrows and enemies.

```
this.allies = this.game.add.group(this.isoChars);
this.enemies = this.game.add.group(this.isoChars);
this.enemies.findNearest = this.findNearest;
this.arrows = this.game.add.group();
this.arrows.enableBody = true;
this.arrows.physicsBodyType = Phaser.Physics.ARCADE;
```

The enemy group has a special method added to it called findNearest. This is a function that will find the closest enemy to a given point. Here is the implementation of findNearest. Because this function is applied to the enemy group object, the "this" property in this function will be a reference to the enemy group.

```
findNearest(xc, yc) {
  var lowestChild = null;
  var lowestDist = null;

  this.forEach(function(child) {
      var dist = Phaser.Math.distance(xc, yc,
        child.x, child.y);

      if(!lowestChild) {
          lowestChild = child;
      } else {
          if(dist < lowestDist) {
              lowestChild = child;
              lowestDist = dist;
          }
      }
  }, this, true);
  return lowestChild;
}
```

To find the object nearest the given point, this function loops through all
the objects in the enemy layer and calculates the distance between that
enemy and the point. If the distance is the lowest distance yet found, the
function stores that enemy in the "lowestChild" variable and the new, lower
distance in the lowest distance variable. The loop will go through every
enemy, continuously selecting the closet enemy if there is one nearer than
the current "winner." Once the loop completes, it returns the closest enemy
of the group to the given point.

7.9.3.2.5 Pathfinder Setup

With the world setup and the enemies placed, the next step is to find a
path for the enemies to follow. We'll be using easystar to accomplish this
task, which needs some setup before it can find a path through the world.
The grid that will be used for the pathfinding is the 2D array of numbers
that was loaded in with the JSON file. For this game, the only acceptable
walkable tiles are the tiles with indices with value of "1". Next, we bind the
callback function to the state object so it will be able to access the enemies
in our enemy group in the state. Then, we start the game on finding a
path, from the first tile in the path (1, 0) to the final tile (0, 4). We will have
to tell easystar to continue calculating every frame, which will occur in our
update function.

```
this.easystar = new EasyStar.js();
this.easystar.setGrid(this.mapData.tileMap);
this.easystar.setAcceptableTiles([1]);
this.boundFound = this.pathFound.bind(this);
this.easystar.findPath(1, 0, 0, 4, this.boundFound);
```

The pathFound method will run when easystar returns with a path. First, the
handler checks to make sure a walkable path exists. If there is a valid path
through the world, the path is translated from the simple x and y indices of
the path to the actual tiles that the path will need to walk. This will change
the path from a series of map values like (3, 2) to world space values like
(165, 110). The world space values will make our tile-walking system in the
skeleton work as desired. These translated tiles are pushed into their own
node list, which will be handed to the enemies to walk.

```
pathFound(path) {
    if (path != null) {
        this.convertedPath = [];
        var curPoint;
        for(var i = 0; i < path.length; i++) {
            curPoint = this.gameTiles[path[i].y]
              [path[i].x];
            this.convertedPath.push( { x:
              curPoint.isoX, y: curPoint.isoY } )
        }
    }
}
```

219

7.9.3.2.6 Final Lines of Setup

The last bit of the create method creates an object that will contain the point of the cursor in isometric space. It then starts the spawn gate running, choosing a time in the future for the next enemy spawn to happen.

```
this.cursorPos = new Phaser.Plugin.Isometric.
    Point3();
this.nextSpawn = this.game.time.now  + this.
    spawnTime;
```

7.9.3.2.7 Update Method

The update method handles collisions between arrows and the enemy, responding to the user input, spawning enemies, calculating the enemy path through the world, and sorting the enemies.

The first step in this process is giving the user some feedback about which tile their cursor is currently over. This is done by translating the pointer's position from the 2D screen space to the iso world space. Once the position is translated into the isometric space, we can check to see if the point is sitting over any of the tiles in the world and store that as the active tile for purchasing purposes, which is done with the checkTiles method.

```
this.game.iso.unproject(this.game.input.
    activePointer.position, this.cursorPos);

this.isoGroup.forEach(this.checkTiles, this, false);
```

The checkTiles method iterates over each tile and checks to see if the cursor is on each individually. It checks to see if the pointer's iso position is inside of the tile using the containsXY method of the isometric plugin. If the pointer is within the bounds of the tile, we know that it is currently over that tile. If it is and the tile isn't already selected, the tile will have the selected flag on it set to true and it will be tinted and animated upward a little to show that it is the currently active tile. The game state will also store a reference to this tile under "selected tile," so it can easily be found when buying objects later.

Should the pointer no longer be over a tile that was once active, it has its colorization and position reset, and sets its active value to false. This will return it to the starting point and it will wait for the pointer to return.

```
checkTiles(tile) {
        var inBounds = tile.isoBounds.containsXY(
            this.cursorPos.x, this.cursorPos.y
        );

    if (!tile.selected && inBounds) {
        tile.selected = true;
        tile.tint = 0x86bfda;
        this.game.add.tween(tile).to(
            { isoZ: 4 },
```

```
        200, Phaser.Easing.Quadratic.InOut,
            true
    );

    this.selectedTile = tile;

}

else if (tile.selected && !inBounds) {
    tile.selected = false;
    tile.tint = 0xffffff;
    this.game.add.tween(tile).to({ isoZ: 0 },
        200, Phaser.Easing.Quadratic.InOut,
        true);
    }
}
```

Next in the update method, the game handles any clicks on a tile. If there is
a tile selected when the player clicks, the game will verify that tile is both a
place where the player can buy something and that there is no occupant in
that tile. Should those conditions be met, the game will attempt to purchase
a unit to place on the tile. The purchase price of the human is set to 100 in
game "money." If the player has enough money, a new human game object
is created and placed at the location of the selected tile. This human is also
passed the enemy and arrow layers, so it can search for an enemy to fire
arrows at. Once created, the human is added to the allies' layer with the rest
of his compatriots. The selected tile is then set as having a character in it,
and the money for the human subtracted from the player's account. The UI is
updated to reflect this change in money.

```
if(this.game.input.activePointer.isDown && this.
  selectedTile) {

  if(!this.selectedTile.occupant && this.
    selectedTile.buyable) {
      if(this.money >= 100) {
              var human = new Human(this.game,
                  this.selectedTile.isoX, this.
                  selectedTile.isoY, this.enemies,
                  this.arrows);
              this.allies.add(human);
              this.selectedTile.occupant = human;
              this.money -= 100;
                  this.scoreBox.setValue(this.
                      money);
        }
    }
}
```

Next the update function checks to see if any arrows are hitting the enemy
and handles that hit with the arrowHitEnemyMethod. While dealing with the
enemies, the game also checks to see if it is time to create a new enemy. If it
is, the spawnEnemy method is called, and a new time in the future is selected
for the next time an enemy should be created.

```
this.game.physics.arcade.overlap(this.arrows, this.
  enemies, this.arrowHitEnemy, null, this)

if(this.game.time.now > this.nextSpawn) {
    this.spawnEnemy();
    this.nextSpawn = this.game.time.now + this.
      spawnTime;
}
```

The last two lines of the update method tell easystar to continue its calculation and sort the enemies on the enemy layer so they appear correctly on top of one another using their isometric positions. If they weren't sorted, the most recently added skeleton would appear on top of the others, which would look quite off considering the skeletons are added at the back of the line.

```
this.easystar.calculate();
this.game.iso.simpleSort(this.enemies);
```

7.9.3.2.8 Arrow Hit Enemy Method

This method responds to an overlap between an arrow and an enemy. The arrow is removed from the game and the enemy damaged. If the enemy's HP has fallen to zero, it will kill itself. Killing enemies in this game is the way to earn money, so if the enemy is no longer alive, the player earns the reward for killing that enemy and the money UI is updated for the game.

```
arrowHitEnemy(arrow, enemy) {
    arrow.kill();
    enemy.damage(1);
    if(!enemy.alive) {
        this.money += enemy.worth;
        this.scoreBox.setValue(this.money);
    }
}
```

7.9.3.2.9 Spawn Enemy Method

The spawn enemy method creates a new skeleton based on the spawn gate that is checked in the update function. The enemy is placed at the start position of the game path and told the path to walk via the "setPath" method. To start it walking, it is told to advance to the next tile. The advance tile is part of the path-walking code we wrote, so once the skeleton gets to the next tile, it will keep walking until it hits the end of its path. The skeleton has a signal that it will fire when it hits the end of the path that will cause this state to run the enemyAtGoal method. Finally, the enemy is added to the enemy layer, making it visible and sortable.

```
spawnEnemy() {
    var skel = new Skeleton(
    this.game, this.convertedPath[0].x, this.
      convertedPath[0].y
    );
```

```
        skel.setPath(this.convertedPath);
        skel.advanceTile();
        skel.pathFinished.addOnce(this.enemyAtGoal, this);
        this.enemies.add(skel);
    }
```

7.9.3.2.10 Enemy at Goal Method

This method is run when the enemy fires its path finished signal. This
signal only fires after it has reached the goal and played through its attack
animation. The player loses one bit of life and the UI is updated to reflect their
current health status

```
enemyAtGoal(enemy) {
    enemy.kill();
    this.playerLife --;
    this.healthBox.setValue(this.playerLife);

    if(this.playerLife <= 0) {
        this.gameOver();
    }
}
```

If the player has lost too much health, the game over function runs, which
changes the state to the game over screen.

```
gameOver() {
    this.game.state.start('gameover');
}
```

7.9.4 Conclusion

Tower defense games that implement animations, signals, pathfinding,
and world targeting are complex but interesting games. With the
added difficulty of dealing with isometric graphics and depth sorting
these wind up being a great projects to study game world simulation.
If the concepts seem a bit difficult to understand, it can help to take time
to play with each of the small parts in turn. After playing around for a
bit, returning to the full implementation will help you see how they all
fit together.

As with other examples in this book, one of the safer places to play with a
game's code is to deal with numbers. Some easy points to play with numbers
to get a feel for the game system include the following:

- Change the damage the player does to the skeleton or the skeleton hp.
- Adjust the cost of buying a new archer.
- Change the firing rate of the humans.
- Figure out how to make the skeleton faster or slower.

If you are feeling more adventurous, then there are a number of areas
where the game can and should be improved to make it a more complete

game experience. All of these Improvements will take a bit of thought and experimentation but the result will be very rewarding.

Things that are typically in a full-featured tower defense style game include the following:

- Predetermined waves with set enemies
- Different enemy types that can be faster or slower or with varying strengths
- Attacks from the player units that might slow or damage a range of units
- A UI to enable the player to buy different sorts of defenses

Each of these additions presents new challenges that will need to be creatively solved and will require some testing before they are good to go. This isn't to dissuade you from trying to add them. Rather they should act as inspiration, now that you have a framework to work on. The next games are going to be targeted more for mobile devices and casual play, so if you're looking for a break, head on to the final two examples in this book.

7.9.4.1 Slicer Game Example

So far the game examples in this book have been programmed with an assumption that they would be played primarily on a desktop computer. These examples were made for the desktop mainly because it is easy to create and test games in that environment. When targeting mobile devices, any keyboard interaction needs to be removed and the games need to be programmed so that simple taps can trigger the majority of the gameplay. In order to give users the best experience on a mobile device, games built for handheld devices are going to need to take up the full size of the phones display (not matter what that size may be). There are some technical hurdles that need to be overcome to properly display a game in full screen on the many different resolutions and display ratios a device may have.

The game example in this chapter will be a version of the "object slicing" games that popped up with the rise of touch-screen devices. These games were a take on the twitchy sorts of games that require good attention and reaction speeds. Because buttons don't work quite as well on a flat screen, these slicer games took advantage of the fact that people are generally really good at the rather inaccurate work of swiping fingers across targets.

7.10 Gestures

A swiping game requires some sort of gestural input to the device. There are a number of different gestures that have become standard for phones and tablets. A quick survey might include a swipe (in either general or specific directions), a two-finger pinch or rotate, and a long press on an object.

This game is only going to tackle the swipping gesture, but the general idea of translating time into input will apply to the other gestures one may want to implement as well. Because Phaser does not have a built-in gesture library, this section is going to cover the basics of implementing gesture handling (see Figures 7.27 through 7.35).

Gestures need to take an aggregate of input from a user and decide if the user is trying to trigger a reaction. They need to be forgiving for the fact that humans are a little slow and inaccurate about our motions. In general, gesture input systems listen for the presence of a pointer and the motion of the pointer. The motion of the finger is used to check to see if the user's pointer has moved a *substantial distance* in order to trigger a gestural interaction. There is a necessity for a substantial distance because there's always a chance that the player had intended for a tap or a long press but their finger waivered slightly when they executed the input. Once the finger is moving, the gesture handler will need to wait until either the speed of the pointer moves below a certain threshold or the finger is lifted from the device. Once the user has slowed down their finger to a speed that could be considered a "stop" (with only perhaps a small bit of waiver), the gesture is ended, and a response to the input can be calculated (See Figure 7.30).

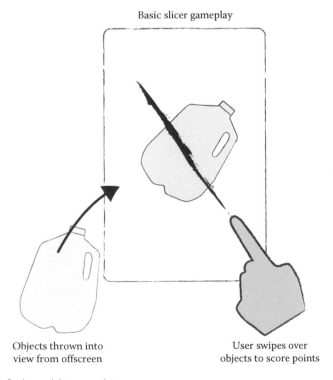

Basic slicer gameplay

Objects thrown into
view from offscreen

User swipes over
objects to score points

FIG 7.27 Fundamental slicing gameplay.

The stages of a gestural input system are as follows:

1. Listen for a pointer to be down.
2. Continuously check to see if the pointer starts moving quickly.
3. Once the pointer starts moving quickly, assume a swipe has been initiated and start watching for when the pointer comes to a "stop" or release.
4. Once the pointer comes to the stop, fire a gesture event for any objects listening to the gesture handler and begin listening for a new gesture.

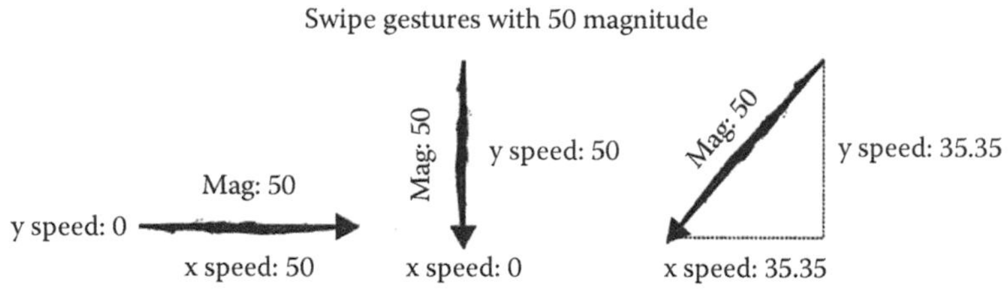

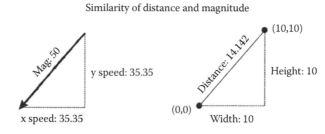

Swipe gestures with 50 magnitude

FIG 7.28 Swipe gesture directions and the impact of both speed and magnitude.

Similarity of distance and magnitude

FIG 7.29 Stages of a full swipe gesture.

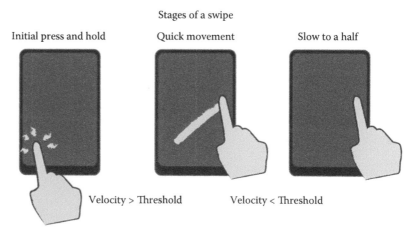

Stages of a swipe

FIG 7.30 Comparison of possible deployment screen sizes.

Target resolution compared to
other common resolutions

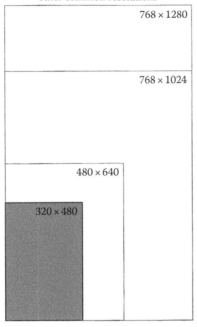

768 × 1280

768 × 1024

480 × 640

320 × 480

FIG 7.31 Overflow region of different screen sizes.

Different device ratio effects on display

Device two (shows more of world)

Device one

FIG 7.32 Issues with positioning objects at absolute pixel values.

Positioning of UI elements on different device resolutions

FIG 7.33 Screenshot of the finished slicer game.

FIG 7.34 Screen shot of Tech Slicer in action.

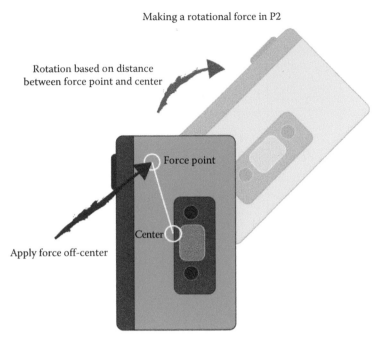

Making a rotational force in P2

Rotation based on distance
between force point and center

Force point

Center

Apply force off-center

FIG 7.35 Effect of applying a force on an object's center of mass.

7.10.1 Creating a Gesture Manager for Phaser

Since gestures are something that one might want to use in other games, it will
be helpful to pull the code for a gesture recognizer out into its own component.
For this game, we will be writing a fairly simplified version of a swipe handler
that only recognizes swipes based on speed and cannot limit the swipes to only
vertical or horizontal input. Here is the SwipeHandler in its entirety, and we'll take
a moment to break down some of the more critical parts in a moment.

```
export default class SwipeHandler extends Phaser.Group {
    constructor(game) {

        super(game);
        this.game.input.onUp.add(this.inputUp, this);

        this.swipeStart = new Phaser.Signal();
        this.swipeEnd =  new Phaser.Signal();

        this.swiping = false;
    }
    update() {
        if( this.game.input.activePointer.isDown ) {
        if( !this.swiping ) {
          if( this.game.input.speed.
            getMagnitude() > 20 ) {
            this.swiping = true;
            this.swipeStart.dispatch(this);
          }
```

```
            } else {
              if(this.game.input.speed.
                getMagnitude() < 10 ) {
                this.swiping = false;
                this.swipeEnd.dispatch(this);
              }
            }
          }
        }
      }

      inputUp() {
          if(this.swiping) {
              this.swiping = false;
              this.swipeEnd.dispatch(this);
          }
        }
      }
    }
```

7.10.1.1 Create Phase

```
this.game.input.onUp.add(this.inputUp, this);

this.swipeStart = new Phaser.Signal();
this.swipeEnd =  new Phaser.Signal();

this.swiping = false;
```

The create method sets up much of the functionality of the class as a whole. The swipe handler keeps a Boolean toggle that is used in this update method. If the component is currently in the swiping state, it will be checking for a swipe end. Conversely, if it does not currently sense a swipe, this component will be checking to see if a swipe has begun. To keep this object self-contained, it will dispatch events when a swipe that has started or stopped. Finally, the handler also responds to fingers being removed from the screen in order to halt the gestures when a pointer is lost.

7.10.1.2 Update

```
if( this.game.input.activePointer.isDown ) {
    if( !this.swiping ) {
      if( this.game.input.speed.getMagnitude() >
        20 ) {
        this.swiping = true;
        this.swipeStart.dispatch(this);
      }
    } else {
      if(this.game.input.speed.getMagnitude() <
        10 ) {
        this.swiping = false;
        this.swipeEnd.dispatch(this);
      }
    }
  }
```

The update method of the swipe hander will continuously check to see if a gesture has begun or halted. If a pointer is down, the cursor's speed is checked to validate if it is over a certain limit. Once the speed limit is exceeded, the swipe state is set and an event is fired to tell any other objects listening that a swipe has been initiated. If the component is already in the swiping state, then the cursor's speed is still checked to see if it has slowed enough to complete the current gesture. When the swipe is over, the swiping toggle is set to false, and the swipeEnd signal is dispatched indicating a full swipe gesture occurred.

7.10.1.3 Pointer's Speed and Velocity

Every update of the game loop Phaser calculates the speed of a pointer based on how many pixels it is moving per frame. This speed is calculated as the pure change in pixels from the current frame compared to the last frame. The speed is calculated for both the x and y properties of the pointer.

Frame	Position	Speed
1	(10, 10)	—
2	(13, 20)	(3, 10)
3	(7, 17)	(−6, −3)

This chart shows how speed is calculated per frame. On frame two, the values from the previous frame {x:10, y:10} are subtracted from the current position of the pointer {x:13, y:20}. The resulting x speed (13–10, or 3) and y speed (20–10, or 10) are then stored as {x:3, y:10}, which is accessible wherever one may need to know how many pixels the pointer moved since the last frame. Note that on the third frame, the player had moved their pointer to the upper left that creates a negative speed in both the x and y directions.

Users never swipe in a pure horizontal or vertical direction that makes relying and either of the axes a precarious idea. A swipe at an angle, especially near a 45° angle, would have a decent chance at not moving fast enough in either direction to trigger a swipe gesture (See Figure 7.29).

Instead of relying on the speeds in any one direction, a number that represents their combined speeds would be preferred. In most game systems, this number would be the magnitude of the pointer motion. The magnitude is the length of the line that points in the direction the cursor is moving. It is always a positive number that represents how strongly the pointer is moving. "Magnitude" is a term borrowed from vector math that may seem scary but it is really just a fancy word for "distance" (See Figure 7.29).

```
//sample code, this is already implemented in the
  speed.magnitude method
var magnitude = Math.sqrt(
        pointer.speed.x*pointer.speed.x +
         pointer.speed.y*pointer.speed.y
        );
```

Because the speeds are multiplied before calculating the distance of that vector, the final magnitude is perfect for use in a gesture system because it will always be a positive number, so the limits for starting and stopping a gesture only need to be positive as well. Keep in mind when coming up with numbers for the swipe code (in the future, or when playing with the code later on), the distance will always be a larger number than any of the other pixel distances moved, so larger numbers will need to be used for the "trigger" states to start and stop the gesture recognizer.

7.10.1.4 Up Handler

```
inputUp() {
    if(this.swiping) {
        this.swiping = false;
        this.swipeEnd.dispatch(this);
    }
}
```

The up handler runs when the user pulls their finger from the screen. If the gesture handler was in the "swiping state" when the finger is removed, this function will stop the gesture and fire the end signal, ensuring that when the user presses their finger down on the screen next time, the component will be ready to start a new gesture.

7.11 Dealing with Stage Scaling

Most mobile games are going to be built to scale to fill the screen of any device. Once one decides to support different resolutions and ratios, they will need to figure out how to make the graphics responsive and reposition themselves based on the width and height of the game. The most common approach to creating a game where the graphics reposition themselves for different views is to decide on a base resolution and ratio for the game. Once the game has been made for this resolution, the graphical assets are programmed to allow for the width and height of the view into the world to grow or shrink by about 20% in either direction. This means your assets should allow for a bit of "overflow" beyond the base ratio. This base display resolution and ratio that you should target will change over the years as devices change in size and shape, preferences change, or display technology gets more powerful.

Step one is then to figure out what your base target will be. This will require some research to find some data on current usage statistics. There is no "master resource" for this information because different companies gather the information in different ways and different developers may be targeting different devices. If you're looking to deploy your game only on Apple devices, then looking at the different resolutions of Apple devices are important (and much easier due to the limited types of devices). For other devices, there are groups that keep their statistics on the resolution and capabilities of the different devices out there. Searching for "mobile screen

resolution statistics" typically will find a page or two with reports from
different groups about their findings. Try to find the most recent statistics
possible, and keep in mind that these findings are taken from only a sample
of the population coming to their site or using their tools. The nature of
the people drawn to the site or app will influence the statistics toward the
audience that uses those tools that might not match your own audience.

Currently, the most popular resolution for a mobile device is 320 × 480.
Figure 7.31 compares the different common display sizes and ratios to the
"base" of 320 × 480.

7.11.1 Challenges of Stage Scaling

Because we're going to make a flexible display ratio game, we're going to
have to figure out how to scale the stage. There are two challenges that come
with scaling the stage: scaling assets and properly repositioning assets.

The first challenge is rescaling a game to fit a different display. Simply scaling
everything to a new width and height has a chance at distorting the game
significantly, unless the ratio of the new display is the same as the base.
Keeping the ratio while scaling upward or downward helps, but there is a
chance the new device has a bigger or smaller display ratio that will cause
parts of the display to be lost or overflow (See Figure 7.32).

The next challenge is the placement of UI elements on the screen of smaller
sizers. An element placed at an absolute pixel value to the far right of the
screen will actually be off the screen when a phone with a smaller display
tries to play the game (See Figure 7.33).

7.11.2 Phaser Scale Modes

The first step into getting a game scaling correctly to the different screen
sizes is to understand the different ways that Phaser can scale a game. There
are five different ways to have Phaser scale a game automatically.

7.11.2.1 EXACT_FIT
An EXACT_FIT game will have its dimension and ratio modified so that it
takes up all the space it has been given to fill. If this means that sprites need
to be distorted, then they will be. A game that is put into an exact fit on a
device that doesn't have the same display ratio the game was built at will take
on a squashed or stretched look.

7.11.2.2 NO_SCALE
This scale mode does not actually scale at all. Instead, it will simply show
black pixels for any place where content was not originally intended to be.

7.11.2.3 SHOW_ALL
This approach will scale the game but preserve the game ratio in order to
ensure the game will never look squashed or stretched. The game is scaled

up to maximum in the direction that it can take up the most space with (either vertically or horizontally) and any space that can't be used displays black pixels instead.

7.11.2.4 RESIZE

This is the preferred mood for responsive scaling.

Resize works like show all, but instead of black pixels where there is overflow, the view into the game world is increased. This will begin to show elements in the world space that were previously off camera. Care must be taken to make sure that the objects are off camera to show this bleed properly.

7.11.2.5 USER_SCALE

The hard way, user scale simply relies on the developer to go through the scaling calculations. It can be immensely useful for custom solutions.

7.11.3 Resize Callback and Positioning Elements

Because the scale mode we will be relying upon actually changes the display ratio, it is impossible for a responsive game to position its UI elements at absolute positions. When there is a high chance that a device with a different display ratio is used, then absolutely positioned UI objects like aiming reticles at the center of the screen might appear off-center on other devices (See Figure 7.33).

Responsive UIs typically solve this problem by positioning objects relative to pin points that act as landmarks on the screen. The five most common pin points are the four corners of the screen and the very center of the screen.

When the display is resized and extra space is added to the game's view, the positioning of any pinned elements needs to be recalculated and set again based on the new location of their pin points on the display. The first step in this process is to be able to react to a screen resize. The following is the general code that should be added into any state that needs to handle a resize.

```
function resize(width, height) {
  //reposition elements based on the new 0,0
    position, and the new width and height
}
```

A relatively positioned element will always reference its pin for its final position. For instance, let's assume there is a game (with a display of 480 × 320) with a UI element (size 100 × 40) positioned at the lower right corner. In an absolutely positioned game, this UI element will have its x position set to (380, 270), making it appear in the lower right. If the game is resized and the new display has a ratio of 4:3 instead of 3:2, this element will actually wind up appearing close to the center of the display. The original position was calculated simply by getting the far right of the screen and subtracting the width and height of the asset before positioning. In a responsive application, the positioning of elements is typically done inside that resize function doing the calculations in code instead of in one's head.

The following is an example of positioning some elements based on the pin points when a window resize occurs. Resizing can occur when a user first launches a game, if they resize their browser window, or if they rotate their device after first loading your game.

```
function resize(width, height) {
        //top left pin point
        this.score.x = 10;
        this.score.y = 10;

        //middle pin point
        this.aiming.x = width / 2;
        this.aiming.y = height / 2;

        //bottom right pin point
        this.healthBar.x = width - healthBar.width - 10;
        this.healthBar.y = height - healthBar.height - 10;

        //'custom' pin point - middle center
        this.warning.x = width / 2;
        this.warning.y = 10;

}
```

In general, design a UI with a certain display ratio in mind and try to support only small changes on that ratio. UIs designed for landscape modes will probably not scale well to the tall format of a portrait mode. When you've designed a game for a certain ratio, it will be important to enforce device orientation so players are playing the game in a view that has been scaled appropriately.

7.11.4 Enforcing Device Orientation

On the web, it is not possible to enforce a certain orientation, and the view into your game will reorient to a different display ratio if the user turns their phone about. The only solution is to pause the game when it is in the wrong orientation and display a message to the user telling them to rotate their device to the right orientation before they begin or resume gameplay. When building an application for one of the app stores, it is possible to enforce an orientation. An app with a forced orientation will still display in the original orientation intended even when the phone is tilted from portrait to landscape.

The forceOrientation method can be used in Phaser to specify a certain orientation a game should appear in. In the setup we're using throughout the book, the optimal place for this method to be executed is in the boot state, before moving into the rest of the application. This bit of configuration will move over to other states and it will pause the game when it is not running in the right orientation. The method takes two Booleans. The first is if landscape should be allowed, the second is for portrait. If only one of the two is set to true, then that orientation will be the only one the game will run in.

```
game.scale.forceOrientation(true, false);
```

While the aforementioned code will work on mobile devices where the game has been delivered as an app, it will not work perfectly on the web. When a player is running your game inside their web browser, you will also need to listen for the change of orientation and inform the user that they need to rotate their devices back to the correct orientation when they are in an incorrect orientation.

```
create() {
        this.scale.enterIncorrectOrientation.
          add(this.enterIncorrectOrientation, this);
        this.scale.leaveIncorrectOrientation.
          add(this.leaveIncorrectOrientation, this);
}

enterIncorrectOrientation() {
        //Show "please rotate your device" image
}

leaveIncorrectOrientation() {
        //Hide "please rotate your device" image
}
```

7.11.5 Restricting Resize Zones

The second issue that arises when attempting to create a responsive UI is that there is a point where it would be harmful to resize to the device's resolution. Devices with a very small display simply won't be able to render all the elements correctly because everything would be squished down too tiny. Large displays have the opposite problem of spacing everything extremely far out.

Most responsive pieces of digital media address this issue by choosing a maximum and minimum resolution that is supported. After hitting either of the extremes, the media will stop to scale any further and will become fixed at the closet resolution it can render inside its acceptable range. This will result in parts of the game being obscured on small resolutions, most likely making them unplayable. The larger screens will still be playable but there will be some empty space to the side of the game where the game stopped scaling to fill the screen.

The setMinMax method will let a developer specify these extremes. The first two numbers are the minimum width and height and the second two are the largest width and height for the game's scale.

```
this.scale.setMinMax(480, 260, 1024, 768);
```

7.12 Making 80's Tech Slicer

Next, we're going to take the concepts of responsive layout and gestures and implement them into a game. This game, 80's Tech Slicer, challenges a player to swipe over as many pieces of cool retro technology as possible. These devices will be launched on a regular interval and will come from different sides of the screen. When sliced, the tech will be split into two halves, and another point will be added to the player's score.

Create the basic project structure described in chapter five. We will be adding to that base throughout this exercise. Should you need to see the finished code or to get the assets for the game, you can find the full source at https://github.com/meanderingleaf/PhaserBookExamples/tree/master/slice.

7.13 Slicer HTML and CSS

The game is going to use a custom font to display the score to the user. There are two ways to approach custom fonts in Phaser. One way is to include a bitmap font, which is a font that has been laid out in a grid like a sprite sheet, wherein Phaser copies these images on the stage to form full strings. This is a custom approach and tends to be used by games that are looking for a "retro" look. The second approach is to use fonts that were designed for computer use like TTF and include them in the game as a webfont. This is the approach that will be used for this game that requires work to be done on the HTML and CSS for this project.

7.13.1 CSS File

To begin with, create a new folder in the project root with the name "css" and add a "style.css" file inside of it. Open the style.css file in your code editor of choice and add the following code to include a webfont. It is a bit complex because there is still not one accepted font face for browsers to use, so several different font files will be included and the browser will decide which one it needs.

To make this game fill the whole screen, a few other styles are applied to the document and the node that contains the game. The width and height of 100% will force the game view to scale to fill the whole screen, and the border and padding of zero on the body will remove any bit of a border. Any resize of the window will change the size of the element that contains the game. This resize will then get picked up by Phaser's scale manager and we can run a resize method in our gameplay code to resize and reposition all the UI elements on the screen.

```css
@font-face {
    font-family: 'dymaxionscriptregular';
    src: url('../assets/fonts/DymaxionScript-
      webfont.eot');
    src: url('../assets/fonts/DymaxionScript-
      webfont.eot?#iefix')
      format('embedded-opentype'),
        url('../assets/fonts/DymaxionScript-
          webfont.woff') format('woff'),
        url('../assets/fonts/DymaxionScript-
          webfont.ttf') format('truetype'),
        url('../assets/fonts/DymaxionScript-webfont.
          svg#dymaxionscriptregular') format('svg');
    font-weight: normal;
    font-style: normal;
}

#game {
      width: 100%;
```

```
        height: 100%;
}

body {
        margin: 0;
        padding: 0;
}
```

7.13.2 HTML File

Next, this style will need to be included in the html, so in the head tag of the HTML, add a link to the stylesheet.

```
<link rel="stylesheet" type="text/css" href="css/
  style.css" />
```

7.14 Slicer Boot State

The boot state for this game needs to be modified to take into account the resizing that the game will need to handle. Here is the new create method for the boot state that will scale the game in between resolutions of 360 × 480 up to 768 × 1024 and has an orientation forced to portrait mode.

```
create() {
        this.scale.scaleMode = Phaser.ScaleManager.
          RESIZE;
        this.scale.setMinMax(360,480,768,1024);

        if (this.game.device.desktop == false)
        {
                this.scale.forceOrientation(false, true);
        }

        this.game.state.start('preload');
}
```

7.15 Slicer Preload State

Phaser sometimes will fail to render a web font correctly the first time the font is used in a game. In order to force this font to load in early, a text field with the font is created in the preload state placed onto the stage with its alpha set to zero to hide it from the player's view. This will trick Phaser into loading up the font early on, making it ready to use in the game state. Since this is technically a sort of preload as well, this trick is done in the preload state along with the other loading of assets.

```
var style = { font: "65px dymaxionscriptregular" };
this.instructionText = this.add.text(-20, -20, ".",
  style);
this.instructionText.alpha = 0;
```

Otherwise, the assets for this game are a number of images on a texture atlas that contains all the images for the tech to be sliced up.

```
this.load.atlasJSONHash('devices',
                    'assets/images/sprites/devices.
                        png', 'assets/images/sprites/
                        devices.json');
this.load.image('gamebg', 'assets/images/gamebg.png');
this.load.image('triangle', 'assets/images/sprites/
    triangle.png');
this.load.image('zoid', 'assets/images/sprites/zoid.
    png');
```

7.16 Slicer Game State

In order to implement the gameplay, this slicing game needs to

- Generate and launch new devices to be sliced
- Detect (and show on the screen) the swipe inputs of the user
- Determine if a user's swipe gesture overlaps a device
- Destroy any devices swiped over and increment score

7.16.1 Game State Prefabs

For this game, we're going to tap into the power of Phaser's P2 physics system and its ability to automatically process collisions. In order for Phaser to process these collisions, there will need to be game objects for both the objects to be sliced and the paths the player draws on the screen via swiping.

7.16.1.1 Device Sprite Prefab

The device sprite represents the different targets for the player to slice. In order to configure these targets correctly, they need to know what image they are going to display, be able to be launched into the game, and destroy themselves once they are off screen again. Also these devices should collide with the user input, but not with other devices. If they collide with each other, then after the first few waves of devices, the screen would be filled with objects continuously hitting each other, which ruins the smooth arc motion that makes these games fun to play.

The constructor this game object as a sprite that will render from the "devices" atlas in the asset cache. This asset is actually an atlas with many different images that it can render. In order to select the sprite to render, the frameName property is specified, which will cause it to render one of the four devices in our device array that was randomly picked and sent to this prefab. Next in the constructor, the sprite is set up to rotate from its center, which will come into play when it is thrown into the air, forcing it to rotate believably around the center of its mass instead of from its upper left. Finally, the device is placed into the device collision group that will be configured for custom collisions. The only objects we want the devices to be able to collide with are the bodies of a user's slice, so that it is set as the only collision group that Phaser should check for and respond to collisions with.

Launch is the other method of device. This is the method that will position the prefab out of view and then send it flying upward toward the screen, so the user can swipe over it. If this device is being revived, it actually already has a velocity and rotation, so those are wiped at the start of the method by resetting both velocities. A chance roll will decide if the device should be launched from the right or the left and the object will be placed just beyond and below the edge of the visible area of the screen.

The actual launching is done via the applyForce method of the sprite's body. One can think of this method as hitting the sprite with a baseball bat. It is an instant increase of motion. The force is applied at a specific location on the target and pushes in a direction. Combining location, direction, and force of push can result in very different reactions from the body. Think about the difference between a light tap at the edge of a boat (or rubber ducky) on the water and a strong hit at its center back. The tap at the edge won't send it moving very far away, but it will start spinning. The shove to the back of the boat will get it moving forward but with little to no rotation.

This application of force to this device is set up to hit the edge of the object with a strong force upward. It will send it flying upward toward the screen and give the object a bit of a spin (see Figure 7.35). The upward and screenward motion is set by the force itself, a vector that is pointing toward the center of the player screen. To get the spin, the force is applied somewhat off-center. The end result is a nice upward toss to the device that grants it a lazy arc across the screen, eventually getting pulled back down via the acceleration of the game's gravity.

```
export default class Device extends Phaser.Sprite {
  constructor(game, x, y, frame, collisionGroup,
    sliceGroup) {
      super(game, x, y, 'devices');
      this.frameName = frame;
      this.anchor.setTo(.5,.5);

      this.game.physics.p2.enable(this);
      this.body.setCollisionGroup(collisionGroup);
      this.body.collides(sliceGroup);
  }

  update() {
      if(this.body.y > 3000) {
        this.kill();
      }
  }

  launch() {
```

```
                this.body.setZeroVelocity();
                this.body.angularVelocity = 0;

                        if(Phaser.Utils.chanceRoll(50)) {
                                this.body.x = this.game.width;
                        this.body.y = this.game.height + 100;
                                this.body.applyForce( [800, 2500],
                                   this.body.x + 20, this.body.y );
                        } else {
                                this.body.x = 0;
                        this.body.y = this.game.height + 100;
                                this.body.applyForce( [-800, 2500],
                                    this.body.x - 20, this.body.y );
                        }

                        this.life = 20;

                }

        }
```

7.16.1.2 SliceBody Prefab

This is going to be a unique prefab to work on because it does not extend a sprite or group like the other prefabs in this book. Instead, this prefab extends just a P2 body, because it doesn't need to display anything on the screen. It only needs to collide with other objects. This prefab is to be added to the world the moment a full slice gesture has been recognized. It takes the start and stop positions of the gesture (as shown on the screen by a yellow line) and creates a body that hangs in space that will collide with any devices on the screen. This prefab will destroy itself quickly to ensure it doesn't destroy objects long after a slice gesture has faded.

A physics body by default does not actually have any shapes in it, so once the body is positioned at the start of the line the user had drawn, a rectangle shape is added to this body. It is of the same size as the user's swipe and can then be rotated so that it is facing the same way as the swipe via ray.angle. Then this body is set so it will only collide with the devices prefabs that are flying about the screen, by adding it to its own collision group and setting it to only collide with the device collision group.

The P2 physics system works with collision handlers differently compared to the arcade physics system. In P2, all collisions are handled automatically by the engine. If you want some custom code to run when a collision occurs (like destroying the object or playing a sound), then you will need to respond to the body's onBeginContact signal. The onBeginContact handler destroys any item that hits this slice and fires a signal if it hits something.

Finally comes the life property in the constructor and the method update life. We don't want this body to sit in the world forever but it does need a few frames of life to give the physics system a chance to detect any collisions and to give the player a bit of flexibility on how accurate their swipes need to be. The life property is reduced by one each frame until it hits zero and the object is destroyed.

```
export default class SliceBody extends Phaser.
  Physics.P2.Body {

  constructor(game, ray, collisionGroup, sliceGroup) {
    super(game, null, ray.x, ray.y, 1);

    this.ray = ray;
    this.addRectangle(ray.length,2,0,0,ray.angle);

    this.setCollisionGroup(sliceGroup);
    this.collides(collisionGroup);
    this.addToWorld();
    this.static = true;
    this.onBeginContact.add(this.sliceHit, this);
    this.life = 10;
    this.success = new Phaser.Signal();

  }

  updateLife() {
    this.life --;

    if(this.life <= 0) {
      this.removeFromWorld();
      this.group.remove(this);
    }
  }

  sliceHit(other) {
    other.sprite.kill();
    this.success.dispatch(this, other);
  }
}
```

7.16.2 Game State

The next step is to bring these prefabs into the game state and implement the full gameplay. This state will also be using the swipe handler from the earlier discussion of gestures, so you can go back and refer that component when working on this code. The threads that will be followed in this state include tracking the start and stopping point of a swipe, setting up the physics of the world, responding to collisions between objects, and drawing the swipes the user inputs.

7.16.2.1 Game State Imports

```
import SliceBody from "../prefabs/SliceBody.js";
import Device from "../prefabs/Device.js";
import SwipeHandler from "../components/
  SwipeHandler.js";
```

Note that the swipe handler has been added into a new "components" folder that was not in any other games, so you'll need to make that folder before adding in the script.

7.16.2.2 Game State Constructor

To get this game ready, an array is established with the different names of the devices that can be spawned, and a method is attached to this array that will return one of the three device names at random.

```
constructor() {
    this.deviceTypes = [ "boy.png", "box.png", "phone.
      png" ];
    this.deviceTypes.getRandomEntry = function() {
        return this[ Math.floor( Math.random() * this.
          length) ];
    }
}
```

How Does `getRandomEntry` **Work?**

One of the great things about Javascript is that it can add new methods and properties to any of its objects at runtime. In this example, a new method, `getRandomEntry`, is added directly to the device types array. Whenever the method is invoked from that array, it will run as if the keyword "this" is the array itself when inside of the function. This is great for attaching little utility methods that might be single use items in a game.

To break down the math of `getRandomEntry`, Math.random multiplied by a number will be some value between zero and the number acting as the scalar. Because the getRandomEntry method is on the array, "`this.length`" is the number of entries in that array. Math.floor rounds the number down to the nearest full number. This will give a range between zero and the highest index number of the array. This random number can then be used to get a random entry in the array every time the method is called.

7.16.2.3 Create Method

The create method begins by adding the visual items to the stage. Among the visual items are the background and the groups for the devices and finger trails. It also will create a particle emitter and a text field to show the user's score. Note that the score field is using the custom font, and has its registration set to the center, which will be useful when repositioning it later.

```
this.add.sprite(0, 0, 'gamebg');
this.devices = this.add.group();
this.trails = this.add.group();

this.emitter = this.game.add.emitter(0,0, 200);
this.emitter = this.emitter.
  makeParticles(['triangle', 'zoid']);

this.score = 0;

var style = {
```

```
font: "70px dymaxionscriptregular",
       fill: "#ff0044",
       align: "center"
       };
this.txtScore = this.add.text(
        this.game.width / 2, 30, this.score.
            toString() + " pts", style
);
this.txtScore.anchor.set(0.5);
```

The next task of the create method is to set up the physics and world space of this game. By default, the world is as big as the game window, which will cause some issues with the swipe targets. Because they are set to collide with the world bounds but are generated outside of the bounds, the moment they are created they would be shoved into this tiny world and sit there, pinned. To give the devices some breathing space, the game world is made quite large. Then the physics system is started and gravity is added to the world.

This game uses collision groups to ensure that the only collisions that happen are between the swipe target and the actual slice bodies. Just like display groups, they are made before adding any objects to their list.

```
this.game.world.setBounds(-15000, -15000, 30000,
    30000);

this.game.physics.startSystem(Phaser.Physics.P2JS);
this.game.physics.p2.gravity.y = 750;

this.deviceCollisionGroup = this.game.physics.
    p2.createCollisionGroup();
this.sliceCollisionGroup = this.game.physics.
    p2.createCollisionGroup();
```

One other important task of the create method is to create the swipe gesture recognizer. The game will respond to the start and stop signals. For it to work properly, it needs to be a part of the display list, so it is added to the world state.

```
this.swipeHandler = new SwipeHandler(this.game);
this.swipeHandler.swipeStart.add(this.swipeStart,
    this);
this.swipeHandler.swipeEnd.add(this.swipeEnd, this);
this.add.existing(this.swipeHandler);
```

Finally, to start the game off, the first wave is spawned, which will continue to spawn more waves as the game progresses.

```
this.spawnWave();
```

7.16.2.4 Spawning Waves
The wave spawner is a simple bit of code that implements an object pool for the slice targets. If there are no free devices, a new one will be made.

When creating the device, a random asset is selected from the atlas, and the collision groups for the devices and slices are passed into the constructor so that the device can properly handle what it will, collide with.

```
spawnWave() {
    var d = this.devices.getFirstDead();
    if(!d) {
      d = new Device(this.game, 300, this.game.
        height + 100, this.deviceTypes.
        getRandomEntry(), this.deviceCollisionGroup,
        this.sliceCollisionGroup);
      d.launch();
      this.devices.add(d);
    } else {
      d.revive();
      d.launch();
    }
}
```

7.16.2.5 Simple Responsive UI
When the game is resized, Phaser will automatically call the resize method that is attached to the currently running state. Here, we move the txtScore text field to the center top of the screen again, which is its pin location. Then the background is repositioned to the center of the screen. Because this game will only play in portrait mode, the height of the background will always be scaled to take up the full height of the game, but the width will stay constant. The background is set up to "bleed" a little, so minor changes in widths will show a little more or less of the game world, but not enough to substantially change the user experience.

```
resize(width, height) {
    this.txtScore.x = width / 2;

    this.bg.x = width/2;
    this.bg.y = height/2;
    this.bg.height = height;
}
```

7.16.2.6 Slice Segment Life
The creation and management of the player's slice attacks is a feature of the physics system, the gesture handler, and two functions that respond to the gesture handler's start and stop signals. These functions will show the input of the user through a graphics object that we will draw into at runtime and create the sliceBody when the gesture is successfully executed.

The first method, startSegment, is called when a gesture is started. It prepares a new graphic to draw into while the user is dragging their finger across the screen. New graphics objects are created for each swipe so they can be faded away when the gesture ends.

```
startSegment() {
    this.sliceStart.x = this.input.activePointer.x;
    this.sliceStart.y = this.input.activePointer.y;
    this.curGraphics = new Phaser.Graphics(this.game,
        0, 0);
    this.curGraphics.lineStyle(10, 0xffd900, 1);
    this.trails.add(this.curGraphics);
}
```

The second method, endSegment, is called when a gesture finishes, and it fades away the line the user was drawing with their gesture. This method will also create a slice body that will impact any of the items that are flying about the screen. In order to create this body, a Phaser ray (or line segment) is created that has the same start and stop points as the yellow line that was on the screen. This ray is sent into the new SliceBody, which will handle generating a box and rotating it to fit with the user's input. The slice will fire a success signal when it hits something; the game state will need to respond to that success and is configured to run a method "sliceHit" when it hears that signal. Finally, the slice is added to a sliceBodies array set so it can have its life updated for each game loop.

```
endSegment() {
    var ray = new Phaser.Line(this.sliceStart.x,
        this.sliceStart.y, this.input.activePointer.x,
        this.input.activePointer.y);
    var sliceBody = new SliceBody(this.game, ray,
        this.deviceCollisionGroup, this.
        sliceCollisionGroup);

    //add the line to it
    sliceBody.group = this.sliceBodies;
    sliceBody.success.add(this.sliceHit, this);
    this.sliceBodies.add(sliceBody);

    this.game.add.tween(this.curGraphics).to({ alpha:
        0 }, 800, Phaser.Easing.Quadratic.Out, true);
}
```

7.16.2.7 Slice Hit Method

When the slicebody fires a signal saying it has hit something, the slice hit method will run. The major tasks here are increasing score, generating some particles along the length of the slice for visual effect, replacing the sliced object (or objects) with two halves to make it look like they have been "cut," and disabling the slicebody.

The approach to generating the particles in this game is unconventional. The slice has occurred on a rotated body, but it is impossible to rotate an emitter. The following code is one way around the problem. It takes the line that the user had drawn (stored as the ray that hits the slice in the sliceBody object) and requests a series of 20 points on that line. All of these points will be equidistant from each other and will start and stop at the two end points of the ray. For example, if the ray started at (0, 0) and ended at (20, 0), a set of points would be returned with the x-value moving up by one each time. Then, iterating through that array of points, one particle is emitted at each point. The end effect is a rotated line of particles that appear along the line the user sliced.

The second new chunk of code here is the creation of the sliced halves of the object that was hit by the player. To make the halves, two new sprites with the same image as the impacted device are added to the stage. These new sprites are cropped to only show half of their entire sprite. The top has its registration point put on its bottom center, while the bottom slice places its registration point to the top center. Then these cropped sprites are rotated and positioned to the center of the target sprite. Since they are positioned in the dead center of the target sprite, they will appear "whole." Finally, each has their collisions disabled and given opposite rotational velocities. The end result is an image that appears momentarily solid until the two halves begin to fall and slowly rotate away from each other, showing the disastrous aftereffect of the user's actions.

```
sliceHit( sliceBody, device ) {

    var coords = sliceBody.ray.coordinatesOnLine(20);

    for( var i = 0;  i < coords.length; i++) {
        this.emitter.x = coords[i][0];
        this.emitter.y = coords[i][1];
        this.emitter.explode(2000, 1);
    }
    this.score++;
    this.txtScore.text = this.score.toString() +
        "pts";

    var sliceSprite = this.slicedPieces.
        create(device.sprite.x,device.sprite.y,device.
        sprite.key,device.sprite.frameName);
    var halfHeight = Math.floor(sliceSprite.
        height / 2);
    sliceSprite.crop(new Phaser.Rectangle(0,0,
        sliceSprite.width, halfHeight));
    this.game.physics.p2.enable(sliceSprite);
    sliceSprite.anchor.setTo(.5, 1);
    sliceSprite.body.rotation = device.rotation;
    sliceSprite.body.setCollisionGroup(this.game.
        physics.p2.nothingCollisionGroup);
    sliceSprite.body.angularVelocity = -1.2;

    var sliceSprite2 = this.slicedPieces.
        create(device.sprite.x,device.sprite.y,device.
        sprite.key,device.sprite.frameName);
    sliceSprite2.crop(new Phaser.
        Rectangle(0,halfHeight, sliceSprite.width,
        halfHeight));
    this.game.physics.p2.enable(sliceSprite2);
    sliceSprite2.anchor.setTo(.5, 0);
    sliceSprite2.body.rotation = device.rotation;
```

```
sliceSprite2.body.setCollisionGroup(this.game.
  physics.p2.nothingCollisionGroup);
sliceSprite2.body.angularVelocity = 1.2;

}
```

7.16.2.8 Update Method

The update method has two concerns: to draw the path of any current swipe gesture and to update any of the slicebodies that are sitting in the worldspace.

Since the user's finger might not always draw the straightest of paths, whatever path was drawn last frame is cleared. Then a 10 pixel thick, yellow line is drawn to the current graphics object. This line starts from when the swipe gesture was first recognized to where the finger currently is. It provides a nice "trail" to show the user where their gestures will hit on the screen.

Unfortunately, because the slice bodies are not display objects, they do not get their update method called automatically like our other prefabs. We use a feature of Phaser's ArraySet that will let us call the updateLife method on every sliceBody in the array.

```
update() {

  if(this.swipeHandler.swiping) {
      this.curGraphics.clear();
      this.curGraphics.lineStyle(10, 0xffd900, 1);
      this.curGraphics.moveTo(this.sliceStart.x,
        this.sliceStart.y);
      this.curGraphics.lineTo( this.input.
        activePointer.x, this.input.activePointer.y );
  }

  this.sliceBodies.callAll("updateLife");
}
```

The following is the entire game state in full for your reference:

```
import SliceBody from "../prefabs/SliceBody.js";
import Device from "../prefabs/Device.js";
import SwipeHandler from "../components/
  SwipeHandler.js";

export default class Game {

  constructor() {

    this.deviceTypes = [ "boy.png", "box.png",
      "phone.png" ];
    this.deviceTypes.getRandomEntry = function() {
      return this[ Math.floor( Math.random() * this.
        length) ];
    }
  }

  create() {
```

```
      this.add.sprite(0, 0, 'gamebg');

      this.game.world.setBounds(-15000, -15000, 30000,
        30000);

      this.game.physics.startSystem(Phaser.Physics.P2JS);
      this.game.physics.p2.graviity.y = 750;
      this.game.physics.p2.restitution = 0.8;

      this.drawingSlice = false;

      this.devices = this.add.group();
      this.trails = this.add.group();

      this.sliceStart = { x: 0, y: 0 };
      this.sliceBodies = new Phaser.ArraySet();

      this.timer = this.game.time.create(false);
      this.timer.loop(1000, this.spawnWave, this);
      this.timer.start();

      this.score = 0;

      var style = { font: "70px dymaxionscriptregular",
        fill: "#ff0044", align: "center" };
      this.txtScore = this.add.text( this.game.width /
        2, 30, this.score.toString() + " pts", style);
      this.txtScore.anchor.set(0.5);
      this.emitter = this.game.add.emitter(0,0, 200);
      this.emitter = this.emitter.
        makeParticles(['triangle', 'zoid']);

      this.slicedPieces = this.add.group();
      this.deviceCollisionGroup = this.game.physics.
        p2.createCollisionGroup();
      this.sliceCollisionGroup = this.game.physics.
        p2.createCollisionGroup();

      this.swipeHandler = new SwipeHandler(this.game);
      this.swipeHandler.swipeStart.add(this.swipeStart,
        this);
      this.swipeHandler.swipeEnd.add(this.swipeEnd,
        this);
      this.add.existing(this.swipeHandler);
      this.spawnWave();
  }

  update() {

    if(this.swipeHandler.swiping) {
        this.curGraphics.clear();
        this.curGraphics.lineStyle(10, 0xffd900, 1);
        this.curGraphics.moveTo(this.sliceStart.x,
          this.sliceStart.y);
        this.curGraphics.lineTo( this.input.
          activePointer.x, this.input.activePointer.y );
```

```
    }
    this.sliceBodies.callAll("updateLife");
  }

  endSegment() {
    var ray = new Phaser.Line(this.sliceStart.x, this.
      sliceStart.y, this.input.activePointer.x, this.
      input.activePointer.y);
    var sliceBody = new SliceBody(this.game, ray,
      this.deviceCollisionGroup, this.
      sliceCollisionGroup);

    //add the line to it
    sliceBody.group = this.sliceBodies;
    sliceBody.success.add(this.sliceHit, this);
    this.sliceBodies.add(sliceBody);

    this.game.add.tween(this.curGraphics).to({ alpha:
      0 }, 800, Phaser.Easing.Quadratic.Out, true);
  }
  sliceHit( sliceBody, device ) {

    var coords = sliceBody.ray.coordinatesOnLine(20);

    for( var i = 0;  i < coords.length; i++) {
      this.emitter.x = coords[i][0];
      this.emitter.y = coords[i][1];
      this.emitter.explode(2000, 1);
    }

    this.score++;
    this.txtScore.text = this.score.toString() + "
      pts";

    var sliceSprite = this.slicedPieces.create(device.
      sprite.x,device.sprite.y,device.sprite.
      key,device.sprite.frameName);
    var halfHeight = Math.floor(sliceSprite.
      height / 2);
    sliceSprite.crop(new Phaser.Rectangle(0,0,
      sliceSprite.width, halfHeight));
    this.game.physics.p2.enable(sliceSprite);
    sliceSprite.anchor.setTo(.5, 1);
    sliceSprite.body.rotation = device.rotation;
    sliceSprite.body.setCollisionGroup(this.game.
      physics.p2.nothingCollisionGroup);
    sliceSprite.body.angularVelocity = -1.2;

    var sliceSprite2 = this.slicedPieces.
      create(device.sprite.x,device.sprite.y,device.
      sprite.key,device.sprite.frameName);
    sliceSprite2.crop(new Phaser.
      Rectangle(0,halfHeight, sliceSprite.width,
      halfHeight));
```

```
        this.game.physics.p2.enable(sliceSprite2);
          sliceSprite2.anchor.setTo(.5, 0);
          sliceSprite2.body.rotation = device.rotation;
          sliceSprite2.body.setCollisionGroup(this.game.
            physics.p2.nothingCollisionGroup);
          sliceSprite2.body.angularVelocity = 1.2;
        }

        startSegment() {
          this.sliceStart.x = this.input.activePointer.x;
          this.sliceStart.y = this.input.activePointer.y;
          this.curGraphics = new Phaser.Graphics(this.game,
            0, 0);
          this.curGraphics.lineStyle(10, 0xffd900, 1);
          this.trails.add(this.curGraphics);
        }

        swipeStart() {
          this.startSegment();
        }
        swipeEnd() {
          this.endSegment();
        }

        spawnWave() {
          var d = this.devices.getFirstDead();
          if(!d) {
          d =  new Device(this.game, 300, this.game.height +
            100, this.deviceTypes.getRandomEntry(), this.
            deviceCollisionGroup, this.sliceCollisionGroup);
          d.launch();
          this.devices.add(d);
        } else {
          d.revive();
          d.launch();
        }
      }
    }

  }
```

7.16.3 Conclusion and Future Additions

Presented in this chapter was the basics of a gestural object slicer game. Like the other examples in the book and just about any project you may tackle in your life, this is only the beginning. Once you understand all the basics, this game will most likely feel incomplete and you may want to play with it and make it your own. There are several places where numbers can be safely played with, but a few of the more interesting ones are listed here:

- Change the spawn rate on the timer at setup.
- Adjust the gravity scale of the world at setup.
- Change the forces applied to the devices when they are launched.
- Modify the angular velocity of the device halves.

Each of these points will give you a good opportunity to get a real sense of how the game is working. Adjustments to the middle two will change how quickly a device appears and remains on the screen and will affect the gameplay the most.

To be honest, this is not a very challenging game. When looking at other quick slicing games that one can find for mobile devices, the challenge isn't just cutting the object in half, but prioritizing motions and building up specific combos. Adding in the ability to launch the objects from more than two directions with varying speeds would be the next step for this slicing game. It seems simpler than it actually will be, and so approach this puzzle with caution and be prepared for a rewarding, struggle to implement those two additions.

7.16.4 Launcher Game

Our final game in this book is going to be a "destruction/launcher" type game that plays around with the physics capabilities of Phaser. Perhaps the most famous of game in this genre is Angry Birds, which is a game that tasks you with launching some cartoony orblike birds at some shockingly resilient structures. The eventual goal of the game is to collide enough birds with the structures and hopefully take the structure down (along with killing some pigs that happen to be within those houses). In order to make a move in the game, the birds are pulled back from a center point on a rubber band slingshot. The player can adjust the angle of release and tension by moving the bird up and down behind the slingshot and closer to the weapon itself for a less powerful throw. Once angle and power are decided, the input to the screen is released, and a force is applied to a bird to send if flying in the direction the slingshot would throw it.

There are a number of other games that rely on the gameplay elements of applying an impulse to an object in order to send it hurtling toward some targets off to the right. Some variants of the launcher-type game might go less for destruction and focus on distance traveled. There is also another variant of "archer" games, where accuracy of the shot is the critical consideration for the player. See Figures 7.36 through 7.39.

Our game, Comet Crusher, is going to be a simple launcher game. The goal of Comet Crusher is to launch a comet from the left of the screen into a series of asteroids that are on the far right. If the comet manages to shove the asteroids off the screen the player is rewarded with a point and the field is reset for next comet launch.

A quick listing of the features of this game includes the following:

- A comet that can be launched by clicking on it and pulling it back to establish a tension that will launch it when it is released.
- A line that indicates the direction and potential force of the throw while the player is pulling back on the comet
- Asteroids that can be hit by the comet and can be thrown off screen
- A reset to the game state after each play has been made
- Physics controlled by the P2 Physics system

Basic launcher style game

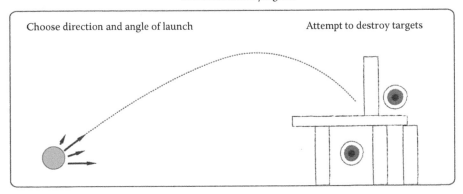

FIG 7.36 Template of a launcher game.

FIG 7.37 Custom positions for the comet's center point and circular body.

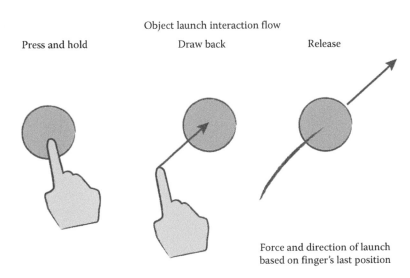

FIG 7.38 Interaction required to launch a comet.

create the basic project structure described in chapter five. We will be adding to that base throughout this exercise. Should you need to see the finished code or to get the assets for the game, you can find the full source at https://github.com/meanderingleaf/PhaserBookExamples/tree/master/crusher.

Creation of the projectile impulse force

1. Get relative sizes of the sides of the force

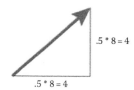
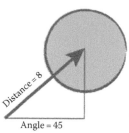

Math.sin(angle) = .5
Math.cos(angle) = .5

2. Start a force with those ratios

force.x = .5;
force.y = .5;

3. Multiply the sides of the force by the length of the line

force.x = force.x * line.magnitude();
force.y = force.y * line.magnitude();

4. Adjust for game units and apply force

force.x * = 10;
force.y * = 3;

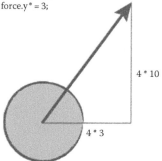

FIG 7.39 Launch force creation process.

7.17 Additions to App.js

There will be an extra scene added to the states, and the size of this game will be increased for a larger view into the game world.

```
var game;

import Boot from "./states/Boot.js";
import Preload from "./states/Preload.js";
import Game from "./states/Game.js";
import HomeScreen from "./states/HomeScreen.js";

window.onload = function () {
  game = new Phaser.Game(1024, 768, Phaser.AUTO,
    'game');
  game.state.add('boot', Boot);
  game.state.add('preload', Preload);
  game.state.add('game', Game);
  game.state.add('homescreen', HomeScreen);
  game.state.start('boot');
};
```

7.17.1 Preload State

Only images will be needed for this game. There will be an image for the background, comet, asteroids, particles, and the foreground.

```
this.load.image('bg', 'assets/images/smasherBG.jpg');
this.load.image('particle1', 'assets/images/comet_
  particle1.png');
this.load.image('particle2', 'assets/images/comet_
  particle2.png');
this.load.image('comet', 'assets/images/comet.png');
this.load.image('asteroid', 'assets/images/asteroid.
  png');
this.load.image('fg', 'assets/images/
  smasherForeground.png');
```

7.17.2 Game State

Everything for this game is going to come in the game state, making it one of the more simple game examples in this book, even if the end result looks like a complex game.

7.17.2.1 Create Method

The create method does most of the important work in this game. This setup work will be split between this create method and the resetBoard function. The following is the create method in its entirety, and the different sections will be examined in detail afterward.

```
create() {

    //object level properties
    this.pulling = false;
    this.launched = false;
    this.round = 0;
    this.score = 0;

    //start physics
    this.physics.startSystem(Phaser.Physics.P2JS);
    this.world.setBounds(0, 0, 3000, 768);

    //add game bg
    this.bg = this.add.sprite(0,0,'bg');
    this.bg.fixedToCamera =true;

    //impulse chain
    this.forceLine = this.add.graphics(0,0);

    //create and configure comet
    this.comet = this.add.sprite(300,330,'comet');
    this.comet.anchor.set(.5, .5);
    this.physics.p2.enable(this.comet);
    this.comet.body.setCircle(40, 140, -10);
    this.comet.inputEnabled = true;
```

```
//setup asteroids
this.asteroids = this.add.group();
this.asteroids.enableBody = true;
this.asteroids.physicsBodyType = Phaser.Physics.
   P2JS;

//emitter
this.trail = this.add.emitter(this.comet.x, this.
   comet.y);
this.trail.makeParticles(['particle1',
   'particle2']);
this.trail.start(false, 3000, 50);
this.trail.setAlpha(1, 0, 3000);
this.trail.setScale(0.4, 1, 0.4, 1, 4000);

//foreground
this.add.sprite(0,0, 'fg');

//Text
var style = { font: "30px Arial", fill: "#FFF" };
this.txtScore = this.add.text(20, 20, "Round 0,
   Score 0", style);
this.txtScore.fixedToCamera = true;

//follow that comet
this.camera.follow(this.comet);

//setup game board
this.resetBoard();
}
```

The start of the create method establishes several object-level properties
that will be used throughout the lifespan of the game. Pulling and launching
are the states of the comet set to true if the users are readying their throw by
tugging back on the graphic or if the comet is currently flying. The score and
round are simple numbers to keep track of the progress of the game and will
be shown in a text field later on.

```
//object level properties
this.pulling = false;
this.launched = false;
this.round = 0;
this.score = 0;
```

Next, the physics system is started. The P2 physics system has been chosen
because this game has irregular shapes and we're looking for fairly realistic
reactions to the collisions that do occur. As an added benefit, the collisions
are processed automatically in P2, meaning there is less code to write in the
update function. The world for this game needs to extend far to the right, so
the bounds are changed to take up a much larger expanse in that direction.
This will give us space to place the asteroid targets and for the comet to fly off
toward its target.

The first image added to the game is the background and it is then fixed to the camera so it won't move. This will give it a bit more of a feeling of depth compared to the quickly moving foreground that will appear above. The last item added is the force line graphic, which will be used to show the player the power and direction of their launch. It is a graphic so we will be able to draw into it using the graphic API calls at runtime.

```
//start physics
this.physics.startSystem(Phaser.Physics.P2JS);
this.world.setBounds(0, 0, 3000, 768);

//add game bg
this.bg = this.add.sprite(0,0,'bg');
this.bg.fixedToCamera =true;

//impulse chain
this.forceLine = this.add.graphics(0,0);
```

The next game object to get configured is the comet that the player will be throwing around. It is a sprite, and its center point is repositioned to the center of the mass of the comet, instead of the center of just the image. While this won't affect its rotations from collisions, it will be used as a position for a particle system, so it is put in a place with enough heft that particles would reasonably fall away from the comet at the location. After the comet is added to the physics system (via p2.enable), its rectangular body is replaced with a 40 pixel radius circle that more accurately represents the shape of a comet (See Figure 7.37). This new circular body begins center of the sprite, which isn't quite where the comet's mass is, so the center of the circle is offset 140 pixels to the right and about 10 pixels upward (see Figure 7.37). Finally, the comet is enabled for input so it can respond to the user pressing down on it to begin the slingshot motion on the comet.

```
//create and configure comet
this.comet = this.add.sprite(300,330,'comet');
this.comet.anchor.set(.5, .5);
this.physics.p2.enable(this.comet);
this.comet.body.setCircle(40, 140, -10);
this.comet.inputEnabled = true;
```

After the comet, the asteroid group is readied. The actual asteroids won't be added to the game until the resetBoard method is invoked. For now, their group will be created and configured to add its children to the P2 world.

```
this.asteroids = this.add.group();
this.asteroids.enableBody = true;
this.asteroids.physicsBodyType = Phaser.Physics.
  P2JS;
```

The next object added to the game is a particle emitter with two particle sprites in its potential particle pool. The sprites will grow from about half their size and fade out during their lifespan, thanks to the setAlpha and setScale method calls. Then the emitter is started with the first argument of "false" forcing it to continuously emit particles. This emitter will generate particles with a 3 s lifespan, and it will create a new particle every 50 ms. Later in the update method, we will write some code to cause the emitter to follow the comet as it moves, making it create a trail of debris that the ice ball leaves in its wake.

```
this.trail = this.add.emitter(this.comet.x, this.
    comet.y);
this.trail.makeParticles(['particle1',
    'particle2']);
this.trail.start(false, 3000, 50);
this.trail.setAlpha(1, 0, 3000);
this.trail.setScale(0.4, 1, 0.4, 1, 4000);
```

Next, in the create method, the foreground is added. This sprite is not fixed to the camera and will move quickly as the comet flies, which will provide a sense of space and speed to the game.

On top of the foreground, the score is added with some default values to start with. This score field is also fixed to the camera, so it will always stay in its place as the camera moves through the game world.

```
//foreground
this.add.sprite(0,0, 'fg');

//Text
var style = { font: "30px Arial", fill: "#FFF" };
this.txtScore = this.add.text(20, 20, "Round 0,
    Score 0", style);
this.txtScore.fixedToCamera = true;
```

The last bit of the create method starts the camera following the comet object. Just like in the platformer, the camera will follow this comet as it moves, so long as there is space in the world for the camera to display.

Finally, the board is reset. Resetting the board will place all the objects in their places and get the round ready for play. This is a fairly long, and important, function that is covered next.

```
//follow that comet
this.camera.follow(this.comet);

//setup game board
this.resetBoard();
```

7.17.2.2 Reset Board

The reset board function will place the objects when the game starts and will later be used to reset the game to its starting state after every round. Because it resets objects after they have moved and had their statuses changed, some extra work needs to be done to ensure that the objects are starting from pristine starting point. Here is the reset board function in its entirety.

```
resetBoard() {
    this.comet.body.reset();
    this.comet.body.rotation = 0;
    this.comet.body.motionState =  Phaser.Physics.
      P2.Body.STATIC;
    this.comet.events.onInputDown.addOnce(this.
      startPull, this);
    this.comet.body.x = 300;
    this.comet.body.y = 370;

    this.asteroids.removeAll(true);
    this.asteroids.create(2800, 400, 'asteroid');
    this.asteroids.create(2500, 200, 'asteroid');
    this.asteroids.create(2200, 500, 'asteroid');
    this.asteroids.create(2200, 200, 'asteroid');
    this.asteroids.create(2600, 600, 'asteroid');
    this.asteroids.create(1800, 600, 'asteroid');
    this.asteroids.create(1600, 300, 'asteroid');

    this.asteroids.forEach(
      function(asteroid) {
        asteroid.mass = .7;
        asteroid.checkWorldBounds = true;
        asteroid.body.setCircle(75);
        asteroid.events.onOutOfBounds.addOnce(this.
          killedAsteroid, this)
      },
      this
    );

    this.round ++;
    this.txtScore.text = "Round: " + this.
      round + " Score: " + this.score;

}
```

The first object to be reset is the comet. After it is launched by the player and the round ends, the comet will be moving quickly, not positioned at its starting point, and potentially rotated from its original orientation. In order to reset it, it will be brought back to its original position (300, 370), the forces and velocity on the body are removed by running the reset method on its body, and its rotation is set back to zero. This will put the comet back into its pristine state.

Unfortunately, any remaining forces on the comet body will continue to act on it once it gets repositioned. The comet will eventually fall off screen unless something is done to negate the actions of the forces on the comet. Setting its body to static will cause it to be unaffected by collisions and forces. While the body is static, it will effectively be pinned in place. This body type will be returned to dynamic once the comet is launched. When the comet has a dynamic body, it will be affected by gravity and will collide with the meteors again. Also added to this comet is an event listener that will fire when a user presses the pointer down on the comet. The handler that runs on depress will begin the process of drawing the visualization for the force on the comet and also start listening for the pointer to be removed from the screen.

```
this.comet.body.reset();
this.comet.body.rotation = 0;
this.comet.body.motionState =  Phaser.Physics.
  P2.Body.STATIC;
this.comet.events.onInputDown.addOnce(this.
  startPull, this);
this.comet.body.x = 300;
this.comet.body.y = 370;
```

The next items to be reset are the asteroids. Here, the existing ones are explicitly destroyed with the call "removeAll(true)," so that there is a completely clean asteroid group to begin with when placing the new objects. These new asteroids are placed into fixed locations that will ensure they are not overlapping in any way. If they were not positioned this way and some of the asteroids overlapped with each other, the physics system will attempt to separate them once they are placed. The separation process would unintentionally add a significant amount of velocity to the asteroids, causing them to explode away from each other and leave the game world before the player had a chance to hit them with the comet.

After being placed, the asteroids need to be configured. The forEach method of a Phaser group function is used to loop through all the asteroids in the group. For each asteroid in that group, the anonymous function will execute with a reference to the current asteroid being passed into the function as the argument "asteroid." The second argument that comes after the array comprehension function, "this," tells the forEach to act as if it were a method on this current state object.

Using the "asteroid" reference that is passed into the function, the square hitbox on each asteroid is replaced with a circle that more accurately represents the shape of the asteroids. The mass of the asteroids is also reduced. Their lower mass means the comet will be slowed down less by any asteroid it hits. Finally, the asteroid is set to collide with the bounds of the world and to run a function when it exits the world space. Because the goal of the game is to knock the asteroids out of the game space, this method is the one that will run when the player makes a successful launch of the comet.

```
this.asteroids.removeAll(true);
this.asteroids.create(2800, 400, 'asteroid');
this.asteroids.create(2500, 200, 'asteroid');
this.asteroids.create(2200, 500, 'asteroid');
this.asteroids.create(2200, 200, 'asteroid');
this.asteroids.create(2600, 600, 'asteroid');
```

```
this.asteroids.create(1800, 600, 'asteroid');
this.asteroids.create(1600, 300, 'asteroid');

this.asteroids.forEach(
  function(asteroid) {
    asteroid.mass = .7;
    asteroid.checkWorldBounds = true;
    asteroid.body.setCircle(75);
    asteroid.events.onOutOfBounds.addOnce(this.
      killedAsteroid, this)
  },
  this
);
```

The final bit of the reset board method increments the game round and updates the text on the screen to give the player some information about how many times they have chucked the comet and the number of asteroids that have been shoved away from the screen over the course of those rounds.

```
this.round ++;
this.txtScore.text = "Round: " + this.round +
  " Score: " + this.score;
```

7.17.2.3 Start Pull Method
The start pull method is called when a player presses down on the comet. It toggles the state's "pulling" variable to true (which will be used in the update function to draw the line of the force input) and starts the game listening to when the input is released. This is the start of the press, draw back to determine force at an angle, and release sequence of a launcher game. Setting the pulling property to true will put the game into the "draw state" so that the player can set the direction to launch the comet. To give the user a sense of force and angle, setting "pulling" to true will also begin drawing a line from the pointer's current position to the center of the comet (See Figure 7.38).

```
startPull() {
this.pulling = true;
this.game.input.onUp.addOnce(this.endPull, this);
}
```

7.17.2.4 End Pull Method
The end pull method, fires when the user releases their pointer (a mouse up or pulling their finger off the screen). Because the listener is added in the pointer down handler, this method will only run after the player presses the input down on the comet. While the intention is for the player to press, draw back, and release, this method actually will run if they simply tap on the comet as well. First, the method toggles two variables that move the game out of the "pulling" state and into the "comet-is-flying" (launched) state.

In order to send the comet flying off to the right at the force and angle the user indicated, we'll need some extra information about the line the user had drawn. We'll use Phaser's line object to create the data for the line. Into the line object's constructor, we'll pass in the current position of the user's pointer as the start of the line and the center point of the comet as the end of the line.

Before applying any forces, the body of the comet is changed from static to dynamic. With its dynamic body, it will react to the forces we apply to it and also collide with the asteroids. Then, forces are added to the object. The forces take the amount the line is "pointing" in each direction by getting their ratio (via trigonometric functions) and scale those amounts upward. Using Math.sin on the angle of the line will return how much the line is pointing in the y direction as a number between zero and one. Math.cos will do the same, but for the x direction. These numbers are really small, and if they alone were used as the force on the comet, it would barely move. In order to make the force a bit stronger, these basic directions ratios are multiplied (scaled) by the length of the line the user had drawn. Longer lines will result in bigger forces applied to the comet. Even if the user pulled their force back as far as possible, the comet would not get moving very fast. There is an additional bit of scaling applied to the forces to make that comet really soar (See Figure 7.39).

After the forces are applied, the force line that the user was drawing is removed. The last line in this handler tells the game to wait for 5½ s and then run the reset board function again. This gives the player that 5½ s for each round to hit some asteroids off screen. After that timespan, the round is over and the board is reset, ready for another launch.

```
endPull() {
    this.pulling =  false;
    this.launched = true;
    var forceLine = new Phaser.Line(this.input.
      activePointer.x, this.input.activePointer.y,
      this.comet.x, this.comet.y);

    this.comet.body.motionState =  Phaser.Physics.
      P2.Body.DYNAMIC;

    this.comet.body.velocity.x =
      Math.cos(forceLine.angle) * forceLine.length * 6;
    this.comet.body.velocity.y =
      Math.sin(forceLine.angle) * forceLine.length * 2;

    this.forceLine.clear();

    this.time.events.add(5500, this.resetBoard, this);
}
```

7.17.2.5 Update Function
The final bit of the gameplay code is the update method that has three sections. One part will always execute, the other two sections only run when the game is in a certain states (either "pulling" or "launched").

The first state the game can be in is the "pulling" state. This state is active when the user is deciding in what direction and how hard to launch the comet. While in this state, the force line graphics are cleared every update, and a new white line is drawn from where the user's pointer is located to the center of the comet.

The next state, "launched," is active while the comet is flying. For the duration of the flight, the comet will have some gravity applied to it via the body.force.y property. Larger numbers will pull down on the comet with a greater strength.

Finally, at any point in the game, the particle emitter is repositioned to be at the same location as the comet. This will make the particles for the comet follow it as it flies around the screen.

```
update() {
    if(this.pulling ) {
        this.forceLine.clear();
        this.forceLine.lineStyle(10, 0xffffff, .8);
        this.forceLine.moveTo(
            this.input.activePointer.x, this.input.
              activePointer.y
        );
        this.forceLine.lineTo(this.comet.x, this.
          comet.y);
    }
    if(this.launched) {
        this.comet.body.force.y = 270;
    }
    this.trail.x = this.comet.x;
    this.trail.y = this.comet.y;
}
```

7.17.3 Conclusion

With the addition of the update function, the code for Comet Crusher is finished. Go cause some celestial mayhem and marvel at how fun a physics sandbox can be. This example game gives you a lot of room to grow and play with the features of Phaser and P2. Play with the numbers, especially the masses, forces, and velocities for the game, to see how you can change it to make it easier or harder for the player (or just more hilarious). Other interesting areas to tackle for this game include more accurate shapes for the models and different levels. The comet and asteroid shapes could be made using programs like PhysicsEditor and imported into Phaser. The levels would need to be carefully laid out like our current one is, but would give you a chance to create more objects for the player to contend with (perhaps including objects that have higher mass, are completely immobile, or even explode upon impact).

CHAPTER 8

Game Deployment

Once your game is complete and polished up to your standards, the next step is to get that game out to the people who matter: the players. These players can be just about anywhere. They just need access to a capable device and an Internet connection. Once the user gets to the page and downloads the assets, your game can run. Other times, perhaps for financial reasons, it may also make sense to package a game up for distribution on mobile app stores like Google Play or the Apple app store. Each deployment target will differ in the issues that will need to be overcome to correctly package the game up and ready it for deployment. The stores themselves also have different hoops to jump through to get things properly set up. Even when deploying to the web, the original intended deployment area for Phaser, there is a set of optimizations and precautions that should be taken before releasing the game to the world at large. In this chapter, we're going to step through the process of readying a finished game for some of the different deployment targets of the web and app stores.

8.1 Web Deployment

The first and easiest way to deploy a game is to put it on the web. In order to do this, you will need to have a working webhost that can serve the files up when a user requests them. This is the original intended location for an HTML5 game and is the fastest way to get your game out to potential players.

The ease of deployment comes with several drawbacks. Firstly, if it's a game that you are hosting on your own website, the cost to get the game to users starts out fairly high compared to other deployment methods and will increase significantly if the game gets popular. Secondly, due to the open nature of the web, it will be very easy for any person who happens upon the game to get access to all the code and assets that make up the game. While some might be okay with their blood, sweat, and tears being stolen and repurposed in other places across the web, many developers might be less than happy with this. If you have a unique game and with a decent amount of polish that gets enough notoriety, expect it to be stolen in some way. There are ways to mitigate the damage, but it is impossible to keep your game completely locked up. One final issue when deploying to the web is the trouble of your games discoverability. Unlike app stores that list all the games and show new games that have been submitted, if you just upload your game to the web and leave it there, people will never hear about it. Any game deployed to the web will need to have some amount of advertising and marketing to get people to come to the site, and the methods and approaches to getting users to these pages are a set of skills that will need practice and study beyond the scope of this book.

There are a number of affordable hosts that can easily serve a game up to an audience, if self-hosting appeals to you as a developer. Entering "web hosting" into a search engine will return a number of companies that will host websites that can work as hosts for small games. Often these companies can scale (or "up" their capabilities) a certain degree to serve games that get more popular. However, if a game gets too popular, you may need to move to a more robust host that is willing to devote large amounts of resources or even dedicate a server to distribute your game files to the players.

Once hosting has been secured, the game will need to be prepped for transfer to the server. The first issue that needs to be dealt with is that not all the files that are in your development directory need to be transferred to the server. The files downloaded by node package manager (NPM) are so numerous and large that it would take an inordinate amount of time to transfer them to your server. The two folders that need to be excluded from the final build are the `src` folder (which contains the unused source code) and the `node_modules` folder that contains a lot of scripts only used for the development process. Other files that should most likely be left out of a production deploy include the `bower.json`, `package.json`, and the Grunt file.

The second consideration before transferring files to the web server is the state of the game's code. In order for a game to run correctly on a user's machine, all of the code will be transferred to from the server to the client machine. With our current Grunt build script, this code is generated with a bunch of whitespace and comments that are lovely for developers but are unnecessary for a final file to run. Most JavaScript files that are transferred across the web are modified to remove any unnecessary characters that aren't required for the script to run. This process, called "minification," winds up making a file that is difficult to read but has a small file size that gives your game a quicker load time and a lower memory footprint. While the minification process makes the code hard to read, it doesn't make it impossible for others to reverse engineer your code.

> **Why Back Ends**
>
> Many HTML5 games have "back end" portions of the game that are only run on the server. While it may be frustrating to the player that they cannot play this game offline, it makes a lot of sense for the developer to create a game with a back end. This back end code is never transferred to the player's machine and that makes it somewhat more difficult for nefarious individuals to reverse engineer the game.

While it is possible to go through all these actions by hand, it will quickly become a pain to remove files and minify Javascript manually to make a final build. Thankfully, these are all tasks that Grunt can automate. Throughout this book, Grunt has been stuck running our development task, but it can actually run many different tasks for different use cases like building a final project. Knowing that the project needs to be cleaned up and minified, we're going to add a few more packages and one new task to the Grunt file. Once configured, the command `grunt build-production` entered in the command prompt in the project root will make a final build of your game to a fresh folder.

8.2 Creating the Grunt Production Task

(Note that if you're using the Yeoman generator, you only need to skim this section to understand how the project works.)

We're going to head back to the command prompt in the project root and then into the Grunt file to create a new task that can move all the essential files into a new folder that can be easily deployed. The new packages that will need to be downloaded are the `clean`, `uglify`, and `copy` commands. In your command prompt at a project root, execute these commands.

```
npm install grunt-contrib-copy --save-dev
npm install grunt-contrib-clean --save-dev
npm install grunt-contrib-uglify --save-dev
```

Once these three packages have been added to your project, the Gruntfile.js needs to be configured to be able to run these tasks to export a "clean" version of the game. There are two additions to the Grunt file: the new package configurations and the new command.

The configuration comes first. Add a comma after the connect task, and add these new lines of configuration for the new packages.

```
copy: {
    build: {
        files: [
            {expand: true, src: ['assets/**'], dest:
                'build/'},
            {src: ['index.html'], dest: 'build/index.
                html'}
        ]
    }
},
uglify: {
    build: {
        files: [{
            expand: true,
            cwd: 'scripts',
            src: '**/*.js',
            dest: 'build/scripts'
        }]
    }
},
clean: {
    build: ["build"]
}
```

Note that all of these new commands have the "build" property inside of their configuration objects. This specifies to Grunt that this particular configuration of the package should only be run when Grunt is run with the "build" command (typing "Grunt" into the prompt will not run these packages, but "Grunt build" will).

8.2.1 Clean

Clean is a fancy term for "delete." For this particular command, the final export will be pushed to a folder named "build." To ensure that nothing is left in an export of your project from a previous build, everything is wiped away from the export directory before the new build is copied over.

8.2.2 Copy

The copy command will copy files from one folder to another. It is configured to copy all the files from the entire assets folder (and its subfolder) to the build directory. It will also copy the index HTML file into the build root.

8.2.3 Uglify

The final task to configure is uglify. This is the task that takes a JavaScript file and removes all the unnecessary whitespace and comments from it and generally makes it as small as possible. It comes with the option of doing some simple obfuscation which will make your code somewhat harder to steal and modify. This script is set up to work its magic on every file in the scripts folder, so the Phaser script and any plugins installed via bower will also go through the transformation if they weren't already minified.

8.3 Build Task

```
grunt.registerTask('build', [ 'clean', 'bower',
  'copy', 'uglify' ]);
```

This task should be added right beneath the main Grunt task. It runs the tasks in the order they are specified in the array, starting with the clean task to delete any old files and folders from the previous build. The Bower command executes next to make sure to bring any new front-end packages over to the scripts folder. Then the html and assets folder are copied into the build direction. Finally, all the scripts are minified and placed into the build/scripts folder.

The last step of this process is to actually run the task. This is done in the command prompt at your project root by entering this command.

```
grunt build
```

This second argument will tell Grunt to run our configured build script instead of the main Grunt command. You will need to enter this command every time you want to build a final export of your game. The resulting 'build' folder will contain the contents that you will need to upload to a web server in order for your audience to be able to play your game.

8.4 App Deployment

It is common to build HTML5 games as "hybrid" apps. These hybrid applications are games or media that were built with web technologies but packaged up and distributed as applications for mobile devices. There are some advantages to making hybrid apps. When working with web technologies, one doesn't need to invest in the specific technologies that each operating system requires—Java for Android and Objective C for Apple devices. The apps that are made with web technologies are, to a certain extent, cross-compatible with all of those devices. Perhaps more important for game developers, more and more people use their phone's app stores to discover and play games. While marketing will still be necessary for a game on the app stores, it will at least be in a place where people know to look for it.

Not everything is rosy when it comes to hybrid application development. A major drawback to this approach is that HTML5 games are not terribly efficient. Even with the best optimizations, there is still a significant gulf between JavaScript and native code performance. Users of these apps won't care what was used to build the game. They will expect app-like performance and will be unhappy if the game does not meet those expectations. A second issue with creating a hybrid application is that, while HTML5 is supposed to be write-once run-everywhere, it is never the case that the code will be cross-compatible for every device. Testing will still have to be done with different devices, and device-specific fixes may have to be added into the code, which has a tendency to produce some ugly and difficult to read scripts.

The two most common technologies used to create hybrid applications are Apache Cordova and Ludei's CocoonJS. Both of these will wrap up HTML, Javascript, and CSS and place them into an app file that will run on the major mobile operating systems. Each has a different community of support and different goals for the usage of the generated hybrid applications. In general, CocoonJS is the best choice when making games because Ludei is focused on making the best wrapper for HTML5 games, not just HTML5 apps in general.

Cordova is most commonly used to make apps that are not meant to be optimized gaming experiences. Instead if focuses on creating an easily managed app experience for text and limited graphics. It gives the developer access to more of the mobile device's capabilities and strives to make the display and transitions between pages fluid and quick. There are guides for building applications with Cordova at https://cordova.apache.org/. To get Cordova working on your computer, you will need to install a set of Node packages and other programs on your computer. For those that don't want to go through the process of setting up and using the build tools on their command prompt, Adobe hosts PhoneGap (a variant of Cordova) at https://build.phonegap.com/. PhoneGap gives web developers the capability to upload a zip file of their project to Adobe's servers, which will turn that zip file into app files with only minimal setup. The simplicity of the process does come with a cost and you'll have to pay to compile more than one app when using Adobe's build servers.

CocoonJS is another hybrid app creator that is built to do hybrid game creation. Like Cordova, Cocoon will wrap your code into a small web browser that displays your game when your app is launched. Unlike Cordova, Cocoon has a specialized build of a browser that takes out a lot of the capabilities that an HTML5 game would not need and optimizes the browser for WebGL graphics rendering. The easiest way to create a game using Cocoon is to make use of their build servers at https://cloud.ludei.com.

8.5 Testing with CocoonJS

Before building your final application, you may need to do some testing on the mobile device to make sure everything is working as intended. Because Cocoon runs on a modified version of a normal web browser, there is always a chance that something will go wrong. To help you test, the CocoonJS team has created an app called the "Cocoon JS Launcher" that will let you test your game without having to actually build an application file. The development project files can be placed either on the phone's file system or on the web for the launcher to find. The launcher is currently available for the Android, Apple, and Amazon app stores.

The first step in the testing process is to register an account at https://cloud. ludei.com/. This account will be needed to log into the Cocoon launcher, so take note of the username and password you create.

To start testing, either FTP your project to a website or place the files onto the file system of the device you want to test. With the files placed and an account registered, it is time to download and install "Cocoon JS Launcher" from your device's app store. After launching the Cocoon JS launcher, click on the "your app" button and log in. You can either then enter the URL of the index html file on the web or point the app to the files on the phones file system. Three buttons enable testing on a normal webview, a webview+, and a canvas+. Exiting and returning to this view can allow you to reload the game files.

- Webview is the closest to running a game in a normal web browser. It has all the bells and whistles of a web browser, including the DOM and CSS processing. It will use the device's built-in web browser to display the game (but without the look of a browser, so the user can't tell they're actually inside of a webpage).
- Webview+ is Cocoon's customized browser that includes a few optimizations meant to speed up games. Because it is Cocoon's browser, it gives a game developer a standard deploy target, so they don't need to deal with the quirks that exist across the different browsers and devices.
- Canvas+ is a specialized view that runs by default in a WebGL context. This view does not have *any* DOM surrounding the game, only a canvas to draw graphics. It is a very fast mode, but UI will have to be done strictly within the game.

In general, it is good to go with Canvas+, so long as your game doesn't run into any issues with testing. The Canvas+ view does not actually work with Phaser's WebGL because it will only speed up 2D canvas calls using its custom implementation of a WebGL canvas. When building a game for this view, make sure to set Phaser's render mode to CANVAS when creating the game object.

8.6 Debugging Cocoon Apps

There are several approaches to debugging CocoonJS Javascript applications, some of which are included on the launcher and others on your browser.

The first way to debug an app is to use the built-in tools in the launcher. There is actually a pretty nice suite of tools for testing and evaluating game performance that is included with the CocoonJS launcher. They can be accessed by clicking on the FPS icon at the upper left corner of the screen when running a game in the launcher. This will launch a view that is similar to a web browser console. This view shows different outputs from the console, along with specific errors and warnings from the Cocoon application. There is also an additional profiler tab that will export information about memory usage throughout the game. This will help to narrow down areas that might be major problem points in your application, whether it is a sprite, a tween gone wrong, or some objects that were not getting properly cleaned up (see Figure 8.1).

Another option that can be used to debug any app running on a Chrome web browser on an Android device is to use Chrome's remote debugger. This will let you debug any instance of Chrome open on your device that is attached via USB. Unfortunately, Android phones are not set up for debugging over a USB cable by default. In order to enable this option, open up the phone's settings and find the build number of the phone (typically under "about device," which sometimes can appear in a submenu). Tap on this build number seven times, and the developer options will be enabled. Inside the developer options menu, there is a toggle for USB debugging. Activating that option will let you phone debug applications over USB. Now, once the device is attached and the game is playing in Cocoon,

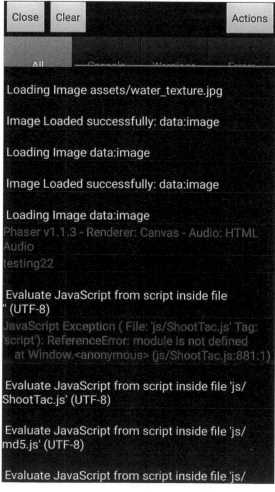

FIG 8.1 Cocoon JS debugger.

FIG 8.2 Using the chrome device inspector.

open up the Chrome web browser on your desktop computer and type "chrome://inspect" into the browser address bar. This will open up a listing of all attached devices and the chrome pages that can be debugged (including your game). Clicking on the "inspect" button of any of the attached Chrome pages will open up Chrome's basic web console for that Chrome instance, along with all the tools you are used to having in a web developer console (see Figure 8.2).

Can't See Your Device?

Sometimes Chrome isn't properly set up to discover USB devices on a computer. If this is the case for you, a few more steps will be necessary to get the whole thing up and running properly. You will need to manually run the "Android debug bridge." The first step is to download and install the Android SDK tools from https://developer.android.com/sdk/installing/index.html.

Once installed, find the folder with the "adb" executable and run that file. Inside of the and prompt, type in "devices" to start the debug server. Now that the server is started, you should be able to find your device's pages in the chrome://inspect tab.

8.7 Building with Cocoon JS

With the game finished, tested, and polished, the final step is to actually build the mobile packages. There are different packages that will need to be built for the different app stores and each needs to be configured before the app can be built and deployed. In order to build your final apps, you can either use the command line tools provided by Ludei to create and package the app, or use the cloud build tools. The second method requires going to Ludei's site and uploading files to their servers to take advantage of their preconfigured build systems. Which approach you take depends on whether you prefer the convenience of the cloud or whether you would rather keep your entire process to yourself.

8.7.1 Using the Cocoon Cloud Build

In order to use the cloud build system, you will need to head to https://cloud.ludei.com and log in using your CocoonJS credentials. Once you do, you should be presented with a view that looks similar to Figure 8.3.

Clicking on the "new project" button will start the process of creating a new app. The next screen is a series of options that are generally shared between all of the app stores. Once the project is created, there will be a chance to edit more of the specific properties for the different targets of iOS and Android. These basic options include the following:

Name: You should enter the full name of your app.

Bundle id: This comes in reverse-URL format, typically starting with a "com." In general, the id is named according to this template: "com.companyName. projectName".

Version: A version number. If you don't know where to begin with versioning, start with a ".1" or ".0.1" and work your way up from there. Every update of your game that you push to the store will need to have its version number changed to be larger than the one that is currently on the store, so make sure to change this version number when making a new build of your app with any updates.

Orientation: This is the orientation of the application that should be displayed in. For most games, this will always be of the same value (either portrait or landscape left).

Scale method: This method defines how the application will scale to take up the different ratios of the screens. This is done automatically and does not interact with Phaser scaling, so if you want to use Cocoon's scaling, you will need to take some time to play around with the settings and see how it interacts with your game.

Splash scale method: This is the same as the aforementioned orientation field but applies to the splash screen that appears while the application is launching and being initialized.

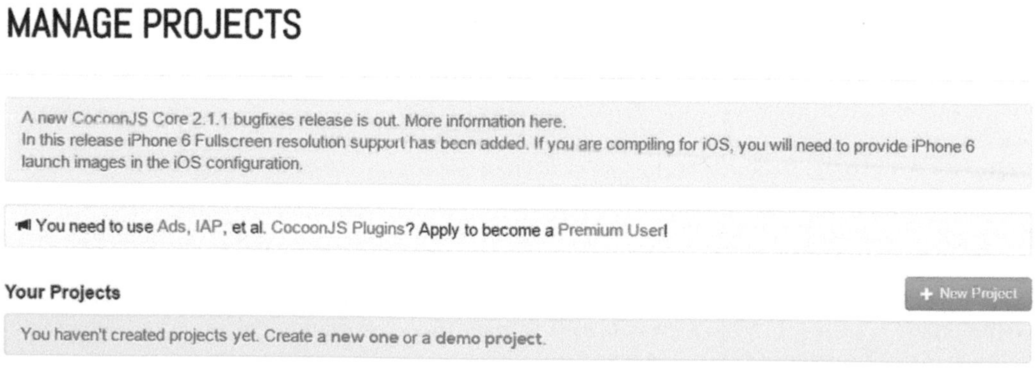

MANAGE PROJECTS

A new CocoonJS Core 2.1.1 bugfixes release is out. More information here.
In this release iPhone 6 Fullscreen resolution support has been added. If you are compiling for iOS, you will need to provide iPhone 6 launch images in the iOS configuration.

📢 You need to use Ads, IAP, et al. CocoonJS Plugins? Apply to become a Premium User!

Your Projects   + New Project

You haven't created projects yet. Create a new one or a demo project.

FIG 8.3 Location of the new project button for cocoon.

Once you fill in your application information, you will be presented with the "compile project" page. In order to compile your project, you will need to zip up your project folder and upload it to this site. Because of the file size limit of the upload, it will be impossible to upload the original project due to the number of Node package files that are sitting in your project directory. You will need to follow the instructions in the "building for web" section that covers how to make a final, clean export and zip up that exported folder to upload to this site to be built into the final application files. This is also the page you can return to create new version of your application.

If you are using the free plan, your project will be limited to thirty megabytes in total, so make sure to keep your assets and file sizes minimal. Once your zip file is uploaded, select the platforms you want to deploy to and hit the "build button."' The build will start after a few minutes (based on resource availability and the status of your user account). When the build completes, your mobile app files will be sent to your email address you provided when registering for the CocoonJS services. The files that you get from the cloud build platform are ready for testing on a device, but not yet ready to submit for display on the stores.

If you are targeting iOS you will need to open the generated IPA application files up in a program named XCode (Apple's developer program available on the app store) and configure XCode to install the IPA on your apple device. The process of getting the app to run on that device is call provisioning, and it is a multiple-step process where you provide information about the game you are making, the computers you are using to build the game, and the devices you want to test the game on. Once you provide all this information, Apple will generate a file that will authorize your computers and devices (and only the ones you registered) to build and run your game. These provisioning files can only be created by Apple developers, so you will need to sign up for their developer program at https://developer.apple.com and pay their yearly enrollment cost. The developer portal will have detailed instructions on how to generate these provisioning files and install applications to your device.

For Android, the cloud build platform will email APK files. The first is a debug application file. This is an APK that can be installed on any Android phone giving you the ability to test on any device that is set up to allow unsigned applications. This file can even be uploaded to the web and shared with anyone who downloads it via the link. Unfortunately, that debug APK will not be accepted when submitted to the Android app store. The second APK is an unsigned application that can be uploaded to the app stores after it goes through a verification process that acknowledges that the application was created by the developer who has uploaded it. This verification process is called signing and is typically done using command line tools. Before you can upload your app to the app store, you will need to sign up for a Google Play developer license. At this time, the license is a one-time fee that grants access to the ability to upload as many applications as one desires.

8.7.2 Using the Cocoon Command Line Tools

Cocoon's command line tools wrap Cordova's tools. The process of working with the tools and many of the commands entered into the prompt are the exact same as Cordova's. The major advantages of using Cocoon over Cordova's command line tools include the ability to keep your whole build process on your own development machine, access to the cloud API build provided by Ludei, and access to all of the Cocoon plugins for your game.

8.7.3 Configuring the Cordova/ Cocoon Command Line Tools

Unfortunately, for the Cordova tools to work properly the development environment you will need to configure the development environment for each target. The Android and Java developer tools will need to be present for Cocoon to be able to build Android games. For iOS games, XCode will need to be installed and you will need to have your provisioning ready to go.

You will need to have NPM and Node.js installed on your computer to get the Cordova/Cocoon tools. Assuming NPM is installed on your computer, these are the steps that need to be followed in order to get the Cocoon command line tools ready:

1. Install Cordova tools via `npm install cordova`.
2. Configure Cordova to build your target platform.
3. Install Cocoon js tools via `npm install cocoonjs`.

8.7.3.1 Configuring the Command Line Tools for Android
In order to get the Cordova tools set up for Android, the tools for standard Android development need to be downloaded, set up, and installed.

The primary tool for Android development is the Android SDK, which can be found at https://developer.android.com/sdk/installing/index.html?pkg=tools. Before you can install the SDK, you will need to install its dependency, the Java Developer kit (or JDK). The JDK can be found at http://www.oracle.com/technetwork/java/javase/downloads/index.html. Once the JDK and SDK are downloaded and installed, make sure the JDK bin folder and the Android SDK's tools and platform-tools are in your computer's path variable, so the Cocoon tools can invoke them from the command prompt.

8.7.3.2 Configuring the CLT for iOS
In order to use the command line tools for iOS, you will need to get an Apple Developers license from www.developer.apple.com (it will cost around a hundred dollars, yearly). Once you have the license and are able to log into the developer portal, download and install the XCode command line tools. With these tools installed, Cordova will be able to build iOS applications from your command line.

The Most Up-to-Date Configuration Methods

Technology moves fast and there is a chance that the way Cordova is configured has changed since the time of this writing. If something isn't going quite as planned when following these directions, the Cordova docs will most likely still have the most up-to-date information on its setup and configuration. The docs for the most recent version can be found on the webpage http://cordova.apache.org/, under the section "documentation."

8.7.3.3 Building an Application File

Once the Cordova and Cocoon command line tools have been installed and configured, the next step is to build the application files. This is done by creating a project folder via Cocoon, specifying the deploy targets that you want to build for and adding the webview+ plugin (which is that custom version of Chrome that runs on every device) to the project. Once everything is properly configured, the command "cocoon run" will build the application for you. This will take a few moments, so be patient.

```
cocoonjs create MyProject com.ludei.test LudeiTest
cd MyProject
cocoonjs platform add android
cocoonjs plugin add com.ludei.webview.plus
cocoonjs run
```

8.7.4 Creating an App Store Ready Package

Once you have your unsigned APK or an IPA without a deploy provisioning file, there is only one last technical hurdle that needs to be jumped before the app can be submitted to the store directories. Each app will have to go through a signing process to verify you are the one who built and readied this app for the store.

8.7.4.1 Signing for iOS

Creating the final application for iOS requires a new provisioning file to be created and used to sign the final application. The process is nearly the same as it is for creating the debug provisioning file. Follow the directions on the Apple Developer portal related to creating a deployment provisioning file and use it to sign the application in XCode.

8.7.4.2 Signing for Android

The process of signing an APK for release in Android requires you to create a key that is unique to you. This key will be stored in a ".keystore" file in which you should keep in a safe place where no one else can get to it, and you can't lose it. If you lose it, you will not be able to upload the updated versions of you game in the future. You will need to use that key to sign your APK using a tool called jarsigner.

1. Create a key and a `keystore`. Entering this command into your prompt will have you generate a `keystore` and a key (you will need to create passwords for each). This particular key will be valid for 10,000 days, and will be stored in a file called `my-release-key.keystore` in the folder where you executed this command.

   ```
   keytool -genkey -v -keystore my-release-key.keystore
   -alias alias_name -keyalg RSA -keysize 2048
     -validity 10000
   ```

2. Sign APK using `jarsigner` and the key you just made in that `keystore`. This command assumes that the key and your app are in the same folder. You will need to enter your `keystore` and key passwords.

   ```
   jarsigner -verbose -sigalg SHA1withRSA -digestalg
     SHA1
   -keystore my-release-key.keystore my_application.apk
     alias_name
   ```

8.8 Conclusion

Once you have built an application for a device, tested it, and signed it, you are ready to submit your game to the stores. Each app store has its own submission and management process that is typically described and detailed in their respective developer portal's help and documentation sections. In general, for each app store, you will need to upload some additional information for the application, including the app description, images of the app in use, and the application icons to be used in the store. After submission, your game will be reviewed. If your game is not breaking any of the app store rules, your game will be accepted into the store and placed onto the market for others to download to their devices and enjoy. Where you take it from there is up to you. If you go to update your app, remember to have your key on hand and to increase the version number to something higher than it was before. Putting your games onto the app store may feel like a big step, but in the end it is simply a small move into the larger world of game development.

CHAPTER 9

Conclusion

Through the course of this book, you have learned about new and upcoming features of JavaScript and another execution environment of Node and NPM, which are robust tools that just about any modern web developer will have on their computer. You played with the Grunt task runner that you can use to customize your project workspace to work for you (or you can find others who have done this already via Yeoman). Your introduction to these tools was in the context of making games using Phaser, an ever-evolving library built for making spectacular HTML5 games that work across a range of devices. As you progressed through the examples, hopefully, you finally got a good taste of what it takes to make a game in this particular environment. The HTML5 game development world is a challenging one because it is still in a state of flux and evolution. Even as you read this book now, new approaches, techniques, and tutorials will have been released on the Internet that cover Phaser or other HTML5 game engines. Even Phaser itself will most likely be updated and will probably even receive updates if you keep working with it past the scope of this book.

The pace of the web is fast but the rewards for working with web technologies can be worth it. Though the technologies presented in this book may seem complex, they will become easier and give you access to a toolset that has broad applications beyond just video games. While in the future you may move on to find new approaches and techniques that you prefer for making video games in HTML5, I hope that this book served as a good introduction to the production of web-based games that you can rely on to get working quickly.

One of the problems that game developers have is finding the right tools to express themselves with. We have so many technologies we could use to implement all of the cool ideas we have in our heads, and we take forever to start because we feel like we need to choose the latest, greatest, and most perfect technology for our applications. This is true to a point, but the paralysis of choice is lost time—time that could be spent making games. Sometimes you don't need the latest and the greatest. You need that familiar tool that feels good in your hand, and this book has hopefully given you that familiarity. Now that you're hopefully filled with energy and confidence, it is time to return to the reasons you picked up this book in the first place. Before you get distracted again, Start a project now, before a new and shiny technology distracts you again. Go make some new art. Go write some code. Go make games.

Index